Psychosocial Basis of Medical Practice

Second Edition

Psychosocial Basis of Medical Practice

AN INTRODUCTION TO HUMAN BEHAVIOR

Second Edition

Charles L. Bowden, M.D.

Nancy U. Karren Professor
Department of Psychiatry
The University of Texas Health Science Center
at San Antonio Medical School
San Antonio, Texas

Alvin G. Burstein, Ph.D.

Professor and Chief,
Division of Psychology, Department of Psychiatry
The University of Texas Health Science Center
at San Antonio Medical School
San Antonio, Texas

with 3 contributors

THE WILLIAMS & WILKINS COMPANY
Baltimore

Copyright © 1979
The Williams & Wilkins Company
428 E. Preston Street
Baltimore, Md. 21202, U.S.A.

Made in the United States of America

Library of Congress Cataloging in Publication Data

Bowden, Charles L
  Psychosocial basis of medical practice.

  Includes bibliographies and index.
  1. Physician and patient. 2. Sick—Psychology. 3. Developmental psychology. I.
Burstein, Alvin George, 1931–   joint author. II. Title.
R727.3B63 1979   616'.001'9   78-23658
ISBN 0-683-00992-3

Composed and printed at the
Waverly Press, Inc.
Mt. Royal and Guilford Aves.
Baltimore, Md. 21202, U.S.A.

PREFACE TO THE SECOND EDITION

Our returning with a second edition is a testament to the favorable reception of the first edition. The audience for the book has been broader than anticipated, with students using it as a text in undergraduate courses preparatory for health careers and in social work, dental, allied health and nursing school courses. We are pleased that students and instructors have seen the general importance of psychosocial variables and relationship skills in patient care and realized that we were not addressing only medical students, but all health professionals. Physicians in practice, especially those in primary care fields and those working with patients with chronic diseases, have also shown an interest in the book. The book's main impact has been on behavioral science courses in medical schools, where to some degree it has helped to define the field of study.

We prefer to keep the second edition reasonably short rather than to try to treat a subject area comprehensively. The brevity of the text is such that most instructors will want to amplify on materials in certain sections. We believe instructors can better complement this core material with the most recent findings or with material relevant to their particular setting and objectives.

Aside from the basically highly complimentary responses of readers and reviewers, two criticisms of the first edition stand out. We are viewed as male chauvinists and the publishers as money gougers. We have reviewed the use of pronouns and eliminated sexual references where the syntax did not suffer. In some cases we have continued use of the generic *he,* because alternatives seemed stylistically awkward. We intend no sexual implications by the use, and hope the reader will be charitable toward our dilemma.

Price is the publisher's dilemma. Costs have greatly risen in the publishing field in recent years. As authors, we have avoided the use of illustrations and graphs in the text, which raise publishing costs, and have tried to make every word count.

Many sections of the text have required only minor modification. The childhood development sections have been expanded in terms of common adaptational problems of specific age periods and the psychosocial history. We have added some of the ethological data which offer firm scientific support for human behavioral principles. Issues of patient compliance, stress disorders, disorders of habit and sociocultural factors which influence health and health economics are elaborated on. Ethical aspects of patient care are considered in more detail.

The references were selected for their particular relevance as further readings, because specific reference is made to them or because material in the text has been taken from them.

We are again pleased to acknowledge the contributions of our colleagues, Doctors Leon, Meyer and Turnbull. We have taken responsibility for most of the alterations in sections which they initially wrote, to bring greater cohesiveness to this second edition. In this context, we are, of course, responsible for any shortcomings of outlook, scope or execution.

We especially thank Dr. Harry Martin, Professor and Chief of the Division of Sociology, who, as director of the first-year medical student course in behavioral science in San Antonio, has had a rich and continuing influence on our views and the emphases in this book. Bertha Freeburn has our special gratitude for coordinating our revision of the text and doing much of the typing. Nancy Migl also helpfully assisted in the manuscript preparation.

CHARLES L. BOWDEN, M.D.
ALVIN G. BURSTEIN, PH.D.

Introduction

One way of perceiving a book's organizational plan is to review its table of contents. This introduction is intended to provide the reader with a different kind of overview—a conceptual one—of our text. We would like to summarize here the main foci of the book, its methodology and its core assumptions.

1. Recognition and management of common emotional reactions among nonpsychiatrically ill patients. This section will focus on improving the student's observational skills and on placing the data that he gathers in an adaptive frame of reference pertinent to concepts of health and disease. The adaptive mechanisms used by patients with common emotional reactions and the early life experiences which predispose to these reaction patterns will be considered. Finally, practical ways the physician can put his knowledge to work in dealing with his patients will be discussed.

2. Understanding all of the factors which influence the doctor-patient relationship. The physician needs to develop his interviewing and observational skills so that he can utilize the personal doctor-patient relationship for more effective patient care. In addition to covering this subject, the factors which influence the doctor's own adaptation to the role of physician will be discussed.

3. Growth and development across the life cycle. This will emphasize stage-specific tasks as a primary developmental concern. Healthy adaptation and minor adaptive dysfunction will also receive attention.

4. Preparation for a richer, more ready understanding of the traditional second-year course in psychopathology. Many of the points touched on in Sections 1 and 3 above will be particularly useful in this regard. For example, the adaptive, or defense, mechanisms are key tools for the understanding of the psychiatric disorders.

Methods

1. By focusing on characteristic emotional responses of patients, the text encourages and is compatible with early patient exposure at a level commensurate with the stage of knowledge and the needs of the first-year student.

2. The focus on common emotional reactions in nonpsychiatrically ill patients, and relating those reactions to early life experiences, as well as the attention to adaptive dysfunction across the life cycle, makes the relevance of growth and development more obvious. It also naturally emphasizes the importance of having a holistic view of the patient within his biopsychosocial environment.

3. The approach described allows the student to learn "without realizing it" in certain areas. There is often considerable resistance to the recognition of the existence of unconscious mental processes and adaptive ego mechanisms. A baldly intrapsychic, didactic approach is not very effective. Describing these processes and operations in real patient situations, coupled with giving the student an opportunity to experience them in the relationship with a patient, then relating what he has learned to psychodynamic concepts minimizes the resistances.

Assumptions

This text is rooted in the following assumptions. Curriculum time for behavioral science courses has increased in recent years. Part I of the National Board Examinations now includes a behavioral science section. The format utilized here developed from our generally successful experiences in implementing such a course and out of our growing feeling that current texts for first-year courses are not satisfactory.

Basic to the text design is our view of the physician as the person in our society most saliently identified with health and illness care. The role of the physician has changed over the past 50 years from one of concern with acute, life-threatening infectious and traumatic disorders to concern with chronic diseases involving multiple, interactional causative factors. This change necessitates having an approach which recognizes and makes use of the broad interrelationships that affect health. The physician must master behavioral and interpersonal skills which tend to get lost in the technique- and disease-oriented, overcompartmentalized medical curriculum.

Psychiatric material is difficult to learn because it may run counter to a person's own biases, stir up conflicts, evoke painful memories and temporarily diminish some of the security of the embryo physician. A principle of learning which has validity in general, but especially in areas in which repression is operative, is that of working through. Educationally, this requires repeatedly going over the basic material within different contexts and at different points in the curriculum. This text lends itself to that. Aspects of sexuality and anxious patients, to take two examples, could be covered in the first-year course, the second-year course in psychopathology and again in the clinical clerkship. Reteaching could and should also go on outside psychiatry course offerings, for example, in liaison service conferences.

Neurobiological material is presented only when it naturally fits in. In many ways, it fits in much better with the psychopathology course, when it is relevant to learn of the limbic system and sleep centers as they influence schizophrenia and disorders of sleep, respectively.

We are aware of the "softness" of the material in a book such as this. The laboratory has not produced significant support for major theories of the mind. Our approach is to emphasize empirical data where they do exist, to teach action skills and to define terms operationally, such as the adaptive mechanisms.

For the student who has been immersed in a welter of objective facts, and who has learned that the memorization of discrete bits of data makes a successful student, we have three special cautions.

First, do not reify these concepts. We have described and named hypothetical events in a way which can be useful, but these events remain hypothetical, not real. They are best regarded as a useful metaphor, rather than as an underlying reality.

Second, do not reject the notions that we describe, despite their "softness," out of scientific or personal skepticism. If the notions seem plausible, engage in the willing suspense of disbelief long enough to test their usefulness in practice. You will find that the point of view we offer is relevant to and useful in the practice of medicine generally.

Third, do not assume that, because much of the material in this book is abstract or not immediately clear, it is over your head. Do not engage in the "I'm just a country boy" defense. Much of the material is refined, applied common sense, and all of it is relevant to medical practice. You can be optimistic about increasingly full cognitive mastery of it as you work at becoming a physician over the next few years.

In conclusion, we wish to emphasize what the preclinical contribution of psychiatry to the student's first exposure to the study of human behavior in medicine should and should not be. It should not be a summary teaching of basic psychoanalytical concepts or a course in the sociology of medicine. It should not be an introductory course in any one of the other psychological theories—behavioral, common sense, etc.—or a course in the neurobiology of behavior. As we conceive it, it should not be a course in psychiatry per se.

It should be a course exploring the ways in which the physical well-being of patients is embedded in and interconnected with their psychological state and sociocultural condition. It should be a demonstration that the skillful use of one's own observational skills and personality can enhance patient care, whereas ignoring those factors can undo the most carefully planned therapeutic regimen. It should be a course which helps to teach the art of medicine.

CONTRIBUTORS

Charles L. Bowden, M.D.
Nancy U. Karren Professor, Department of Psychiatry, The University of Texas Health Science Center at San Antonio, Medical School, San Antonio, Texas

Alvin G. Burstein, Ph.D.
Professor and Chief, Division of Psychology, Department of Psychiatry, The University of Texas Health Science Center at San Antonio, Medical School, San Antonio, Texas

Robert L. Leon, M.D.
Professor and Chairman, Department of Psychiatry, The University of Texas Health Science Center at San Antonio, Medical School, San Antonio, Texas

George G. Meyer, M.D.
Professor, Department of Psychiatry, The University of Texas Health Science Center at San Antonio, Medical School, San Antonio, Texas

James M. Turnbull, M.D.
Associate Professor, Departments of Psychiatry and Family Practice, The University of Texas Health Science Center at San Antonio, Medical School, San Antonio, Texas

CONTENTS

PART I
Working with Patients

PART 1

WORKING WITH PATIENTS

CHAPTER 1

THE THERAPEUTIC RELATIONSHIP: I THE PHYSICIAN, THE PATIENT AND THE DIAGNOSTIC PROCESS

CHARLES L. BOWDEN, M.D.

A physician's technological, disease-oriented skills must be used within the context of clinical observation and human interaction. Engel emphasizes three aspects of the physician's activity related to patient care. The first is the (1) ability to get the patient to respond appropriately through interview, examination and personal relationship. The second is the ability to observe and (2) accurately record behavior, which yields the history of the patient and his illness and the manifestations thereof. The third is the ability to translate (3) these data into pertinent frames of reference, which constitutes the diagnostic process. As Engel stated, "These skills are basically behavioral and call for scientific strategies that utilize the tools of the behavioral sciences, rather than the traditional laboratory approach to the causes and mechanisms of disease. An essential task of medical education, then, is to develop the physician as the most effective and reliable observing instrument possible."

This chapter focuses on the doctor-patient relationship. The roles of the physician and the patient and the factors that influence each throughout the vicissitudes of the therapeutic relationship are analyzed. The components of the diagnostic process and the concepts of normality and abnormality conclude the chapter.

The Physician

The physician's own personality influences how he will respond to the stresses of the medical profession. A recent study at our institution indicates that only one trait—the need to understand, to seek cognitive closure—is correlated with physician excellence. We did not find any particular personality style or cluster of traits with such a correlation. Many different types of people can make good doctors. Perfectionism and the need to achieve on a high level, which are common in physicians, can cause difficulties in the doctor's personal life when they are coupled with strong external pressures toward overestimations of one's skills and personal importance. In general, the direct patient-care specialities, particularly those in which a sustained, intense relationship with the patient exists, such as psychiatry and pediatric hematology, are associated with such pressures. A more detailed description of factors influencing the physician's own role adaptation is found in Chapter 20.

Factors Affecting the Student Physician

Role Insecurity. Several factors influence the medical student's behavior with patients. Foremost is his insecurity in his new role. He is often torn between his needs to learn and his feelings of being an unnecessary burden to the patient or to the more experienced health-care team members. In fact, the student's educational goals and the patient's needs are usually complementary, not antagonistic. The patient benefits from the opportunity for human interaction. The student, with his ready access to other members of the health-care team, is an important means of communication to and from the patient. Medical students also may serve as a crucial link in transmitting new basic science information to clinical practitioners, to the benefit of the patients.

A student should act confidently, not diffidently or apologetically. In so doing, he will be more successful in establishing the type of relationship that will both further his own learning and provide the best care for the patient. Youth and inexperience are not as much a barrier to an effective relationship as most students think. Some patients are especially able to confide in the younger physician, with whom they are able to relate comfortably and warmly, as they would with a son or daughter.

Embarrassing or Repugnant Areas. Some patients may have symptoms or behave in ways which the student finds conflictful. Frank or covert sexual invitations may generate conflict and embarrassment. Symptoms such as alcoholism may generate disapproval. Social prejudices may be strongly felt; vomits, feces, or odoriferous lesions may generate feelings of disgust. When the student becomes aware that subjective reactions are interfering with his function, he must attempt to rectify the situation. If he is intensely attracted to or repelled by a particular type of patient, a likely source of the feeling is an unresolved personal problem. Predisposition to biases and to unrealistic attitudes is common to everyone; such characteristics can often be diminished through self-assessment and self-discipline. If the inappropriate reaction persists, or if attention is called to it by an instructor, the student should consider seeking advice. Many times, the problem can be alleviated by discussing it with a more experienced physician.

Conflict between the Needs for Closeness and Distance. Student physicians are pulled by emotional crosscurrents in their work with patients. They need to learn as much as they can of the facts of the patient's life and the meaning of his symptoms to him. Yet the closer students come to the secrets and meanings of the patient's life, the more they risk overinvolvement and, with it, the loss of perspective and objective judgment necessary to help the patient. If they are emotionally overinvested in the patient, there is a tendency to avoid questioning or treatment which might cause pain, embarrassment or other distress to the patient and, in turn, to the overinvolved physician. If they have had previous experiences of similar interpersonally shared pain and disappointment, whether in their own childhood, adult personal relationships or with their patients, they may try to shield themselves from these painful memories by being aloof and uninvolved with their patients.

This conflict operates in yet another direction best summed up in the adage "familiarity breeds contempt." To know extensive and intimate details about the patient places physicians in a role of considerable power, a role which they may eschew or may misuse to the detriment of a patient. There are no easy answers concerning these issues, but awareness of the difference between empathy and sympathy and of the different modes of doctor-patient interaction (a topic of Chapter 3) can help the physician toward confident, mature responses in this area.

The Physician Role

The physician has the unique right and the responsibility to make a personal inquiry into the history of his patient's life (including the most intimate and private details), to examine his body and to carry out treatment. He or she is required to be professionally competent and to have special knowledge based on empirical data. Like certain other professionals, he is licensed by the state as a symbol of the social sanction given to his activities and of the responsibilities to society entailed in his professional function. He is expected, in the context of his professional activities, to put the patient's interests ahead of his own and to be motivated by the patient's best interests. This special form of professional altruism is an example of a fiduciary relationship between truster and trustee that is analogous to the relationship that bankers, lawyers, and many health professionals have with their clients. This trustworthiness is an important factor in establishing a basis for the patient's willingness to give the physician access to his privacy—including his bodily privacy—and his willingness to act on his physician's advice. The physician is expected to be primarily motivated by the needs of the patients whom he serves. This loyalty to his patient, including the ethic of medical confidentiality, is an important factor in establishing a basis for the high level of trust desirable within the relationship. He is expected to maintain emotional neutrality toward those he treats, lest his personal involvement impair his medical judgment. He is authority, healer and succorer, as well as technical expert.

The public esteems the physician for several reasons. There is drama in the life of the doctor, with emergencies, long hours and involvement with the mysteries of birth and death. The scientific advances of the 19th and 20th centuries have literally invested physicians with the power of life and death. To feel secure in his relationship with his physician, the patient naturally tends to make him omniscient, that is, to endow him with the qualities of a parental figure who will care for and protect him. Some try to "demythologize" these aspects of medicine by viewing the physician as "just another member of the health-care team." But, in fact, pride in membership in an elite profession based on learning, humanity and dedication is an appropriate attitude.

The Hippocratic oath, formulated almost 2500 years ago, recognizes the power inherent in the doctor-patient relationship. The ethical principles regulating the relationship between physician and patient have relevance today.

> I swear by Apollo physician, by Aesculapius, by Hygeia, by Panacea and by all the gods and goddesses, making them my witnesses, that I will carry out, according to my ability and judgement, this oath and this indenture. To hold my teacher in this art equal to my own parents; to make him partner in my livelihood; when he is in need of money to share mine with him; to consider his family as my own brothers, and to teach them this art, if they want to learn it, without fee or indenture; to impart precept, oral instruction, and all other instruction to my own sons, the sons of my teacher, and to indentured pupils who have taken the physician's oath, but to nobody else. I will use treatment to help the sick according to my ability and judgement, but never with a view to injury and wrongdoing. Neither will I administer a poison to anybody

when asked to do so, nor will I suggest such a course. Similarly, I will not give to a woman a pessary to cause abortion. But I will keep pure and holy both my life and my art. I will not use the knife, not even, verily, on sufferers from stone, but I will give place to such as are craftsmen therein. Into whatsoever houses I enter, I will enter to help the sick, and I will abstain from all intentional wrongdoing and harm, especially from abusing the bodies of man or woman, bond or free. And whatsoever I shall see or hear in the course of my profession, as well as outside my profession in my intercourse with men, if it be what should not be published abroad, I will never divulge, holding such things to be holy secrets. Now if I carry out this oath, and break it not, may I gain for ever reputation among all men for my life and for my art; but if I transgress it and forswear myself, may the opposite befall me.

The Patient

For the purposes of discussion, it is convenient to sort the factors which influence the patient's behavior into two general categories: personal factors and sociocultural factors. Personal factors are considered here and more extensively in Chapters 5 through 11. Sociocultural factors will be considered in Chapter 2.

The Patient Role

Social role expectations and realities exert a profound influence on the doctor-patient relationship. The patient comes with preconceived expectations about his own and his physician's behavior. He may expect a certain dress, decorum, language and appearance. He expects to submit to an examination without fear of exploitation, including sexual or financial exploitation. He expects to be told what, if anything, is wrong and what to do about it, including receiving appropriate treatment with drugs. He also expects personal concern from the physician.

The "sick role" is generally assumed by the patient who considers himself ill. In our culture, five aspects are basically important: (1) the person is considered incapacitated through no fault of his own; (2) he is viewed as having a right to have his need for care by another person met; (3) his incapacity may exempt him from his usual social obligations; (4) he must recognize that he is ill and must desire to "get well" and return to social functioning within the limits of his capabilities; (5) he is expected to cooperate with his physician and to adhere to the treatment regimen.

Personal Factors in Health and Illness

Personal factors are those related to the particular event or time which influence the patient's behavior. Common examples of such factors are described in the following pages.

Resistance to Disease. A small percentage of the population receives the bulk of medical care, suggesting not only that the delivery of care is influenced by the patient's economic status and geographic locale but also that health and illness are not evenly distributed across the population. Persons who have experienced traumatic events in the preceding 6 months to 2 years are significantly more likely to develop chronic diseases than are those who have not. The recent book by Lynch details the epidemiological link between interpersonal loss and a variety of disease states. The studies by Hinkle and Wolff have also demonstrated the temporal clustering of life stress and illness. Neurosis, peptic ulcer and proneness to infection have been associated with upward mobility.

Hospitalization. This is a special facet of the patient role which has been studied extensively. The patient enters a system which effectively strips him of much of his outside identity. He does not wear his own clothes, he must conform to a time schedule much different from his usual one and he gives up personal controls and authority to a much greater degree than in most ambulatory patient roles. The alien and dehumanized environment in the coronary care unit or intensive care unit may cause the patient to suffer from sensory deprivation which can cause confusion, disordered thinking and perceptual abnormalities.

Prognosis for Recovery. Recovery from disease is correlated with two major psychological factors: *lack of depression* and *high ego strength*. The latter indicates the ability to meet problems without undue internal stress, without undue avoidance and without employment of regressive defenses.

Two prospective studies found that patients who, preoperatively, had shown severe depression and inability to discuss postoperative plans had a mortality rate during or after open heart surgery of over 80%, compared with a 20% average mortality rate for the total patient groups. Prognosis for recovery from myocardial infarction is highly related to emotional factors. Patients in one study showed a uniform tendency to avoid taking sedatives, minimize symptoms and retain harmful habits during the convalescent phase of their illness. This suggests the great difficulty which integrating a major change in physical self-concept poses for patients. The studies by Rahe et al., indicating that small group process has a substantial effect on recovery from myocardial infarct and on knowledgeability about the disease state, show the importance of emotional factors in useful assimilation by patients of important data about their physical status. These examples underscore the importance of psychological and social-cultural factors in the development of and recovery from illness and of the careful assessment of these areas during evaluation of the patient.

The Patient's Past Experiences Relating to Other Persons. In the doctor-patient relationship, the patient is likely to manifest reaction patterns which reflect his expectations about authority figures. Similarly, his past experiences in the patient role will affect his behavior and expectations. The repetition in the therapeutic relationship of attitudes the patient has had toward parents, teachers, physicians and other authority figures who have been important in the person's life is termed *transference*. The patient is often unaware of this tendency to repeat the same feelings and behavior when faced with a similar stress. By recognizing the tendency of patients to identify physicians with earlier important persons in their lives, the physician can avoid taking such reactions personally and can use his understanding in the management of the patient. This issue is explored in the following chapters.

The Patient's Discomfort. The patient may consult a physician because pain, discomfort or disability has become intolerable. In doing so, he is acknowledging that he is not as self-sufficient as before. The range of tolerance for discomfort is great. Some of the variables within the social role of the patient which affect tolerance have been considered earlier in this chapter.

The category of pain deserves special attention. It is discussed in detail in Chapter 8, but some general remarks should be made here. The patient's assessment of pain and the doctor's appraisal of it can be widely divergent. One reason for this divergence is the misconception that, in order to hurt, the patient must have an organic basis for his complaints. The experience of pain is subject to wide variations even within the same individual. We have no instrument to rate the intensity of pain objectively. Beecher found that two-thirds of the men badly wounded at the Anzio beachhead during World War II did not complain about pain or want medications for it. In contrast, 80% of a group of male civilians undergoing major surgery wanted pain medication even though they had far less tissue damage than the men at Anzio. The important variable in both events is the circumstances in which the traumatic event occurred. To the combat soldier, a wound meant respite and a possible chance to go home. No similar gains accompany surgery during peacetime. Neither the presence nor absence of organic pathology provides much of a guide to the amount of pain an individual is suffering.

It is also important not to use the model of acute pain for all pain. Visible signs of distress, such as sweating, crying or facial contortions, are less likely to occur with chronic pain, where adaptation occurs. Even a patient with severe pain can appear untroubled, through a combination of stoicism (suppression), distraction and relief by medication.

The placebo effect is also a misunderstood response, especially in the area of pain relief. Placebo response is the patient's tendency to respond favorably to suggestion, apart from any specific pharmacological effectiveness of the drug or treatment. It is a common response, occurring in about one-third of the population and even more often under situations of stress. It can be used to positive advantage in many therapeutic relationships. Conversely, there are circumstances in which the use of placebos is unwarranted. It is no substitute for careful diagnosis. Giving a patient an injection of saline and observing his favorable response has no relevance in terms of separating psychogenic from organic pain. An additional disadvantage of such a procedure is that the patient is being tricked, and his discovery of this could undermine the therapeutic relationship. A placebo should not be used to justify or express one's annoyance with or dislike for a patient.

In the case of pain of uncertain etiology, a psychiatric consultation may be useful to identify or to rule out those psychiatric conditions which often have pain as a major symptom: conversion neurosis (hysterical type), depression, malingering, compensation neurosis, schizophrenia and hypochondriacal neurosis.

The Patient's Fears Concerning His Illness. The patient may consult a physician not because his symptoms are causing distress, but because of their implications. A lump in the breast, a small hemoptysis or blood in the stool may fall into this category. Physicians who classify consultations for episodes of this kind as necessary or unnecessary are making the mistake of assuming that the patient's knowledge of illness is equivalent to their own. Only when a patient with a harmless or imagined disorder fails to respond to reassurances and education should his behavior be considered inappropriate; in that case, he should be considered in the next category.

Problems of Living Presenting as Symptoms. The use of medical services may be a result not so much of symptoms but of life events. A man may complain of a backache because of the extra stress of his wife's illness. A woman may seek an operation for varicose veins, which she has had for 20 years, primarily to win back the affection of her husband. In such cases, the most important question is not "What is the diagnosis?" but "Why does the patient come or keep coming with this particular symptom?"

Administrative and Preventive Contacts. McWhinney has proposed a useful taxonomy of factors determining a patient's coming for medical care. Among these factors is that a patient may come for a solely administrative purpose—for example, to obtain a certificate of disability or a medical report for a driver's license. The patient may also come for reasons unrelated to ongoing illness, but for preventive reasons. Services in this category include such contacts as well-baby care and annual physical examinations.

Social and Interpersonal Triggers. A person's decision to see a physician about a problem is more influenced by several social and interpersonal events than by the severity of the disorder. Perceived interference with social or personal relations is one such trigger. Another is perceived interference with vocational role or physical functions, such as gardening, dancing and jogging. It is the point at which the person himself senses the interference which is important, not that point which physicians, as objective experts, might consider critical. Sanctioning by a close friend or relative is another catalyst. The "Yeah, you'd better go see a doctor about that" may impel the person to seek care even though actual symptomatology remains unchanged. A temporal clustering of symptoms is another factor. A patient's stomach pains, anxiety, family conflict and work pressures may be nothing new, but their appearance within the same day may cause the person to attend to his symptoms and need for treatment with a new sense of urgency.

The central point is that physicians should not focus solely on symptoms in evaluating patients but on the factors which precipitated their coming. These catalysts have more to do with the patient's subjective motivation than do the symptoms per se. With knowledge of these factors, physicians are in a position to use them motivationally to improve the patient's compliance with planned treatment.

The Diagnostic Process

Identification and Localization of Problems

Diagnosis is a multifaceted process which includes the identification of problems and the localization of those problems in anatomical terms. The approach to this is discussed in detail in the next chapter.

Analysis in Structural and Functional Terms. The physician must next analyze the symptoms reported by the patient and the signs that he has observed in terms of abnormalities of structure and function. The physician makes an attempt to visualize what is going on in terms of his scientific knowledge. A thorough knowledge of preclinical and clinical disciplines is essential for such diagnostic thinking. The competent physician who hears a patient report tiredness and apathy, feelings of sadness and worthlessness, recent weight loss, frequent crying and wakings during the night will consider a functional disturbance in central nervous system biogenic amine metabolism. This thinking has therapeutic implications, if the diagnosis of a primary depressive disorder is borne out. Similarly, from symptoms of dyspnea and orthopnea and signs of edema, rales and an enlarged liver, he will infer inadequate function of the heart.

The first step in the diagnostic process, personally interviewing the patient, usually contributes more information toward determination of the medical problem than any other aspect of the examination. Of the various facets of the diagnostic process, such as laboratory studies and x-rays, the interview is the only one which is entirely human and done without instruments. Furthermore, studies indicate that experienced clinicians usually quickly reduce their uncertainty about the patient's problem in the early moments of history taking, primarily by recognition of patterns. This process involves storing a series of disease pictures in one's brain and recognizing similarities in the patient, without initially needing to look at all details of the picture. Experienced clinicians are able to do this partly because they learn to note physical changes, attitudes and other cues which enable them to assign a value to the information obtained and to focus on the crucial aspects of the clinical presentation.

Causal Factors. The next stage involves the elucidation of causal factors. Two levels of pathological process must usually be considered simultaneously: the disease and the illness. Pneumococcal pneumonia of the lower lobe of the lung is a specific *disease*. The pathological process can be understood in technical, impersonal terms, and it involves a specific etiological agent, *Diplococcus pneumoniae*. But the physician does not treat that disease in vacuo. Rather, he treats a person with an illness: pneumonia.

This means that he needs to evaluate all of the factors which may have played a role in the development of the illness or which may contribute to the person's recovery therefrom. In the case of pneumonia, this may include such considerations as other diseases which predispose to infection, the patient's age, the physical care he gave himself and the risks to which he exposed himself, his alcoholic drinking pattern, the adequacy of heating in his home and his willingness to acknowledge and seek medical care for significant distress.

The Classification of Disease

The classification of disease is the next phase of the diagnostic process. There are several conceptual levels in the classification of disease. Syndromes generally are the least clear and exclusive of diagnoses. These are groupings of characteristic signs and symptoms which are often of diverse etiology. Examples are the nephrotic syndrome and organic brain syndrome. Other diseases are named for the man or woman who first described the disorder or for the first patient or family in whom the disorder was described. Examples in the latter category are Parkinson's disease, Graves' disease and Down's disease. Such names often are confusing, for to be explicit they should refer only to disease states which have all of the characteristics of the original description, whereas refinements and increased complexity in evaluation procedures often have changed the bases of diagnosis. Other names are based on actual or assumed characteristics about a disease process. Lupus erythematosus, which means, literally, the condition of the red wolf, is named for the characteristic red facial skin lesions. The term schizophrenia was based on a belief that a splitting of the mind occurred in the disordered person (*schizo*, split; *phrenia*, mind).

In addition, some diseases are listed in functional terms (nutritional diseases, the neuroses versus the psychoses), others in terms of organ systems (cerebrovascular insufficiency, hypertensive cardiovascular disease, degenerative joint disease) and still others in terms of etiology (infectious disease; diseases from specific toxins, such as lead poisoning).

The issue of nomenclature is thus a confusing one. It is presented here with the aim of helping the student to be aware of the presumptions behind various diagnostic systems and not to be a slave to them. His mind should be free to question and he should be able to reorganize his thinking when facts warrant. As a rule, he should choose the most accurate, explicit and complete diagnosis. In general, a standard diagnosis should be used—"latent schizophrenia" is better than "borderline personality"—although the second term may be used as an adjunct for explanatory value. Attaching men's names to diseases is best avoided. Terminology such as chronic adrenal insufficiency secondary to adrenal tuberculosis is preferable to Addison's disease. The need to organize and to name can be carried too far. Many diseases are sometimes incorrectly grouped under one title. The term schizophrenia is an example. Almost certainly the term comprises several disorders totally or in part causally different. Study and discussion of the disease are, therefore, more difficult, and debate is often unnecessarily acrimonious because the term is not even descriptively defined with a high degree of exclusivity.

The response to available treatments can be a strong latent influence on diagnosis. To continue with the example of schizophrenia, the development of the phenothiazines, with their dramatic effectiveness in the disease, resulted in an increased attention to the possibility of the disease and, to some degree, a tendency to err on the side of including the severely emotionally disturbed patient in the schizophrenic category, inasmuch as a rather specific remedy for control existed. At the same time, the availability of a new, effective treatment can set off a study of disease mechanisms to clarify causal factors. This, too, has been the case with schizophrenia; only in the mid-1970's are the fruits of much research concerning etiological, causal and prognostic factors beginning to take coherent shape.

Standards of Normality

The last stage of the diagnostic process is, at least conceptually, the most difficult: the evaluation of the severity and the impact of the illness on the individual. In order to make this estimate, the patient's unique signs and symptoms are compared with a standard of normality. But, as with the confusing classifications of disease, there are many concepts of normality and abnormality. Although the discussion here will primarily be from characterological, social and psychological points of view, in many ways it is relevant to a wide range of medical disorders.

The first three concepts of normality have little to recommend them. Nevertheless, they too easily invade and influence thought about normality, and they need to be known so that one may recognize such assumptions in patients and may guard against them in one's own thinking.

Ideal Fiction. This concept refers to the illusion of the conflict-free man and the perfectly functioning organism. For example, misinterpretation of the tenets and goals of psychoanalysis has led to the belief in the perfectly analyzed person who has no anxiety, fully understands his mental functions and is devoid of conflict. Such a view lacks utility. For one thing, conflict is essential to maturation. Another example is the statement on health in the charter of the World Health Organization: "Health is a state of complete physical, mental and social well-being and not merely the absence of disease and infirmity." If the charter writers of the World Health Organization were to apply their stated criteria exactly, it would be impossible for them to find a single healthy person in the entire world.

The Right or the Good. This view is common among religious fanatics and political zealots. Normality in such cases can serve as a _reaction formation_ against one's own unpleasant wishes and taboos. By reaction formation, we mean that the person represses or denies the unconscious motivation for his "good" behavior. The basis for such a belief usually involves some inarguable premise or revealed truth. Denial, paranoia and polarization are reactions which tend to accompany "the right or the good" view of normality. The prototype of this is the person carrying out a campaign against smutty books in the local library who, in order to know what is smutty, must read all of the salacious, erotic books in the library. The physician, fortunately, seldom makes the mistake of basing his actions on this belief, but it is common among persons whom he must treat or otherwise contend with. Examples are the views of some Catholics about the absolute sinfulness of any abortion and the Bible-based view of Jehovah's Witnesses forbidding transfusions.

What I Am. To some, to be normal is to have the same relevant characteristics as the person making the judgment. This attitude can hold in areas of physical attributes (size, skin color, length of hair), psychological characteristics (spontaneity, sense of humor, perseverence), social customs (religion, child-rearing practices) or politico-economic practices (party allegiance, wealth). Despite the obviously limited utility of such a concept, it is frequent among persons who wish to justify their own behavior and beliefs or who fear any change in those areas. It is in the latter area that the physician may see patients who resist coming for or cooperating in treatment because they have long had the characteristic or problem: "My husband is just a man who has to run around," or "I guess everyone I know gets as anxious as I do, so why should I get help for it?" or "I've smoked this way for 20 years and I figure if it hasn't hurt me by now it ain't a'goin' to."

The next concepts of normality have both utility and limitations.

Health. Health is the absence of disease. We feel "normal" if we do not have a cold, are not anxious, do not hurt anywhere and so on. This view can be misleading in paying attention only to current, surface phenomena. A person may have no symptoms but may have arteriosclerotically clogged arteries which predispose him to a myocardial infarction.

In addition, in the last half-century, emphasis on the study of diseases has moved away from those of a single etiology—such as most infections—to diseases of multiple and often obscure causation. Mental disorders, hypertension, coronary artery disease and cancer are examples. In each, reactions to nonobjective components of the environment play significant roles. These reactions cause us of necessity to place health versus disease on a continuum determined by the balance between those factors _permitting_ effective functioning and those _disrupting_ it. It becomes impossible to assign an absolute worth to any value in terms of where it places one on the continuum; thus the results of a single test, or even a battery of tests, may not yield clear yes or no answers to the questions of a patient's health. This obscuring and complicating of causation contributes to confusion about the too loosely used word "health."

Semantic confusion contributes to some of the false expectations about the health of the public and of ourselves. The use of the word "health" in terms such as health centers, health insurance and health examinations—instead of more accurate terms such as disease centers, disease or illness insurance, etc.—subtly reinforces the notion that it is right or normal to be young, healthy and free of pain and wrong or shameful to be old, sick or uncomfortable. Actually, aging, disease and pain are part of the human condition, and their presence and impact are reducible only in part.

Statistical Normality. A patient is said to be normal if he is 5 feet 9 inches tall, weighs 150 pounds, has three colds per year, plans to have two children and earns $8000 per year. Here we are referring to where a particular characteristic of the patient lies on the bell-shaped curve. But, although statistics can tell us where the person scores, the task of determining at what point we become concerned or when we describe something as abnormal is not always an easy one. It is abnormal, statistically, to be 6 feet 11 inches tall. Yet such an attribute is an asset on the basketball court. In a more medical example, the issue of what limits of the various glucose tolerance tests to consider as normal or, if the patient is beyond those limits, what values necessitate treatment are heatedly argued by authorities.

Molecular Normality. The advances in analytical biochemistry over recent years have allowed the identification of abnormalities at the molecular level. Extrinsically, this may come about through identifying trace amounts of carcinogens in tissues. Intrinsically, genetic protein abnormalities such as sickle cell trait and hemoglobinopathies can be identified. It is not especially helpful to view such molecular data as normal when they represent a statistical majority or have a normal, Gaussian distribution. It is more useful to say that a molecule or gene is normal when it is compatible with well-being, activity, longevity and reproduction of the individual.

Cultural Normality. The practice of breast feedng, the physical distance between persons talking together and the relative spontaneity and expressiveness of feelings vary in terms of cultural norms. It can be normal to be expressive or inhibited. On a spectrum, Italians would be the most gregarious and effusive and the English the most restrained, with Americans somewhere in between. Most cultural patterns are not "normal" or "abnormal." Rather, they are more or less effective in achieving certain goals valued by the culture.

Biological Utility. Sexual discharge, living in groups, the need for close interpersonal ties and the sharing of food are examples of behaviors which seem to be "built into" the human organism. These are not only normative but essential if the society is to survive. Some cultural attitudes breach biological absolutes and are per se abnormal. An example was celibacy among the Shakers in the 19th century. All that remains of those societies are pleasant tourist villages in New England and Kentucky. The 19th century

sexual attitude toward women—the attempt to divorce pleasure and function—is another example. A society which abandoned children would be
abnormal because of the biological necessity for dependent care until 10 to
13 years of age.

Adaptation within the Context of Environmental Change. The adaptational concept of normality is the best single one we have for purposes of
assessing man's behavioral life. Here the measure of normality is the flexibility
and the freedom to learn through experience, to change when internal and
external circumstances change, to be influenced by reasonable argument, to
respond appropriately to rewards and punishments and the ability to cease
responding when satiated. This definition implies: (1) a general happiness, a
pleasure in functioning; (2) adaptation to one's own biological and physiological make-up; (3) adaptation to the external environment; (4) adaptation
to the reality of one's own history; (5) both *shaping* and *being shaped* by the
above; (6) efficiency—some things are best done automatically.

The physician needs to respond largely automatically when treating a
patient in status epilepticus or ketoacidosis, just as the pianist does in playing
the piano. The beginning pianist's finger movements are self-conscious,
deliberate and slow. But the talented pianist plays automatically in terms of
which notes to strike, thus freeing himself to be concerned with the nuances,
emotional overtones and phrasing of the piece, which takes it into the realm
of fine art. This ever-fluctuating balance between attention and automatism
is a characteristic of most complex skills, including most of those which the
physician uses.

Abnormality

From an adaptational point of view, abnormality is the tendency to choose
a type of reaction which represents an escape from conflict-producing situations instead of facing the problem. Extending this definition into the
physiological realm, Engel has referred to disease as a failure of the organism
to cope with forces originating within itself or its environment which disrupt
its dynamic steady state.

Behavior is abnormal if the processes that set it in motion predetermine its
automatic repetition, irrespective of the situation, the utility value or the
consequences of the act. Stereotypy of behavior is the hallmark of abnormality. Rigidity of behavior in some areas may be a cultural norm and, thus, in
some senses not be "abnormal" except that it leads to restriction of function.

*   *   *   *

The diagnostic process is one of the greatest challenges in medicine. To it
the physician can fully apply his power of logic, his ability to empathize with
the patient and his knowledge of disease and of psychological, social and
environmental factors in the patient's illness.

What more may physicians do to optimize the skill with which they approach the patient and apply the diagnostic process to his illness?

In the area of his relationship with the patient the physician should be aware of the limits of sympathy. The danger is loss of objectivity. The physician cannot afford the luxury of being hurt by the patient's slights and inconsistencies, nor can he afford to share in the patient's fears. A proper amount of courage is required to practice good medicine. This does not mean that the physician must proceed coldly and with detachment. He or she can warmly respond and candidly deal with the range of problems a patient may have, if he preserves his own sense of identity.

One reason for including the material on normality is that the physician is often asked to "diagnose" or to rule on things outside his area of expertise. This invitation stems from his status in the community, the wish to give the stamp of professional legitimacy to a decision or a program or to have the physician pass judgment on ethical or political issues over which the public feels inexpert, anxious or even guiltily ambivalent. Thus the physician is asked to promote a fund-raising drive for a chronic disease or a new school, to testify about a man's insanity at the time of a crime or to assess the competence of an elderly man. At times, in particular contexts, these may be appropriate. But the physician should know the limits of his expertise and should have every right to state those limits and not extend his activities beyond them.

This last leads to Homer Smith's comments about the application of the scientific method, with its implications for what I have been writing on these pages about the practice of medicine.

"In essence, the scientific method consists of careful observation of nature, and cautious confirmation of all conclusions to the exclusion of unsubstantiated hypotheses. A scientist is one who, when he does not know the answer, is rigorously disciplined to speak up and say so unashamedly; which is the essential feature by which modern science is distinguished from primitive superstition, which knew all the answers except how to say, 'I do not know.' "

REFERENCES

1. BEATON, L. E. Toward a definition of adequate health care. *Pharos 28:*2–9, 1965. (A moving consideration of physicians' ethical obligations.)
2. BEECHER, H. *The Measurement of Subjective Responses: Quantitative Effects of Drugs.* Oxford University Press, New York, 1959. (A classic on the study of pain.)
3. BOLINGER, R. E., AND AHLERS, P. The science of "pattern recognition." *J.A.M.A. 233:* 1289–1290, 1975.
4. BURSTEIN, A. G., LOUCKS, S., KOBOS, J. C., AND STANTON, B. Psychological characteristics of medical students and residents. *J. Med. Educ.* (in press).
5. ENGEL, G. L. The education of the physician for clinical observation. *J. Nerv. Ment. Dis. 154:* 159, 1972.
6. HINKLE, L., AND WOLFF, H. G. Ecologic investigations of the relationship between illness, life experience and social environment. *Ann. Intern. Med. 49:*1373, 1957.
7. KIMBALL, C. P. The experience of psychological responses to open-heart surgery. *Psychosom.*

*Med. 30:*552, 1968.

8. LYNCH, J. J. *The Broken Heart—The Medical Consequences of Loneliness.* Basic Books, New York, 1977.

9. MARTIN, H. W., AND PRANGE, A. J. Human adaptation: a conceptual approach to understanding patients. *Can. Nurse 58:*234–243, 1962.

10. McWHINNEY, I. R. Beyond diagnosis: an approach to the integration of behavioral science and clinical medicine. *N. Engl. J. Med. 287:*384, 1972.

11. OFFER, D., AND SABSHIN, M. *Normality: Theoretical and Clinical Concepts of Mental Health.* Basic Books, New York, 1966.

12. PILOWSKY, J., AND BOND, M. R. Pain and its management in malignant disease. Elucidation of staff-patient transactions. *Psychosom. Med. 31:*400, 1969.

13. RAHE, R. H., O'NEIL, T., HAGAN, A., AND RANSON, J. A. Brief group therapy following myocardial infarction: eighteen month follow-up of a controlled trial. *Int. J. Psychiatry Med. 6:*349–358, 1975.

14. SMITH, H. W. *From Fish to Philosopher.* Little, Brown and Company, Boston, 1953, p. 230.

15. SUSSER, M. W., AND WATSON, W. *Sociology in Medicine.* Oxford University Press, London, 1971.

16. TUFO, H. M., AND OSTFELD, A. M. A prospective study of open-heart surgery. *Psychosom. Med. 30:*552, 1968.

17. WISHNIE, H. A., HACKETT, T. P., AND CASSEM, N. H. Psychological hazards of convalescence following myocardial infarction. *J.A.M.A. 215:*1292–1296, 1971.

18. ZOLA, I. K. Pathways to the doctor: from person to patient. *Soc. Sci. Med. 7:*677–689, 1973.

CHAPTER 2

THE THERAPEUTIC RELATIONSHIP: II SOCIOCULTURAL AND ECONOMIC FACTORS

CHARLES L. BOWDEN, M.D.

An array of variables beyond the immediate physician-patient relationship influence medical care. These sociocultural factors have assumed greater importance in recent years for several reasons. The direct impact on the physician and patient of private and public policy—through insurance plans, regulation and the like—is greater than at any past time. We are beginning to have data from health planners, sociologists, epidemiologists and other scientists which indicate some specifics of that impact. The health professional is in a position to use this information to motivate patients toward more effective, healthful practices and to influence social policy in these areas.

Sociocultural Factors

When the patient defines himself as ill, the following sociocultural factors influence how he responds to that definition and whom he seeks for help.

Socioeconomic Class. Koos asked individuals to identify, from a group of 17 symptoms, which ones should be brought to the attention of a physician. More than three-fourths of the business and professional classes but less than one-fourth of the blue collar group believed that the following 7 symptoms were important enough to be called to the attention of a physician: persistent joint and muscle spasm, swelling of ankles, loss of weight, bleeding gums, chronic fatigue, shortness of breath and persistent headaches. Among the 17 symptoms offered, none was considered a reason to go to the doctor by as many as .three-fourths of the blue collar group. Obviously, business and professional class patients have a broader view of what problems constitute illness and entitle them to seek medical assistance than do blue collar workers.

Poor and less educated persons have greater morbidity, disability and mortality in general, not just for stress diseases or infections. This difference by socioeconomic class is not new; the basic ratios have not changed since 1900. Furthermore, it is a phenomenon observed all over the world. In the U.S., the mortality of the lowest socioeconomic group is 64% greater in white males and 105% greater in white females compared to the over-all rates for those in the 25 to 64 age group. Although blacks have over-all hypertension rates somewhat higher than the over-all population, those blacks in the lower socioeconomic classes have rates much higher than the average. Access to care does not appear to account for this difference nor does utilization; lower socioeconomic classes actually have higher rates of utilization than do middle and upper groups. Crowding and more toxic environments appear not to account for these differences. Possible factors include the lower literacy and educational levels of the poor, the greater prevalence (six-fold) of obesity, higher smoking levels (twice as high) and a higher frequency of stressful life changes such as moving and job change.

Ethnic Group. Marked differences in response to pain have been observed among different ethnic groups. One excellent study found that Anglo-Saxon Americans de-emphasized pain and reported it unemotionally but described it precisely and differentiated its severity. Jewish patients described pain with great precision but did not differentiate its severity. Italians gave poorly differentiated accounts of both the location and degree of their pain. Both Jews and Italians emphasized pain and described all pain as "very severe." Irish patients de-emphasized responses to pain and gave vague, poorly differentiated accounts of it. Jewish patients promptly consulted their physicians when pain became apparent, whereas Anglo-Saxon Americans delayed seeking help.

Among Mexican-Americans studied in southern California and south Texas, men, in particular, resisted the sick role because seeking help was not "manly." To be sick, especially to be mentally ill, was to risk loss of respect within the barrio. These Mexican-Americans tended to blame external forces for their illnesses or, in the case of emotional disorders, to attribute the cause to organic disease. There is a frequent use of folk medicine, as distinguished from scientific medicine. The curandero, or folk healer, develops a close and trusting relationship with his patient. He is frequently able to help by offering the patient an opportunity to talk and to relate to a wise elder, as well as by suggesting a cause and treatment consistent with the patient's religious and cultural expectations. These examples illustrate how clear understanding and appropriate treatment can be facilitated by awareness of the patient's cultural traditions.

Denial of Illness. Within any culture, persons may ignore or deny even gross symptoms. This is particularly likely to happen when (1) the condition is widespread, (2) there is no effective or inexpensive remedy for it or (3) symptoms are episodic and do not threaten the community welfare. Colds, allergic reactions and menstrually related emotional disorders are frequently responded to in this way in the United States.

Rituals for Episodic Illness. Traditional folk remedies exist for many episodic illnesses. Prophylactically, for example, a mother may give her asymptomatic child a dose of milk of magnesia to "clean him out." Therapeutically, these folk remedies include such generally harmless nostrums as aloe vera for burns, a hot toddy for a cold and various procedures to remove warts or to abort hiccups. Likewise, some consider a penicillin shot as the ritual treatment for colds. It sometimes happens that a folk remedy is found to have a scientific basis.

Disorders of Habit

In discussing the sick role earlier, we spoke of a person's right to have his health care needs met. An equally important counterpart is that the individual should have the social obligation to preserve his own health. Consider the general evidence. The U.S. spends more on health care than any other nation, yet the male life expectancy is lower than that in more than 15 other countries. Although seat belts practically ensure survival in auto accidents occurring below 50 miles per hour, less than 10% of motorists regularly fasten them. Over 50 percent of all deaths are from cardiovascular diseases, frequently associated with obesity, lack of exercise and smoking. Nearly 100,000 deaths each year result from lung cancer caused principally by smoking. The lung cancer rate has increased most dramatically in women, tripling in less than 20 years; this is largely a function of increased smoking among women. The third major cause of death is stroke, contributed to by arteriosclerosis and hypertension, the latter often able to be controlled by weight reduction, exercise, reduction in use of stimulants and quitting smoking. One half of all accidents—the fourth leading cause of death in the U.S.—are involved with motor vehicles. Half are associated with alcohol intoxication.

Although environmental pollutants which we cannot individually avoid such as phosphates, DDT, microwaves and radioactivity pose real health problems, most physicians have never seen a death from one of such causes. By contrast, they daily see death at too young an age by the things people do, or fail to do, to themselves. Eighty per cent of cirrhosis of the liver is due to alcoholism. One-third of all suicides are related to alcoholism or drug abuse. Cigarette smokers have 45 percent more sick time than nonsmokers. Appallingly, the list can be extended almost endlessly.

There are important cautions in interpreting such data. All disease is not disease of habit, auto-pollution or behavioral disease, terms sometimes applied to self-destructive behaviors. Many are multifactorial, with contributing genetic, constitutional and host-vector variables. Some habits were not always known to be self-destructive. A distinction needs to be made between individuals who are ignorant of the health consequences of their behavior and those who are fully cognizant but persist in smoking, drinking and eating excessively.

Our failure to recognize and effectively treat persons with these voluntary disorders is compounded by the subsequent effects on their children. Children are twice as likely to smoke if their parents did and 10 times more likely to be alcoholic if one parent was.

Too often, the approach of physicians, the public and politicians is solely to increase the expenditure for treatment of end-stage diseases. More doctors, greater use of high cost technologies and national health insurance are presented as solutions to these problems of health. It is becoming increasingly clear that crusades to find the cure for cancer are of limited benefit and that, from an over-all population standpoint, much greater emphasis should be given to encouraging habits and life-styles conducive to feeling and remaining well.

John Knowles, President of the Rockefeller Foundation, writes of this objective:

> The barriers to the assumption of responsibility for one's own health are lack of knowledge (implicating the inadequacies of formal education, the too-powerful force of advertising, and the informal systems of continuing education), lack of sufficient interest in the knowledge about what is preventable and the cost/benefit ratios of nationwide health programs (implicating the powerful interests in the health environment, which could not be less interested, and calling for a much larger investment in fundamental and applied research), and a culture which has progressively eroded the idea of individual responsibility while stressing individual rights, the responsibility of society at large, and the steady growth of production and consumption ("We have met the enemy and he is us!").

Imbuing people with healthy attitudes is not easy. It is not known in all cases which behavior patterns do pay off with reduced morbidity. Physicians themselves have tended to view these kinds of problems as not legitimate medical concerns. But in many ways it is more instructive to look upon emphysema and lung cancer as symptoms of the disease of smoking. Because physicians often lack specific treatment skills to deal with such conditions, it is not surprising that many patients fall into the hands of charlatans and pseudoscientists proclaiming new, miraculous and effortless treatments for problems such as obesity. Genuinely effective interventions are likely to require the individual's special effort—going to the dentist, using contraceptives, working to establish a harmonious family life and exercising.

Physicians and others working with them on the health-care team will need to develop skills in the area generally known as behavioral medicine.

Several sections of this book deal with subsets of these skills—how to improve compliance (Chapter 3), modifying the treatment approach based on the patient's personality and applying principles of learning theory. Other areas will need to be further developed. As an example, most smokers begin smoking as teenagers. There is no single moment of decision to become a smoker. Rather a complex induction period over several years leads to an eventual ingrained pattern. Intervention during this transitional period of learning the habit should be more effective than efforts aimed at reversing a smoking habit of 20 years' duration.

Structural Factors in Health Care

Interrelating with the above factors are a host of structural factors involving fees, insurance incentives, public and political attitudes and even language practices.

Physician's Fees. To a considerable extent physician's fees are outside the usual laws of supply and demand. In some cases, fees actually go up as the per capita number of physicians increases. With fewer patients and fewer opportunities for surgery, some physicians raise their fees sufficiently to attain a targeted income level. In 1939 physicians' fees were less than twice as high as those of a broad range of other professional people. In 1975, their earnings were four times as high. It is not anticompetitive practices which account for this, because physicians individually and organizationally have supported the expansion of the nation's medical schools. Most of the fee inflation can be ascribed to the increased percentage of income used for insurance payments and the large degree to which physicians have been able to determine the costs of their services. It is the surgical intervention for end-stage disease which commands the highest fees. Highest incomes accrue to hospital-based physicians, primarily pathologists and radiologists, who, in 1975, earned an average of $138,000 and $122,000, respectively—more than twice the median income of self-employed physicians.

The leveraging of income contributes greatly to cost escalation. This occurs either on the basis of income rising in disproportion to time spent (in the case of hospital-based pathologists) because the number of services billed for determines income or the willingness of insurers and patients to pay fees for surgical procedures which are disproportionately higher than those charged for nonoperative medical services.

Other Medical Costs. Although physician's fees have risen faster than inflation, other medical costs have risen even faster. Health-care costs accounted for 4.6% of the gross national product in 1950 but almost 9% in 1978. Whereas over-all health-care costs rose at an annual rate of 9.5% in the mid 1970's, hospital costs, which accounted for 40% of all costs, rose at a rate of over 17%. One reason for the extremely high cost of the renal dialysis program is that it was established to favor more expensive hospital-based dialysis rather than less costly home-based or clinic dialysis. The number of acute care hospital beds in the country is 10% greater than optimally required, contributing significantly to rising hospital costs.

Number and Distribution of Physicians. The rapid expansion of numbers of medical schools and class sizes appears to have at least ensured that there will be no over-all numerical shortages of physicians. Indeed, some authorities believe that an excessive number of physicians are currently being educated. Problems of distribution geographically and by specialty remain. Relatively few physicians elect to practice in rural areas. The reasons include problems with overwork, lack of colleague stimulation, difficulty in accomplishing continuing education and, until recently, a decline in the number of primary care physicians. A resurgence of interest in primary care fields, especially family practice, has resulted in approximately 50% of current graduates entering family practice, internal medicine and pediatrics. Most authorities believe that an excessive number of surgeons are being trained. The consequences of this are that many surgeons do not perform as many operations as they wish and are able to perform, resulting in difficulty maintaining optimal skills, a tendency to increase per case fees, and the election of surgical intervention when it might otherwise not have been the treatment of choice.

In 1978, the Institute of Medicine of the National Academy of Science made recommendations to deal with some of these problems. They asked for a moratorium on increasing the number of medical students, stating that the expanded enrollments of the 1960's and 1970's had eliminated the doctor shortage and noting that each new physician adds $250,000 annually to the nation's health bill. They recommended that insurers not pay for specialist care unless it had been requested by the patient's primary physician, and that primary care physicians and specialists be paid the same fee for the same work. They proposed that the practice of paying city doctors more than rural doctors for the same service be eliminated.

An additional factor which drives up costs is the illusion that someone else is paying for it. About this, Joseph Califano, current Secretary of the Department of Health, Education and Welfare, has said, "The doctor's ordering a service he's not paying for. In the hospital, the patient's probably not paying for it. The third party carrier pays for 90% of those hospital costs, so there is no incentive at any point except for him to give every conceivable test he thinks might in one way or another be relevant. Even a few that aren't relevant."

Inadequate Evaluation. Various disease treatments are initiated without adequate cognizance of their efficacy or cost. Rarely have any surgical procedures undergone double-blind, placebo-controlled studies. Although such test procedures are often awkward and sometimes unwarranted, they can generally be accomplished. Such pilot testing could have reduced the current controversies over whether breast cancer is best treated by radical dissection or by less invasive, more conservative measures. Similarly such pilot testing might have allowed clarification of the utility of coronary bypass surgery, a $5,000 to $10,000 operation which is currently under heated debate. The nationally funded renal dialysis program for Americans with kidney failure was predicted to cost no more than a few million dollars annually, but costs for 1977 exceeded $1 billion, half of the entire budget for the National Institute of Health. Evaluation either in the way of pilot programs or building evaluation components on a wide scale into newly initiated programs could provide more knowledgeable decisions regarding costs and benefits.

External Regulation. Regulatory agencies have increasingly influenced the practice and the cost of medicine. In all cases these regulations are well intended. We want hospitals which are safe, yet accreditation standards sometimes result in what is obligatory with one agency being forbidden by another. Fetal defects and long term side effects from new drugs need scrupulous identification. However, most authorities believe that excessive bureaucratic documentation and lack of willingness to accept data from even well executed studies performed outside the U.S. are resulting in several-year delays in marketing effective drugs available in European countries and in much more expensive unit costs of drugs, inasmuch as the developmental costs are of necessity passed along to the purchaser. Fully informed consent is a moral obligation which all physicians view as necessary. However, the complexities of obtaining approval for some human studies and the trivialization of some of the required statements result in able investigators not performing potentially beneficial studies and being deterred from developing their research capabilities.

Changes in Public Attitude. The public's attitude toward physicians is less favorable than in past decades. Much of this reflects a disenchantment with all persons in roles of authority and a somewhat cynical distrust of such persons. However, physicians are still held highest in esteem of all professional groups. An exhaustive Canadian report of public attitudes about physicians showed the following responses to the question, "What is the single most important quality you look for in a doctor?" Forty-six per cent said good human relations, 34% said competence, 17% said service and 2% gave other desired qualities.

Even our words can mold our thoughts. "Delivery of care" is used as if medical care were like the mail. "Health-care industry" suggests that medicine is an aggregate of manufacturing enterprises. (To call patients "consumers" implies that they are basically passive, without responsibility for their own health, quite distorting the optimal relationship necessary, especially for patients with chronic disorders.) Awareness of these trends at least allows us to have a chance to control their consequences. These tendencies to cast medicine in business contexts are likely to continue, due to our industrialized, corporate and bureaucratic society. In the main, these trends are to be resisted because they cause those in the medical fields and the public to have expectation sets which either cannot be attained—complete health without personal responsibility—or they mercantilize the doctor-patient relationship just at the first time in history when physicians are indeed able to be both humane and scientific.

This chapter has summarized a host of "public" factors which negatively affect the practice of medicine and the health of Americans. This focus is not intended to gainsay the great strengths of American medicine nor the utility of high technology procedures and equipment. It is to say that decisions as to when and how to use them properly need to be cautiously made. If the private sector does not adequately regulate itself, it is likely that long term forces will impel us toward ever greater governmental regulation. It suggests that the traditional view of equating degree of health with numbers and availability of physicians and hospitals is incomplete and misleading. What is called for if we are to improve our level of health is a greater shift toward individual responsibility for reducing self-imposed risks, emphasis on prevention, improving the environment and advancing our knowledge of human biology and treatment benefits, risks and costs.

*   *   *   *

The physician's direct role may seem limited in these problems, but it is critical. The most effective and easily implemented preventive measures are those which require the least individual responsibility, such as pure water, sanitation and immunization procedures. The most difficult measures, such as controlling smoking, diet and obesity, require more individual responsibility and are less amenable to governmental intervention. Public health education is helpful, but knowledge alone has a very small effect on individual behavior, especially after a harmful behavior is established. Smokers, for example, are much less likely to be influenced by educational media in their comprehension of cancer risks from smoking than are nonsmokers. The potential role for physicians and other health professionals in individual, effectively motivating educational efforts is great.

REFERENCES

1. CULLITON, B. J. Health care economics: the high cost of getting well. *Science 200*:883, 1978. (This entire issue contains trenchant assessments on health in the U.S. from a variety of perspectives.)
2. KNOWLES, J. H. *Doing Better and Feeling Worse: Health in the United States.* W. W. Norton, New York, 1977.
3. KOOS, E. L. *The Health of Regionville.* Columbia University Press, New York, 1954.
4. LASAGNA, L. The development and regulation of new medications. *Science 200*:871–873, 1978.
5. SORENSON, A., AND SAWARD, E. The current emphasis on preventive medicine. *Science 200*: 889–894, 1978.
6. SYME, S. L., AND BERKMAN, L. F. Social class, susceptibility and sickness. *Am. J. Epidemiol. 104*:1–8, 1976.
7. THURLOW, H. J. General susceptibility to illness. *Can. J. Med. 97*:1397–1404, 1967.
8. ZBOROWSKI, M. *People in Pain.* Jossey-Bass, San Francisco, 1969.

CHAPTER 3

THE THERAPEUTIC RELATIONSHIP: III INTERVIEW SKILLS

CHARLES L. BOWDEN, M. D.

The fundamental characteristic of the doctor-patient relationship is the need of the patient to be able to place himself under the care of the physician with trust and confidence. Part of this, of course, comes from the patient's response to such things as diplomas and office atmosphere. More important is that the physician display the characteristics previously described in the social role of the physician. Continuity of care within the therapeutic relationship allows for the building of new information on an old foundation and increases the implicit emotional support in the relationship. The therapeutic relationship is a flexible one, both in nature and depth of contact. As previously discussed, some visits may be made for an annual physical examination or for help for a minor disorder, whereas at other times the contact may be frequent and require detailed exploration of the patient's physical and personal life.

Types of Doctor-Patient Relationship

Szasz and Hollender have usefully described three modes of doctor-patient interaction. The first of these is the *active-passive* mode. In it the physician uses all of the authority inherent in his role, and the patient does not actively participate in his treatment. It is generally applicable to emergent situations, such as the care of a severely injured auto accident victim.

The *guidance-cooperation* mode is one in which the physician still exercises considerable authority, but the patient is expected to cooperate with the effectiveness of his active cooperation being a factor in determining the outcome. This mode is most appropriate to a number of acute diseases, such as pneumonia, and to the recuperative phase of most surgery.

In the *mutual participation* mode the patient is expected to be actively responsible for his treatment. The physician works in a collaborative way with the patient and must use persuasion, not his authority, to obtain the ends both he and the patient desire. The degree of dependence of the patient on the physician is much less in this type of relationship than in the other two. Some dependence is useful and normal in emergent and acute disorders. But, in general, the physician should encourage the patient to take as much responsibility as is appropriate to the kind of disorder and to the stage of treatment. The best physician is able to move freely among these three models as the situation changes. The mutual participation model is especially important in diagnostic interviewing and in the management of chronic disorders.

In the last analysis, patients with chronic diseases must largely be their own physicians. Many studies document the high degree of noncompliance in such disorders as diabetes, hypertension and schizophrenia. Two important, related reasons for this are that physicians tend to neglect education of the patient about his disorder and its management and that they tend to assume a more authoritarian role than circumstances warrant. This is in part a result of clinical learning as a medical student, which predominantly occurs in inpatient settings dealing mainly with the acute phase of illnesses and with serious disease management.

In the 20th century, several other factors make the importance of the mutual participation model greater. First, the "crowd" diseases, such as plague and typhoid fever, have largely been eliminated as a result of epidemiological medicine. The infectious diseases have, likewise, largely come under wider control through a combination of public health measures, vaccination and antibiotics. Thus the major medical concerns of 20th-century man are the chronic diseases, which are multifactorial in origin (with stress a significant factor), and, with our increased longevity, diseases related to the aging process, such as heart disease, stroke and cancer. Second, although doctors 50 years ago had about as much education as they now do, most of their patients had much less than a high school education. That education gap has narrowed greatly. And the gap is likely to be less with the average patient in office practice than it is with those encountered by the medical student. Finally, societal changes stressing the importance of personal freedom underscore the concept of informed consent as a crucial component of the doctor-patient relationship. Legally and morally the patient's decision to cooperate or participate in the treatment process must be as active as possible and made in the light of relevant information.

Interviewing Skills

Within the doctor-patient relationship the single most important activity of the physician is talking with the patient. Much of the data in the rest of this book will help the physician to determine interview strategy on the basis of the person's stage in life, his personality and the particular situation in which the interview is occurring. Before that, there are basic skills which apply to most medical interviews.

Opening the Interview

Much is covertly conveyed by the process by which the doctor introduces himself. Does he acknowledge the appropriateness of introduction at all? Does he stress the patient's "inferior" status by brusquely assuming the right to require cooperation or to unilaterally define the manner in which the patient is to be addressed? It is appropriate to attend to social proprieties during an initial visit—to welcome the patient, make sure you have his name right and, in general, convey that you regard him as a consequential person. For example, "Mr. Braun, I'm Doctor Smith. I'm pleased to meet you. Please have a chair."

With the introduction done, one can begin by asking about the problems which brought the patient to the physician. Appropriate first questions are "Tell me about the problems you have been having" or "What are the troubles which bring you in today?" Such a beginning tells the patient that you are interested in him and his problems and encourages him to discuss anything which he feels may be important. It allows the physician to learn quickly which problems the patient considers most important and gives him information about the way the patient approaches his problems—whether he minimizes, exaggerates, rationalizes or circumstantially evades the real issues. It also says to the patient that the physician wishes him to take as much responsibility and initiative in his own treatment as is compatible with good patient care. This approach to interviewing minimizes bias, which can easily be introduced when questions are detailed and directive. Let us briefly consider the most polar alternative approach to medical interviewing: the interrogative-directive, or the "district attorney" type. This approach is to ask a large number of specific questions, the answers to which are usually brief or are simply yes or no. This approach does not encourage the patient to amplify his responses; rather, the amount of information is largely predetermined by the way the question is asked. Such questioning says to the patient, "I'm in control, you follow my lead." It suggests a rather passive role for the patient. The patient may be so distracted by the rapid-fire questions that he forgets to report important symptoms, or he assumes that the physician is not interested. Some medical situations call for this authoritarian type of interview (for example, the emergency room interview if a patient is in acute pain).

The interview should proceed with the patient telling his story in his own words. This minimizes bias which can be interjected when the words are chosen by the physician in a directive approach. If the patient is having difficulty in going on with his story, several facilitating comments may help. The physician may say, "Tell me more about the pain in your chest," or "You were saying about the pain in your chest" or he may simply repeat in an expectant manner the last words the patient used, suggesting that he continue on the subject " . . . pain in the chest."

The more general and open-ended the question the better, especially early in the elucidation of an area. For example, in obtaining a family history, the first question or request should contain only enough information to make clear the subject on which the patient is expected to respond: "Tell me about your parents" is thus a better statement than "Tell me about your mother," as it allows the patient to select which person he will talk about and it may provide information about the way they interrelate. "What is the pain like?" is a better question than "Is the pain sharp or dull?"

As the interview progresses, specific questions will be called for both to fill in areas of the history which the patient has not covered and to complete the data needed in a particular area. As a rule, move from general, open-ended statements to specific, delineated ones. Do not accept a statement until it is as clear as possible. If a patient states that he is "nervous," one should not accept the statement as sufficient but should inquire how he experiences his nervousness.

General Guidelines Regarding Questions and Instructions

In assessing the patient's problems, the following areas are covered.

Bodily Locations. Most complaints can be localized to a specific portion of the body. Even many emotional complaints, such as nervousness or fear, are usually experienced in portions of the body. Only a few sensations are not localizable and those, such as hunger, joy, anger and sleepiness, do not hamper the characterization of the experience for diagnostic purposes. Inquiry to localize problems can be initiated with questions such as "What part of your head hurts?" or "Where did you feel the nervousness?" or "Does the pain go anywhere?"

Quality. Complaints are characterized as acute or chronic, as sharp or dull and by analogy, such as the pain of myocardial infarction being "like having one's chest crushed," or dyspnea being "like" suffocation. Inquiry in this area is best begun by asking, "What was it like?" If the response is unclear, a statement such as "What do you mean by 'gripping?' " or "Was it sharp, or dull, or aching or what?" can be helpful.

Quantity. The quantitative aspect refers to the intensity of the stress perceived (mild to unbearable), the degree of functional impairment (usually based on a description of everyday activities) and the frequency, volume, number and size of symptoms.

Questions concerning intensity are best framed in personal and comparative terms. The query, "How severe was it?" encourages the patient to elaborate in personal terms. Similarly, the question "Was this the worst it has ever been?" or "How would you compare this with your spell a year ago?" provides an estimate of severity.

Questions which get at functional impairment are best asked concerning everyday tasks: "Are you able to do your housework?" or "Can you fully dress yourself?" or "How far can you walk before you get short of breath?" An especially useful source of data in this and several areas of inquiry is to ask the patient how a full day went for him, starting with when he arose and what he then did in a step-by-step fashion throughout the day until he retired. It is best to ask about a specific day, usually the one before the day of examination, as the response will yield more vivid, clear-cut information. Many physicians will wish to record this as a separate part of the work-up in the problem-oriented medical record.

Questions concerning frequency, volume, number and size should begin with a general statement, such as "How many beers do you drink each day?" Nonspecific answers should always be followed up: "When you say 'a few,' what do you mean? Would you say more or less than six beers a day?" By such a process, the interviewer may gradually have a specific figure as well as some idea of the accuracy and validity of the figure, based on the clarity or haziness of the person's memory and his tendency to minimize or to exaggerate symptoms.

Chronology. The time of onset, duration and frequency and the time course (Does it get better, worse or stay the same with time?) are to be determined. This dimension usually is the one most helpful in organizing and clarifying the patient's symptoms. Question such as "When was that?," "What happened next?" and "Then what?" not only yield important data at the time but also suggest to the patient that he pay attention to the chronology in the spontaneous account of his story.

Setting. Symptoms develop in relationship to (1) some place—at work, at home, in the patient's car; (2) some activity—eating, arguing, walking; (3)

some person—boss, wife, police officer. Understanding these factors can especially help the physician to understand the matrix of the patient's life which influences his disorder and which is, in turn, influenced by that disorder. The physician is then in a position to take these factors into account in his treatment plans. The initial questions in this area are easily put: "Where were you when it began?"; "In what situations do you find yourself getting anxious?"; "Was anyone there to help you when it happened?" As the physician has hunches about possible diagnoses, he may ask questions concerning etiological factors. When concerned about the possible cause of liver damage, he may ask whether the person has worked in an area around, or has used, any cleaning compound such as carbon tetrachloride.

Aggravating and Alleviating Factors. Such questions as "Is there anything you can do to relieve your headache?" or "What did you do for it?" or "Is there anything else that helps?" encourage the patient in this area. In two important instances, the patient may withhold information in this area of the history. Patients with problems primarily in the emotional area may be self-medicating themselves with alcohol, barbiturates or other harmful drugs to alleviate anxiety or to alter their moods. They are often reluctant to relate this. In the second case, the patient may have tried a remedy which, although not harmful, was embarrassing. This especially applies when the person has used folk remedies or has done something on the advice of a friend, pharmacist or relative, or when the person has used a nonmedical healer. (For example, a Mexican-American may have used herbs from a curandero but chooses not to relate this out of fear of embarrassment.)

As the student physician becomes more adept in recognizing clinical syndromes, certain questions will have additional usefulness in this area. For example, the pain of angina pectoris is characteristically relieved within 1 to 2 minutes by sublingual nitroglycerin. So, if the patient is taking nitroglycerin for any chest pains, information about the speed of relief is important. The questions should be phrased so as not to admit bias or suggest the "right" answer. Rather than, "After you took the nitroglycerin did the pain go away within 2 minutes?," the patient should be asked "What happened after you took the nitroglycerin?" or "How long was it before the pain subsided?"

Associated Symptoms. It is rare that one symptom appears in isolation. Usually the patient will report other problems, generally less troubling to him, in other organ systems. As the student of medicine becomes more knowledgeable about symptom complexes, he will learn about what to inquire. For example, the patient who is tearful and depressed may often have a poor appetite, weight loss and diminished interest in sex and may awaken in the middle of the night or be constipated.

Instructing the Patient. Questions and instructions should be as simple and as brief as possible. The patient's educational background, intelligence and attitude toward his illness should be taken into account. Nevertheless, even with a well educated person, the physician will generally do better to use the simpler word when two terms are available. Medical terms should especially be avoided. "Did your skin ever turn yellow?" is preferable to "Did you ever have jaundice?" One reason for this is that the connotation a patient gives a word may be quite different from that which the physician gives it. This suggests two other general guidelines. First, a patient's statement that he had an "ulcer" or a "nervous breakdown" should always be pursued until it is fully clear what symptoms or illness he is actually describing. Second, in the area of diagnosis and instruction, the physician should try to establish a common ground of meaning with the patient. How a patient interprets the term diabetes or arthritis can only be determined (and then not always) through a candid discussion with him. This is essential, because anxiety or denial concerning a disease state (the adolescent's inability to accept the fact that he is diabetic or the schizophrenic patient's difficulty accepting his illness, based in both cases on the life-long implications of the diseases and the damages to self-esteem which the "injury" causes) or misconceptions concerning disease (the patient with a renal infection who stops his antibiotics as soon as dysuria abates) are major factors in patients' failures to follow through with treatment. The physician should be explicit in his instructions to the patient. One patient told to drink "a lot" will drown himself, while another will drink one glassful between meals. Clarification such as "Drink a total of about 16 ounces every 4 hours" minimizes this response range.

When indicated, make a special effort to explain that the patient should continue to take medication even though he is feeling well. It is difficult for many patients to understand that, in many disorders, there is no relationship between feeling better and no longer needing the drug.

Only one question should be asked at a time. Similarly, the patient should be given instructions one at a time and should have an opportunity to ask questions to clarify any points of confusion. It is useful to have the patient recite the intended treatment regimen. This can be done in a statement such as "Let's see if you're clear about taking this new medicine, Mr. Jones," made with the expectation that he will relay his understanding of the number of pills to be taken at what time of day.

Patients usually do not ask about all of their concerns. This is often because the physician appears overly busy to the patient, who is thus reluctant to ask a question. Patients are sometimes awed by physicians and feel they should in no way have a complementary relationship with them. Patients' anxiety, fear and pain may distract their attention from instructions. Poor patients in particular are not likely to express their main worries to the physician. As a group, they tend not to understand technical terms, feel the physician does not expect them to ask questions and sense a greater social distance between themselves and the physician.

There is good evidence that simple efforts to improve communication of information about the illness help with outcome. Actively encouraging the patients' questions can overcome much of this. Those underinformed about their illnesses and treatment are the ones most likely not to comply with the regimen. Pediatric compliance is significantly improved if the child's mother is called by her name and is praised for something she is doing well. Anesthesiologists' telling patients what to expect in the immediate pre- and postoperative periods reduced narcotic analgesic use by one-half. Such kinds of instruction reduce uncertainty and allow the patient to do the "work of worrying" in advance.

Prescription Instructions. One aspect of medical care which is especially prone to misinterpretation by the patient is instruction about prescriptions. Studies indicate that 30 to 70% of outpatients fail to take their medications as prescribed. The rationale for a particular regimen should be discussed with the patient. Indicate what can be expected in terms of speed of response, the time necessary for an adequate trial of the medication and the kinds of steps to be taken if the current medication and dose are not efficacious. Side effects which are likely to occur should routinely be discussed with all patients. The patient should be told about potentially dangerous side effects which should cause him to call the physician or to alter the treatment regimen. Some side effects, such as sedation or diminished alertness, may be only temporary but require restriction in driving or other potentially dangerous activities and should be discussed. Information about side effects should be varied somewhat depending on the personality of the patient. The rigid, obsessive, controlling patient generally benefits from an especially detailed and full disclosure, because greater knowledge increases his sense of control.

Specific times for taking the medication should be indicated. "At bedtime" may be interpreted to mean any time from dinner until the actual moment of retiring, when your actual intent is that the medication be taken 30 minutes before retiring. Vague instructions such as "take as necessary" are to be avoided. Phrases which are self-evident to the physician or nurse may be misunderstood by the patient. "Take as necessary for fluid retention" is misinterpreted by some patients to mean that taking the medicine will produce fluid retention. Even words such as diarrhea and constipation are misunderstood by about one-third of patients. In addition to asking the patient to explain what you have told him, comprehension and thus compliance can be further improved by the use of pamphlets, audio-visual aids and discussion with physicians' assistants.

Clearly indicate to patients that for some genuinely distressing symptoms there are no medications which can safely provide relief. Physicians should feel comfortable in acknowledging the limits of their therapeutic armamentarium. The vain effort to try "one more drug" suggests to the patient that he is right to expect symptom relief from medications when, in fact, this may be unrealistic.

Additional Guidelines. Occasionally, the patient will ramble off the topic. In such cases, the physician may interrupt by commenting, "I'm not following that; could you please go back over it?" Persistent inability to adhere to the topic and to relate a coherent story suggests mental retardation, delirium, organic brain syndrome or psychosis.

When questioning the patient in an emotionally charged area, move from factual data into more subjective and emotion-laden areas. For example, in asking a patient with severe angina pectoris about his illness, factual questions about pain should precede questions about functional limitations, which, in turn, should precede questions concerning the meaning of symptoms to the patient, his fears, hopes, etc. When appropriate, ask questions about the patient's behavior, thoughts and emotions during the physical examination. Questions as wide ranging as ones concerning headaches, visual acuity and auditory hallucinations can often comfortably be asked while examining the head and related organs. This suggestion can be misapplied. It is unlikely that a woman would be most comfortable discussing her sexual life while lying on her back with her feet in stirrups during a pelvic examination.

Information about what is usually called the review of systems can often best be tied into the physical examination, especially when, by this phase of the examination, the physician has a good idea of the range of diagnostic possibilities, he can easily ask questions concerning an organ system while examining that system. This has two additional advantages. It may catch the patient off guard and cause him to relate something of concern which he might not have said during the interview. This is a function of the greater implicit authority and accessibility to information which the physician has when laying hands on the patient. Second, the physical examination of the system usually results in the patient's focusing on that system and may cause him to remember important events which he could not have done in the interview portion of the examination.

We have not provided guidelines for the traditional reviews of the system wherein the physician asks a large number of specific questions to obtain encyclopedic data about the patient's past and present conditions. This seems the least useful application of the physician's skills and time. This class of data is better obtained through self-reporting forms or by paraprofessional interviewers. In either case, the physician can then follow up significant positive or negative findings which emerge from this preliminary and increasingly automated area of data collection.

Caveats. Do not ask the patient "why" questions: "Why did you marry your husband?"; "Why did your arthritis affect your job?" Such questions are almost invariably poor. They ask the patient to give a causal explanation when, if he were able to do so, he might not be seeing the physician in the first place. Such a question puts pressure on the patient to agree with the physician. Persons of lower socioeconomic classes often do not think in terms of intrapsychic processes, and such questions are only upsetting to them. Such questions allow the patient to select a plausible answer which may, however, undermine his appreciation of the multiple factors which may have contributed to the difficulty.

Rabbi's anger

Do not argue with, minimize or challenge the patient. It can be easy to lose sight of the truth that your aim is not to prove the rightness of your position but to help the patient. Most persons react negatively to such an approach—either directly or by responding with the more maladaptive unconscious adaptive mechanisms such as passive aggression. This impasse often occurs when the physician is, in one sense, justifiably angry: The patient has failed to care properly for a wound which the physician had spent time in debriding and suturing, or a mother has not brought her child in for treatment soon enough to make treatment for his rheumatic fever free of danger. But if the patient is aware of his error, he probably already feels guilty enough, and a statement of blame will more likely close off the sense of trust, openness and anxiety-free communication which is a prerequisite to change through the therapeutic relationship. If, on the other hand, the patient was unaware of what he should have done and conflict of motives was not a factor in his behavior, a straightforward educational approach is more likely to be productive.

Specific questions to be avoided, then, are ones such as the following: "Why did you wait so long to bring your boy in, Mother?" (The use of the depersonalized, collective noun "mother" is a stark reminder of the scorn the interviewer feels, in addition to the accusation implied.)

In a similar vein, questions which presume an answer are generally undesirable. "How often do you beat your wife?" presupposes the fact that the person does beat his wife. Only in unusual situations is such an approach justified. An example would be with a patient who is likely to minimize his responses. The physician might well start with the question "How much liquor do you drink?" or "Tell me about your drinking of alcohol," rather than "Do you drink?," which the patient may take as an indecisive gesture which allows him to save face, if he wishes, by saying no and closing off further inquiry.

On the other hand, one should not praise the patient, especially during the first interview. The patient may misinterpret the praise and be falsely reassured. He may not have told the full, embarrassing truth and may find that the praise makes it all the more difficult to be candid in subsequent visits. Or, he may doubt the sincerity of the praise: "If he is this free with his praise when he knows so little about me, how can I be sure of his perceptivity and honesty later on?"

Do not make false reassurances or promises. The patient who asks for such is often laying a trap for the physician: "But you told me it wouldn't hurt." "But you said I would be well within 2 months." The story of the man who asked the physician, who was placing his fractured arm in a cast, whether he would be able to play the violin when the arm healed is a case in point. The physician said, "Why yes, I see no reason why not." To this the patient responded, "That's funny. I couldn't before it was broken." The joke is feeble, but the moral is useful. The meaning of the question to the patient must be understood, as must the knowledge of where the patient is, currently, in regard to the question. To respond to a couple's requests for genetic counseling by telling them that, based on what they have said, you would strongly advise against their having children may not be useful if in fact the woman is already pregnant. The issue of promises in treatment is especially critical with the hypochondriacal person and is discussed at greater length in Chapter 10.

Do not participate in criticism of the patient's parents, mate, children, friends, associates or other physicians. It is not your task in the treatment relationship to do so. The treating physician is often not at a vantage point to know the multiple sides of the story. He hears only what the patient says, filtered through his personal, protecting biases. A person may feel ambivalent toward those he criticizes; rather than be pleased with the physician's siding with him, he may begin to defend the person in question or feel guilty about his own feelings toward them and either withdraw his trust from the physician or turn his anger toward him. Responses that can be useful are "I see that the situation upsets you very much" or "A remark like that would be disturbing." Unsuitable responses are ones such as "Maybe you were prejudiced against that doctor" or "It's a shame that she doesn't realize what she is doing to you." Other suggestions about dealing with criticism can be found in Chapter 4, *The Angry Patient*.

Special Techniques

Maintaining the Flow. Often there will be pauses during the interview. At times the patient will have stopped to collect his thoughts, or because he is embarrassed or anxious concerning something he has not yet related but knows is important or simply to obtain feedback from the physician that he is on the right track. Often the most useful facilitation is nonverbal. A nod of the head says, "Go on, you are on the right track." Similarly, a rotational movement of the hand encourages the patient to continue. A puzzled or quizzical look with furrowed brow says, " I don't understand; can you elaborate to make that clearer?"

Similar encouragement is conveyed by brief statements such as "yes," "mm-humm" or "go on." A particularly useful, facilitating remark can come after a person has alluded to some issue or problem within the context of discussing another problem or organ system. If the physician allows the patient to continue for several minutes until he has completed a particular explanation, the physician can then come back with a statement such as "A little while back you mentioned that your ulcer flared up after you stopped playing golf—can you tell me more about that?" Not only does the remark ask for a reply, but it also conveys the interest and perceptiveness of the physician.

Clarifying Statements. A continuing problem for physicians is that some patients prematurely and mistakenly diagnose their own symptoms. This often involves erroneous attribution of a symptom to disturbance in a specific organ system. It can lead to expensive doctor shopping, unwarranted faith in charlatans and miracle cures, and sometimes fatal delay in beginning effective treatment. The following is a common occurrence. Patient: "And then I get this terrible pain in my heart" (points to the left side of his chest). Doctor: "Can you tell more about when you have these pains in your chest?" The physician has subtly suggested that the pain should not be attributed to the heart per se. Such redefinition can work at practically a subconscious level to help the patient redefine and more realistically comprehend his concerns. Such skills are ones which experienced physicians gradually learn over time without realizing it, but the early and more effective use of such conceptual shifts can be optimized by conscious attention to opportunities for their use.

Confrontation. By confrontation, we mean pointing out to the patient some contradiction between two things that he had said or between his statement and his appearance, or pointing out an emotional response which the patient may either be unaware of or unable to acknowledge. The surgeon who sweeps hurriedly into a room preoperatively and, based on his accurate perception of the patient's appearance, says, "You look scared to death" is practicing a high level skill. Or the physician who says, "You seem awfully sad" may facilitate the person's sharing his sadness, with its tears and meaning, with the physician.

Timing is especially important in the use of confrontation. Confrontation is usually avoided in everyday social interaction, so the physician may feel uncomfortable using it. For certain kinds of situations, timing can be overlooked. When a patient's anxiety is interfering with his responses, it is practically always facilitating to say, "I notice that you are very uncomfortable" or "You appear to be awfully nervous." This acknowledgement often results in an immediate reduction in anxiety, because it suggests that the physician is sensitive and concerned with the way the patient is feeling and, because the patient may have been attempting to hide his anxiety and finds that he no longer needs to do so, his anxiety lessens. Feelings of anger, especially in depressed persons, should be treated cautiously. The physician may be quite accurate in perceiving a patient's anger or resentment, but to confront him with this often makes him feel more depressed and frightened, as his sense that his anger is unjustified and unacceptable may be one factor in his depression.

Communicating Empathy. The patient often needs and deserves support from his physician. This is especially so following his or the physician's disclosing something of strong emotional content, such as the diagnosis of a terminal illness, or the patient's expression of intense feelings, such as crying or voicing his fear or despair. Nonverbal means are often useful—a response of silence, clasping a hand of the patient or putting an arm on his shoulder that says, "Yes, I know how hard that must have been for you." Verbally, a comment can be brief: "I know," "I understand"; or longer: "That must have been very upsetting for you" or "This is hard for you." All of these responses cement the solidarity of the relationship, increase the sense of trust and say to the patient that "I will be with you, and available to you, no matter what."

Periods of silence need present no major problems. As suggested earlier, if brief, they may be useful. And in those situations where the patient, overwhelmed with feeling, cries, silence is essential to show that you care about his feelings and that you are not uncomfortable with them. The expression of such feelings is nearly always beneficial, both in immediately relieving tension and in increasing the sense of trust within the relationship.

Family Interviewing. Certain situations invite or necessitate family interviewing, including premarital evaluation, well-baby care, acute crisis (such as a burn), an evolving crisis (such as renal failure) and chronic illness (such as heart disease and arthritis). Skills in this area will allow the physician to obtain useful information he would not otherwise have and, when appropriate, to utilize the family or a member thereof as a therapeutic tool in his work with the patient. Two common situations are (1) when the family member accompanies the patient and (2) when the family as a unit is interviewed. In the first case, the accompanying person should practically always be interviewed. This person provides a different vantage point regarding the patient's problem. He may be able to corroborate what the patient says or he may allow the physician to observe important interpersonal interaction, such as the patient's efforts to obtain sympathy from the individual or the individual's efforts to scapegoat the patient. Beyond the initial visit, the physician may decide in what context seeing the accompanying person is useful. With the husband of an arthritic woman, full involvement of the man in the interviews will probably be useful. With the mother who accompanies her 20-year-old son for care, it may be better to exclude her from the interview, as her presence implies that her mothering, protective role is still important, a view which is not consistent with the normal emancipation of the adolescent.

In situations in which an entire family is interviewed, several additional observational skills need to be utilized. The physician should observe how the family enters the room and who sits next to whom. Who looks to or away from whom? Who speaks, who listens, who smiles, who frowns? Who appeals to, urges, coerces, blames or praises whom? What issues are covered up? About what issues is there apathy, ignorance, confusion or distrust? In short order, dominant interpersonal patterns will be evident, and the physician will have learned a great deal about the way in which the family members, individually and collectively, face illness and stress and how they respond to ill members within the family.

When interviewing the family as a unit, the physician should seek to transpose conflict and anxiety to the level of active, candid interpersonal exchange. In doing so, the physician should side with healthy adaptation, rather than with a particular family member. He must respect the family's effort to maintain privacy, while encouraging family members to give up pathogenic secretiveness and tacit pacts. This is often seen in families with a member who has a terminal illness. All of the relatives "want to know the truth" but want to "spare Dad, so he can live his time out in happiness." Such an effort to hold in a burden unshared, the anxiety lest one reveal the truth and the emotional isolation of the ill person invariably make such a tacit pact painful and counterproductive.

Empathy and cooperative solutions to problems among family members should be fostered, and any form of scapegoating should be neutralized. Confrontation can be an effective therapeutic tool within the family in a variety of ways. Included are the exposure of maladaptive defenses, the exposure of underlying moods and feelings and confrontation of the family with obvious inconsistencies and contradictions in their beliefs, statements and actions.

Closing the Interview

The physician needs to develop the fine art of appearing not to be hurried. This can be done even while fully acknowledging how busy the physician is likely to be. The open-ended approach to interviewing presented here facilitates the patient's feeling that the physician is intently interested in his problems. Such obvious gestures as fidgeting nervously in the chair, looking at a watch or tapping a finger tell the patient that you are either bored or hurried. Verbally interrupting the patient before he has completed a sequence or saying "mm-humm" excessively says the same thing. Many physicians make these errors based on the erroneous belief that such behavior is necessary to get the patient to stop talking. But the physician is in the seat of authority and, when the allotted time is nearly up, he can state matter-of-factly, "Before we stop, Mrs. Jones, I want to summarize what we've gone over today and what our plans are from here. First, I want to know if you have any questions you would like to ask or get cleared up?" He will do well to make clear that the time is up, and not to exceed it by more than a few minutes, unless the situation is emergent or acute.

Occasionally, patients who present no other untoward personality elements in the interview will be tenaciously prone to hold onto the interview and resist its termination. The importance of limit setting in dealing with angry or hypochondriacal patients is discussed in Chapters 4 and 10. Whether the difficulty in ending the interview reflects dependency, loneliness, a latent depression or fear concerning his illness, it most frequently is symptomatic of a general tendency of the person, once involved in a relationship, to have difficulty giving it up. If the latter is the case, the physician should deal firmly with the patient. As the patient will predictably behave this way on most visits, the physician may find a preventive approach useful. "We only have about 10 more minutes today, and there are a few other things we need to cover before we stop" gives the patient a set time in which to prepare himself emotionally for termination and is considerate, fair and educational for the patient.

If there is a cardinal word about bringing an interview to a close, it is congruence. Evidence is great that failure to understand or agree with the physician's diagnostic impression and treatment plan regarding medications and activities, frequency of visits and length and cost of treatment account for much of the high rate of noncompliance and failure to return for follow-up. Attention to the preceding factors discussed in this section, especially as they bear on moving the patient to the viewpoint and understanding you wish him to have, will materially help in preventing the problem from arising.

*   *   *   *

The student of medicine who develops a mastery of the knowledge and skills discussed in this chapter will have the additional benefit of greater comfort in dealing with difficult patients. He will be able to recognize the psychosocial dimensions of the patient's illness—the fact that the patient has a relevant life outside the hospital bed or clinic office. He will have greater skills in working with the family. He will better appreciate the vicissitudes of the doctor-patient relationship and be able to manage it accordingly. He will have the capability to consider the patient as a whole, rather than fragment his problems.

REFERENCES

1. ACKERMAN, N. W., AND KEMPSTER, S. Family Therapy, in *Comprehensive Textbook of Psychiatry*, Freedman, A. M., and Kaplan, H. I., eds. Williams & Wilkins, Baltimore, 1967, pp. 1244–1248.

2. BOWDEN, C. L., AND GIFFEN, M. B. *Psychopharmacology for Primary Care Physicians*. Williams & Wilkins, Baltimore, 1978, pp. 4–7.

3. BENARDE, M. A., AND MAYERSON, E. W. Patient-physician negotiation. *J.A.M.A. 239*:1413–1415, 1978.

4. CHAPMAN, A. H. *The Physician's Guide to Managing Emotional Problems*. J. B. Lippincott, Philadelphia, 1969. (Excellent, straightforward presentation of the detailed management of common emotional reactions.)

5. ENELOW, A. J., AND SWISHER, S. N. *Interviewing and Patient Care*. Oxford University Press, New York, 1972.

6. HOLLENDER, M. H. *The Psychology of Medical Practice*. W. B. Saunders, Philadelphia, 1958. (Chapter 9, which considers psychological factors in the use of medications, is especially useful.)

7. KORSCH, B. M., GOZZI, E. K., AND FRANCIS, V. Gaps in doctor-patient communication: doctor-patient interaction and patient satisfaction. *Pediatrics 42*:855–871, 1968.

8. MAZZULO, J. M., LASAGNA, L., AND GRINER, P. F. Variations in interpretation of prescription instruction. *J.A.M.A. 227*:929, 1974.

9. MORGAN, W. L., AND ENGEL, G. L. *The Clinical Approach to the Patient*. W. B. Saunders, Philadelphia, 1969.

10. REDLICH, F. C. The doctor and his patient: explaining illness. *Psychiatry Med. 1*:171, 1970.

11. SZASZ, T. S., AND HOLLENDER, M. H. A contribution to the philosophy of medicine—the basic models of the doctor-patient relationship. *A.M.A. Arch. Intern. Med. 97*:585, 1956.

CHAPTER 4

PATTERNS OF DEFENSE AND ADAPTATION

CHARLES L. BOWDEN, M. D.

Differing Roles of Character Traits And Defense Mechanisms

A central theme of this book is that physicians' work is more effectively done if, in addition to diagnosing and treating the patient's illnesses, they recognize the patient's consistent patterns of behavior and his idiosyncratic traits. There are two sets of consistent patterns relevant to personality: "character" and defense or adaptive ego mechanisms. Character traits such as pedantry or competitiveness play a role in the over-all functioning of the personality and in situations not associated with specific conflict. In contrast, defense mechanisms characterize the ways in which persons deal with stress-producing situations.

Although defense mechanisms are often fundamentally involved in the various psychiatric disorders, they are not intrinsically pathological but are present in all individuals and serve several essential functions in maintaining psychological well-being.

Before listing and describing various patterns of defense and adaptation, the following prefatory remarks are in order. First, such mechanisms are not directly observable realities; we infer their operation from the behavior of the person and utilize the concepts because of their explanatory and predictive power. Because these mechanisms are hypothetical concepts, different writers utilize somewhat varying terminology. This lack of uniformity can be confusing to the student. Second, these mechanisms describe processes rather than discrete entities. Third, they are evanescent phenomena, waxing and waning with the degree of stress. Fourth, the operation of a defense mechanism is often so obvious to the observer that he finds it difficult to believe that it does not represent a conscious and deliberate choice. Nevertheless, these mechanisms operate automatically and unconsciously and do not reflect conscious attempts to manipulate. For this reason, attempts to alter these defenses through the use of confrontation often intensify rather than diminish them.

Functions of Defenses

Defenses serve several purposes. First, they may be invoked to keep feelings within bearable limits during a sudden alteration in one's emotional life. Examples include the response to the death of a loved one and the response to sudden awareness of erotic feelings for a person who is considered taboo or off limits.

Second, defenses can restore psychological homeostasis by postponing or deflecting sudden increases in biological drives. We see this in adolescents who deal with aggressive or erotic feelings toward parents by avoiding dependence upon them.

Third, defenses are often useful in providing a "time-out" to master changes in self-image that cannot immediately be integrated. Adaptation to the physical changes of puberty or to the loss of a limb are physical examples. Psychologically, this occurs with job promotions or in adapting to the roles of medical student and physician.

Fourth, defenses are used to deal with unresolvable conflict. As such, they may influence the responses of a black person in a racist society or of an adolescent who learns that he has diabetes.

Defenses do not necessarily reflect mental illness; both the mentally ill and the mentally healthy utilize them. Nevertheless, there are some useful generalizations about the relationship of pathology to defenses. The more successful, adaptive defenses change the object of the impulse rather than the aim and, accordingly, require less inhibition; that is, they allow for some acceptable discharge of the impulse or wish. For example, if one likes to smear, he may become a sculptor. The less successful defenses—reaction formation, reversal, denial, etc.—try to change or deny the basic aim.

Generally, defenses are maladaptive if they are inflexible, mechanistic or lead to avoidance of conflict and unnecessary regression. Adaptive coping behavior is flexible, minimizes regression and leads toward eventual conflict resolution.

Classification of Defenses and Adaptive Mechanisms

The description which follows closely parallels the writing on the subject by George Vaillant. Each mechanism is defined so that it can be clearly distinguished from every other mechanism. Furthermore, the definitions are based on observable behavior. This approach is helpful from the practical point of view in that an understanding of aberrant *behavior* is more important than understanding aberrant *ideation*. The mechanisms discussed are simultaneously arranged along a developmental continuum, which presumes that some defenses are more mature than others, and along a pathological continuum, which assumes that some defenses are more adaptive and less correlated with severe psychopathology than others.

Narcissistic Defenses

Narcissistic defenses are common in healthy individuals before the age of 5 and in adult dreams and fantasies. For the *user*, these mechanisms alter reality. To the *beholder*, they appear blatantly incongruous. They tend to be refractory to elimination, but controllable through psychotropic drugs and environmental manipulation.

Delusional Projection: A *delusion* is a false belief out of keeping with the patient's level of knowledge and his cultural group. It results from unconscious needs and is maintained against logical argument and objective contradictory evidence. *Delusional projection* is a frank delusion about external reality, usually of a persecutory type. It involves attributing feelings which arise in one's self to another person, perceiving the feelings as in the other person, and then acting on that perception. A 3-year-old child who has spilled his milk may say that his brother did it or that his brother forced him to spill it. A diabetic man could not acknowledge his disease because of the threat which awareness posed to his self-esteem. Rather, he believed that the physicians were plotting against him to shield him from his true diagnosis of hypoadrenalism and leprosy. Accordingly, he refused to take insulin or to care properly for a diabetic skin ulcer.

This mechanism occurs in the very young, in psychoses and in deliria. This mechanism can be distinguished from introjection in that responsibility for the feelings is projected to others.

Denial: denial of *external* reality. As here defined, it does not include denial of essentially internal (intrapsychic) feelings and thoughts. Examples are denying the presence of real tears, insisting that a dead person is still alive, that after amputation one still has an arm or that one does not have cancer, despite incontrovertible evidence which has been explained to the patient and would otherwise be understandable by him.

Distortion: grossly reshaping external reality to suit internal needs. It includes hallucinations, unrealistic megalomanic beliefs, wish-fulfilling delusions and feelings of delusional superiority or entitlement. Persistent denial of personal responsibility for one's own behavior is also included. An example is the person who has dropped out of classes while failing in all of them but who continues to play the role of student to himself and his family. The child who converses with an imaginary friend or has her dolls talk to her is using this mechanism. It can be adaptive in adults in religious beliefs—for example, providing the comfort of literally going, after death, to a house of many mansions in a heaven with gold-paved streets.

In contrast to delusional projection, where distress is alleviated by assigning responsibility for offensive feelings elsewhere, in distortion, unpleasant feelings are replaced by their opposites.

Immature Defenses

Immature defenses are common in healthy persons aged 3 to 16 and in adults with character and affective disorders. For the *user*, they generally deal with distress associated with interpersonal intimacy or the fear of loss of intimacy, support or dependency gratification. To the *beholder*, these behaviors appear socially undesirable and may be labeled as misbehavior. They may be altered through improvement in interpersonal relationships (personal maturation, finding a more mature spouse or a physician more comfortable with the open, direct expression of dependency needs) or, occasionally, through long term psychotherapy. The setting of firm expectations and limits of tolerable behavior is sometimes useful in controlling the associated behaviors.

Projection: One's emotionally unacceptable feelings are unconsciously rejected and attributed to others. This mechanism includes excessive vigilance, injustice collecting, severe prejudice and overattention to external dangers.

Schizoid Fantasy: the use of fantasy and solitary withdrawal or retreat for the purpose of conflict avoidance and/or pleasure. It is often associated with

global avoidance of intimacy. Unlike mere wishes, schizoid fantasies gratify
unmet needs for personal relationships and serve to prevent, halt or avoid
overt expression of feelings toward others. Unlike delusional projection, denial
or distortion, the person does not fully believe his fantasies or act them out.

Hypochondriasis: the transformation of feelings toward others arising from
bereavement, loneliness or unacceptable aggressive impulses into complaints
of pain, somatic illness and neurasthenia (lassitude, physical ineptness). The
resultant is perceived as within one's self and causing plausible disease. This
mechanism often permits the patient to belabor others with his pain or
discomfort, instead of making direct pleas to them to satisfy his wish to be
dependent. It does not include illnesses such as ulcer and hypertension. Such
diseases are neither intrinsically adaptive nor defensive (i.e., they do not
diminish conflict). Chapter 10 deals in depth with the hypochondriacal
patient.

Passive-Aggressive Behavior: aggression expressed indirectly and ineffec-
tively through pouting, procrastination, negativism and illnesses which affect
others more than the self. It is closely related to hypochondriasis and is often
found in conjunction therewith.

Acting-Out: direct expression of a conflictful unconscious wish or impulse
in order to avoid being aware of the unconscious affect or fantasy that
accompanies it. More is involved than simple impulsivity; there must be an
element of intrapsychic conflict. It includes some forms of delinquency,
extramartial affairs, exhibitionism, the sexual Don Juan, drug use, sexual
perversion and self-inflicted injury to relieve subjective anxiety. Acting-out
involves chronically giving in to impulses in order to avoid the tension that
would result were there any postponement of expression.

Regression: return to an earlier mode of behavior which was either more
successful or more pleasant. Examples include thumb-sucking, baby talk (as
a result of stress in children who have earlier given up this behavior) and the
wish in frightened adults to be held. Regression has characteristics apart from
the other defenses in this section. First, regression is to some degree essential
to healthy adaptive function, such as in some aspects of play and sexual
intercourse. Second, it is a term with multiple meanings, which can lead to
confusion if one is not aware of the particular assumptions underlying its use.

Turning against the Self: the redirection of feelings and impulses toward
one's self that were originally directed toward another person or object. An
example is the woman who characteristically berates herself for not doing
more for her husband and for being so selfish in her wants from him,
following his having harshly and unnecessarily rebuffed her.

Neurotic Defenses

Neurotic defenses are common in relatively healthy adults, in neurotic
disorders and in mastering acute adult stress. For the *user,* these mechanisms
alter private feelings or instinctual expression. To the *beholder,* they appear as

neurotic hang-ups and individual quirks. They can often be dramatically modified for the better with conventional brief and longer term psychotherapies.

Intellectualization: thinking in a formal, bland way, without awareness of attendant feelings and without acting on the thoughts. This mechanism includes such other defenses as isolation, rationalization, rituals, undoing and magical thinking. An example is the man who plans all week to ask a woman for a date and considers what they would do, and the cost, etc., but never gets around to asking for the date.

Repression: seemingly unexplicable naïveté, memory lapse or failure to acknowledge input from a sense organ. It is often accompanied by behavior which suggests that the repressed material is not really forgotten. Examples include failure to keep an appointment with the dentist and failure to remember the name of a well known acquaintance. The observer of such behavior often feels, "He's not that stupid!" This mechanism differs from denial in preventing the expression of perception of instincts and feelings, rather than in affecting recognition of and response to external events.

Displacement: the redirection of a feeling toward a person or situation more acceptable than the person causing the situation. Practical jokes, sarcasm, caricature, some prejudicial and conversion reactions and most phobias involve displacement.

Reaction Formation: a feeling or behavior which is the opposite of an unacceptable one (unacceptable means that it generates anxiety). Examples include "loving" a hated rival or an unpleasant duty or caring for someone when one basically wishes to be cared for.

Dissociation: temporary but drastic modification of one's character or sense of identity to avoid emotional distress. Examples include amnesia unrelated to brain damage, short term failure to perceive responsibility for one's acts or feelings, drug intoxication to avoid unhappiness or other unpleasant feelings and counterphobic behavior to blot out anxiety or other distressing emotions.

Dissociation is more understandable to others than distortion. It is both less exploitative of others and less prolonged than acting-out.

Mature Defenses

Mature defenses probably emerge gradually during childhood growth, especially during adolescence, as a result of successful identification and the development of an ideal self-image. They reflect and probably require the ability of formal abstract thinking. For the *user,* these mechanisms integrate conscience, reality, interpersonal relationships and private feelings. To the *beholder,* they appear as convenient virtues and character strengths. Under increased stress, these defenses may revert to less mature mechanisms. Because these mechanisms may occur at least partly at the level of awareness and because they are so generally adaptive, many do not include them among the defense mechanisms. The issue of degree of consciousness seems a poor one on which to base inclusion of adaptive mechanisms. Too, even these mature mechanisms may be maladaptive. A physician may channel his energies into his enjoyable professional work to such an extent that he undermines his health and his relationship with his family.

Altruism: vicarious but constructive, gratifying service to others. It includes benign reaction formation, philanthropy and well repaid service to others. It differs from projection and acting-out in that it also leaves the person using the defense at least partly gratified.

Humor: the overt expression of feelings without personal discomfort or immobilization and without unpleasant effects on others. Humor lets one call a spade a spade. Humor involves the ability to laugh at the plights in which we sometimes find ourselves. It can never be applied without some observing ego. Unlike wit and sarcasm, which are forms of displacement, it does not involve distraction away from the issue at hand, nor is it at the expense of others' comfort. It does not exclude other persons, as does schizoid fantasy.

Suppression: the conscious or semiconscious decision to *postpone* paying attention to an impulse or a conflict. It includes minimizing physical and emotional discomfort, employing a stiff upper lip, being unflappable and deliberately postponing but *not* avoiding. It is saying, "I will think about it tomorrow," and, when tomorrow comes, one remembers to think about it. It differs from repression in that the latter results in unconscious inhibition to the degree that the goal is *lost,* not just postponed.

Anticipation: realistic anticipation of or planning for future inner comfort or discomfort. It includes goal-directed planning and worrying and realistic anticipation of death, surgery, separation and taxes. It is involved in the conscious utilization of insight gained from psychotherapy.

Sublimation: indirect expression of drives without adverse consequences or marked loss of pleasure. It includes the expression of aggression in games, sports and hobbies and the romantic attenuation of sexual drives during courtship. So-called regression in the service of the ego is included here. Examples of such include Kekule's dreaming of snakes encircled, tail in mouth, solving the spatial structure of the benezene ring, and the poetry of e. e. cummings.

In sublimation, one's feelings are acknowledged, modified and directed toward a relatively significant person or goal, so that satisfaction results. Unlike the "neurotic defenses," impulses are *channeled*, rather than *dammed* or diverted.

Conflict-free Spheres of the Ego

Man is not merely a grouping of defenses and coping mechanisms. Many ego* functions develop and operate outside of conflict, society or, in some

* The ego is defined as that grouping of functions which mediate between the inner life of the person and the outside world.

cases, even psychological maturation. A listing of these includes the following autonomous ego functions: perception, motivation, thinking, language, memory, productivity, motor development, learning and the synthetic function of the ego. Most of these functions are considered in Chapter 11.

All of the ego functions facilitate man's adaption in three major ways: (1) adapting and modifying the environment to human function; (2) adapting secondarily to the environment which we have helped to create—"You have made your bed, now lie in it"; (3) choosing a new environment which is advantageous. This last adaptive mode is uniquely important for humans.

* * * *

In this chapter we have provided a system of nomenclature which will be utilized in exploring the psychological aspects of patient care as well as the development of the person through the life cycle.

REFERENCES

1. FREUD, A. *The Ego and the Mechanisms of Defense.* International Universities Press, New York, 1953.
2. HARTMANN, H. *The Ego and the Problem of Adaptation.* International Universities Press, New York, 1958.
3. RADO, S. *Psychoanalysis of Behavior.* Grune & Stratton, New York, 1956. (Excellent for considerations of the totality of factors which influence adaptation.)
4. VAILLANT, G. E. Theoretical hierarchy of adaptive ego mechanisms. *Arch. Gen. Psychiatry 24:* 107, 1971.
5. VAILLANT, G. E. *Adaptation to Life.* Little, Brown, and Co., Boston, 1977.

CHAPTER 5

THE ANGRY PATIENT

ALVIN G. BURSTEIN, Ph. D.

The emotional climate in which any personal transaction occurs is an important element, often coloring and shaping the formal transaction. For that reason, professionals who work directly with other people must be knowledgeable, not only about their specialties, but also about the emotional climates in which their work may be carried out. People who see themselves as needy or weak in relationship to more powerful figures on whom they depend are likely to develop strong and volatile feelings. Students often develop crushes on their teachers. Criminals and prisoners of war may develop strong wishes to be liked by their interrogators. Such feelings can become so strong as to compel the prisoner to confess to crimes he has not committed, in an effort to please or impress his questioner. Doctor-patient relationships, particularly those in the active-passive mode (Chapter 3) in which the patient sees himself as weak, helpless and dependent on his doctor, are media in which such feelings can flourish.

Several important points are to be made about such feelings. They can be both strong and volatile, often springing up and dissipating rapidly. They are experienced by the patient as real perceptions, although to the observer the feelings are not clearly justified. Such feelings, even within the context of a relationship which is objectively quite consistent, can range between positive and negative poles. Finally, these feelings can result in a subjective view of the relationship which is strikingly different for the participants. The doctor's sensitivity to these possibilities will greatly increase his effectiveness in anticipating and dealing with his patients' behavior.

The kinds of feelings described above are irrational or unreasonable in the sense that they do not appear to have visible, objective causes within the patient's immediate context. It is equally important to take note of feelings which are rooted in the actual exchange between the doctor and his patient. In this and the five chapters that follow, we deal concretely with the more common emotional reactions of patients, their sources and how they should be handled.

Anger in patients can be particularly troublesome. It can provoke a rejection from the doctor or other members of the health team that sends the patient on a shopping expedition, often wasting valuable prior work. It can lead to expensive litigation. It can be sufficiently abrasive to the doctor to lead him to avoid the patient or, in other ways, to blur his judgment in the clinical situation. Anger on the patient's part can be expressed either in the more readily recognized form of direct challenge and criticism or in a disguised, indirect form.

Openly Expressed Anger

Situational Anger. It is important to note at the outset that these patients may be characteristically angry; they may be angry as part of a temporary process within them; they may be venting, in the current situation, anger stirred up within other contexts; or, not the least important, they may be voicing a legitimate complaint. For example, the patient may say to the student taking a history, "Why do I have to answer all these questions? Why can't you look at my chart?" or "Why do you have to interrupt me when I have visitors?" The student's first recourse, in such a situation, should be to survey his own behavior realistically as a possible source of anger in the patient. Has he, in fact, been inconsiderate of the patient's schedule, or has he been unnecessarily redundant and forgetful in his history taking? It is important that this self-assessment be a realistic one, because some students tend to feel overly diffident in their new roles and to feel that any contact they make with a patient is an unwelcome and unnecessary intrusion. However, when the student feels that he has realistically contributed to the patient's anger, he should acknowledge the merit of the patient's complaint and take appropriate remedial action. Abject apologies are less likely to be helpful than an appropriate modification in the student's behavior. Usually, the patient's anger is a temporary response; if he is given an opportunity to express it fully and if it leads to a constructive change, the most likely outcome is an improvement in the openness and frankness with which the patient can talk with his doctor.

Suits alleging malpractice are an expression of anger in patients which have received increased attention recently. The so-called malpractice crisis is sometimes attributed to rapacious lawyers, naive juries, faint-hearted insurance companies or careless physicians. All simplistic explanations are inadequate, but a few relevant facts stand out. First, malpractice suits are on the increase. Second, most patients recover small amounts, although there are occasional very large awards. Third, a relatively small number of physicians account for almost all the malpractice complaints. Fourth, patient satisfaction surveys indicate that patients are relatively realistic about accepting bad treatment outcomes, if they feel the physician has been honest with them, accessible to them and exercised care. Fifth, malpractice insurance is readily available. In Texas, published rates for malpractice insurance vary from about $500 per year for minimal coverage in low risk specialties (e.g., nonsurgical pediatrics) to $9000 per year for maximum coverage in high risk specialties (e.g., neurosurgery).

Inasmuch as the malpractice phenomenon has multiple causes, a number of approaches are useful in dealing with it. On the individual level, the physician should strive to answer his patients' questions, to be accessible to his patients and to minimize unnecessary risks. On the level of the professional association, pressures should be put on state boards and on individual hospitals to take action against those few physicians who are repeatedly careless. On the level of social structure, the incentive for frivolous suits should be minimized. A Florida hospital, for example, adopted a "no-fault" procedure in which certain untoward events automatically entitle the patient to corrective procedures without the patient having to bear any of the direct or indirect expense.

Displaced Anger. Frequently, the student's behavior has not in itself provoked the patient's anger, but the anger has been carried over from some other situation. This kind of displacement may be an unconscious adaptive mechanism intended to help a patient to vent his anger while maintaining a positive image of those members of the health team whom he sees as more important. It is, therefore, particularly familiar to nurse's aides and students, who must be schooled in how to respond to it most constructively. Placatory attempts or anger in return will have little beneficial effect. The second may further inflame the situation, while the first signals the patient that the student is frightened of the feelings. If the student acknowledges to the patient that he understands the quality and depth of the feelings, this will frequently lead, first, to a shift in focus to the more legitimate sources of the anger and, second, to an abatement in its intensity. To repeat, many emotional states are essentially transitory and, if permitted open expression, leave in their wake a clearer field for communication.

Anger as a Reaction to an Internal Process. A third alternative is that the anger expressed may not be a reflection of current interpersonal transactions, either with the student or his colleagues, but, rather, a reflection of some process internal to the patient. An example that is discussed in some detail in Chapter 11 is the dying patient, who, as part of the natural process of assimilating the knowledge of his situation, is likely to experience and express anger. In general, patients who have suffered an acute reduction in their sense of being competent and adequate, through falling prey to serious illness or for causes unrelated to their illness, are likely to feel anger at some level of their consciousness. In the management of such situations, the worst common error is to abort the feelings by premature and unnecessary reassurance, placatory maneuvers, etc. Such anger should be neither provoked nor avoided, but simply recognized and acknowledged as it emerges, with the understanding, again, that it represents a transitory, although important, stage in a more complex series of responses.

Characterological Anger. The characteristically angry patient may be the most difficult to deal with. This patient is one whose critical early childhood experiences with help-givers have been such as to convince him in pervasive and preverbal ways that parents, teachers, doctors and other helpers are more likely to take advantage of him than to help him. Such patients tend to be rigid in their beliefs (sometimes to the point of arrogance), suspicious of others, hyperalert, uncomfortable, awkward with and contemptuous of tender emotion and self-centered. They rely heavily on the adaptive mechanism of *projection*. The family history is likely to reveal parents who tended to overpower or to humiliate the patient or (as in the case of some disadvantaged minority groups) an environment that is hostile, non-nurturant and experienced as degrading. Such a background can teach a person that ostensible helpers are in reality punishers and that those who offer to help are potentially dangerous.

Dealing with such patients will be most difficult in proportion to the degree of their characterological commitment to this angry posture. In general, such patients respond best to openness and candor—to them, ambiguity equals threat. Second, a cool, consistent and authoritative posture will be helpful, because such patients despise weakness in themselves and in others. Their anger is very likely to erupt in the face of inconsistency or softness on the part of their doctor. Third, maximizing the patient's areas of mastery and competence, while minimizing the occasions on which things have to be done for him, will help to preserve the patient's self-esteem and reduce opportunities for conflict.

In the most extreme clinical cases, patients with the dynamics and characteristics described above can be viewed as paranoid. Even these extreme cases will respond well to the management techniques suggested. However, particularly when delusional projections or psychotic gradiosity are revealed, a psychiatric consultation will be helpful in determining whether psychopharmacological or psychotherapeutic intervention would be helpful.

Disguised Anger

Heretofore, we have dealt with anger expressed openly to the physician. Anger and hostility, of course, often find diffused or disguised expression, and these forms, too, require careful treatment. As illustrations of the less blatant forms patient anger may take, we will discuss the patient who complains about others, the controlling patient and the demanding patient.

The Complaining Patient. One frequently encounters patients who voice complaints about the care received at the hands of others. Sometimes these complaints reflect genuine difficulties in gaining access to health care. At other times, they reflect an attitude of criticality toward health-care workers as representatives of other care-givers in the patient's past. Sometimes they represent deflected anger generated by the doctor's present or recent behavior toward the patient which the patient cannot express directly, either because he has general difficulties with the expression of anger or because he fears that open communication with the doctor will result in his treatment's suffering because of his candor.

Whatever the cause, there is a natural tendency either to protect one's colleagues defensively by explaining away the patient's complaints or, on the other hand, to play the role of the good guy by endorsing the patient's complaints. It is more helpful to the patient when the physician exhibits a willingness to listen and a readiness to acknowledge the fact of the patient's complaints. When this is done, patients who are situationally, rather than characteristically, angry will spontaneously take a more accommodating and constructive stance. On the other hand, as explained above, patients who are characteristically angry are best handled by openness and candor, by a cool, consistent and authoritative posture and by maximizing the patient's areas of mastery and competence.

The Controlling Patient. A more indirect form sometimes taken by anger is seen in the controlling patient. This patient is typified not by angry outbursts but by his struggle to stay in charge of his own treatment. Hence, he may attempt to anticipate his doctor's diagnosis, press for his physician's working hypothesis and then challenge it, quarrel about the appropriateness of the treatment regimen, etc. If these maneuvers stir up the competitive urges of the physician, the struggle can escalate to the point where the patient rejects the physician's valuable advice or the doctor declines to treat the patient who will not listen to him. In patients, this form of antagonism often reflects a lifelong characteristic pattern of relating to potential helpers, and it springs from a basic distrust of parental figures and their surrogates.

When this characterological propensity for suspicion exists, it tends to be potentiated by a strange or poorly understood environment. Medical procedures which are not understood or equipment which is not familiar to these patients represent unconscious threats to be met with a display of strength and mastery. To such patients, accepting help is equivalent to being weak and vulnerable, and they struggle to remain in a position of dominance and mastery. Such a patient is best handled by avoiding direct conflicts, offering the patient the fullest possible explanations of procedures and possible outcomes in advance and maximizing the opportunities for him to exercise options. In short, the greater the extent to which such a patient can be offered the role of a collaborator in his treatment, the less he will feel required to struggle for mastery.

The Demanding Patient. The last type of patient to be dealt with in this chapter, the demanding patient, also represents difficulties which are most often characterological and lifelong. The demanding patient struggles to extract the maximum in attention and care from his physician. He will want to be seen frequently, call frequently in emergency situations, be disappointed at treatments which are not energetic and bombard the physician with multiple minor complaints. We classify such patients as angry because their grasping, guilt-inducing behavior often reflects unconscious anger and a feeling that love and concern are never freely given, but are obtained only by extortion. Doctors and other care-givers often react by avoiding such patients, revealing their own angry responses to such patients in the abusive and slangy names they assign to them (e.g., "crocks"). The difficulty is that the patient's legitimate needs may be overlooked and his health may suffer because his grasping maneuvers stimulate avoidant behavior in his care-givers. With the most difficult of these patients, limits will have to be set, and firmness in setting these limits can free the doctor to be available clearly and effectively within those limits. The physician should realize in such cases that the more evasive he is the more the patient will feel unconsciously impelled to involve him. Therefore, within the limits he has set, he should make himself available to the patient, display interest in his situation and even initiate contacts.

For example, if the physician has decided to speak with such a patient in a hospital setting, the interview will be more successful if the doctor comes into the room and sits down, making himself available to the patient but firmly terminating the interview at the appropriate time. The interview will suffer if the doctor stands by the door, signaling his desire to leave and stimulating the patient throughout the interview to engage him more fully. Similarly, the ending of the interview will go more smoothly if the doctor terminates the interview by referring to the time of the next contact. On an outpatient basis, suggesting that the patient call the physician back to keep him informed of the progress of the treatment can forestall unnecessary emergency calls and emergency room visits.

*　*　*　*

In review, this chapter has tried to clarify the various forms that anger takes in patients and the techniques that are useful in dealing with them. It has also stressed the difference between characterological and situational anger in patients and has pointed out the importance of recognizing the transitory nature of situational reactions and the beneficial consequences of permitting the expression of such feelings.

REFERENCES

1. BLUM, R. H. *The Management of the Doctor-Patient Relationship.* McGraw-Hill, New York, 1960.
2. MORGAN, W. L., AND ENGEL, G. L. *The Clinical Approach to the Patient.* W. B. Saunders, Philadelphia, 1969.

CHAPTER 6

AFFECTION IN PATIENTS

ALVIN G. BURSTEIN, Ph.D.

As we have already remarked, the doctor-patient relationship, like other helping relationships, often serves as a hothouse in which strong feelings flourish. In the previous chapter, we explored the issues involved in understanding and managing the angry patient; in this chapter, we are concerned about the unrealistically affectionate patient.

Sexual Intercourse with Patients

An extreme but not uncommon example of intense and unproductive mutual emotional involvement is sexual intercourse or other erotic involvement between patient and physician. If survey data are to be relied upon, between 5% and 15% of practicing physicians report having had erotic involvement with patients. In such situations, it is commonly the case that the physician will report having intercourse not with only one patient, but with many patients. Most striking, almost all physicians, including those involved, disapprove of such relations. The physician having intercourse with patients is an example of a person emotionally out of control, engaging in behavior of which he himself disapproves. To understand these behaviors, we will turn first to their origins.

Psychosocial Origins

All human beings carry within them residues of an infancy in which being held, touched and loved were necessary for normal psychological development and, indeed, for the maintenance of life. Zoologists are familiar with the problem/of mortality in higher primates deprived of "mothering" but not nourishment. Harry Harlow has demonstrated the need for physical contact and social stimulation in infant monkeys, in his famous studies with terry cloth and wire surrogate mothers. In the human sphere, René Spitz's pioneering study dramatically illustrated the lethal consequences of marasmus, a failure to thrive among infants provided with nourishment and basic physical needs but deprived by circumstance of the opportunity to be "mothered"— to be held, fondled and loved.

At the core, then, of every human's earliest social experiences is a need for contact and love. The contact between a patient who is frightened and in pain and the doctor whose help he seeks can act powerfully to re-evoke these dependent and affectionate needs. These factors have helped to shape a mythology concerning the family doctor in our culture. Kindly, wise, strong and infinitely knowledgeable, he meets his patients' needs for spiritual counsel and personal advice and sees tirelessly to their physical needs. So important is this mythological figure in our culture that it has been given literary expression in the "Dr. Kildare" role played for years on radio and later adapted for television, as well as in the television series "Marcus Welby, M.D." and in the comic strip "Rex Morgan." Such literary forms not only reflect social expectations that doctors will function as superparents, but also powerfully reinforce the likelihood that such expectations will occur in both the patient and his doctor.

The motivations specific to individual patients who are unrealistically affectionate vary with their personalities. In many cases, the affectionate, trusting response is a re-evocation of childhood situations of being cared for by loving parents. In other cases, when the patient has a history of being required to conform, and a general character trait of compliance, positive feelings toward the physician may represent an effort to curry favor with a powerful and potentially punitive parent surrogate and may mask unconscious feelings of anger. In still other cases, the doctor-patient relationship may become heavily sexualized because of the patient's general tendency to relate in a seductive manner to all members of the opposite sex.

The circumstances of the illness also strongly shape the patient's response. Patients who are fearful of the consequences of their treatment or of the prognosis for their illness are realistically insecure, regardless of their more abiding personality characteristics. Patients whose treatment involves them in frequent, intensive and intimate relationships with the physician are also prone to emotional overdependence on the physician. In both cases, the patient is prone to view the doctor as a magical, romantic figure who possesses all of the qualities that a young child attributes to his parents. The more insecure the patient is at the moment, the more intense will be the expectation of help and the more the patient will attempt to win the approval, favor and affection of the physician. Women who are pregnant commonly experience such feelings toward their obstetricians. These feelings also occur frequently in patients undergoing intensive psychotherapy. They are most profoundly seen, however, in the surgical patient. Surgeons, especially those who carry out heroic lifesaving procedures such as cardiovascular surgery, invariably have experiences in which some former patients maintain contact and strive to involve the physician in their private lives.

There are also factors in the doctor's situation which lead him to encourage affection in his patients. The doctor whose altruism or grandiosity leads him to sacrifice his private life to his professional calling thus deprives himself of important sources of love. The normal need to be loved and admired may then lead this physician to encourage or to depend on the affection which his patients will offer.

Such emotional investment occurs in less blatant ways and in less spectacular cases. Consider the case of Alice O. Mrs. O. and her husband were being evaluated for fertility problems. In the course of Mrs. O.'s physical examination, a cyst was discovered on her left breast. The physician believed that the cyst was benign and that the decision to remove it was an entirely elective one. Mrs. O. asked her doctor to arrange surgery, as she felt that getting herself in perfect physical condition would somehow enhance her chances of getting pregnant. She met the surgeon, for the first time, in the hospital the afternoon before the operation. He examined and talked with her for about 15 minutes, explaining the procedure and telling her that she would be discharged the following afternoon, if there were no complications. The surgery was uneventful. Following the operation, the surgeon again met briefly with Mrs. O. to check on her condition and to tell her how the operation had gone. She was discharged that evening, with an appointment to return to the outpatient clinic to have the sutures removed.

Four days after the operation, the surgeon was hospitalized with a myocardial infarct. Mrs. O. was routinely notified that the removal of her sutures would have to be taken care of by another physician and, by way of explanation, was told of the surgeon's illness. She became quite concerned and moderately depressed. She pressed for details of the surgeon's condition and phoned the hospital daily to inquire about his progress. In short, she reacted as though the illness had struck a member of the family, rather than a man with whom she had dealt for only a few minutes. Mrs. O.'s reaction was not pathological, but, rather, it reflects the deep emotional investment which patients often make in the physician treating them, especially if the condition being treated is one in which the patient has a high degree of emotional involvement and concern.

Recognition of Unrealistically Affectionate Patients

Because affection, trust and the wish to please are expectable and desirable aspects of the doctor-patient relationship, it is important to be able to recognize evidence of unrealistic affection in patients. No physician will have difficulty recognizing the patient who is overtly seductive, but what is more important is recognition of subtle signs of overaffection and excessive dependency, realizing that most of these are not specifically sexual. A key point is to note whether the attitudes exist in situations where the patient *is* realistically ill, frightened or insecure or whether they occur in inappropriate medical situations in which they do not facilitate treatment. Such responses are frequently characterized by flattery, ingratiation, subservience or child-like behavior. The patient may say, "Miss Williams told me what a marvelous doctor you are. I know you will be able to help me." These are the patients who show up early for appointments and who couple this with such state-ments as "I know you are busy, doctor. I don't mind waiting, I have all the time in the world."

As with all patients, the physician's assessment of his own behavior and feelings can be one of his most powerful tools. The physician should suspect that he is dealing with such a patient, and is unrealistically meeting the patient on his or her terms, whenever he finds himself feeling overly self-satisfied or embarrassed around the patient or giving extra time to the patient. Similarly, he may find himself being fatherly or concealing the truth in such circumstances.

Effects on Treatment

From a practical point of view, the patient's investment in his doctor has both advantages and disadvantages. It can be an important source of support and can blunt the anxiety of patients caught in a frightening situation. In addition, it can increase that patient's amenability to treatment and the likelihood that he will follow a treatment regimen, even if it is a difficult or painful one. In general, it very much enhances the patient's ability to trust his doctor, curtailing his need to engage in testing maneuvers.

On the other hand, the development of an unrealistic investment in the doctor can be a problem if it results in the patient's insistence on overbur-densome contacts. Substantial problems can also develop if the patient's romanticized view of the physician begins to corrode the doctor's objectivity, encouraging his gradiosity or tempting him to use the patient's investment in him to take advantage of the patient sexually, financially or otherwise. Particularly for inexperienced physicians, involvement with an unrealistically affectionate patient can constitute a seductive hazard.

The Management of Unrealistically Affectionate Patients

Despite the dangers, however, the clinical advantages of facilitating a trusting relationship make it important that the physician understand how to facilitate his patient's investment in him. The doctor should be reluctant to divulge personal information about himself. The social distance induced by the asymmetry in information sharing and the ambiguity about the reality of the doctor's actual likes and dislikes, his personal life, etc. will facilitate the patient's investment in him. Use of the patient's first name is a concrete way in which the asymmetry of the doctor-patient relationship can be stressed.

Willingness to touch patients, particularly when they are frightened or in pain, and the willingness to spend time with them when they feel in crisis will also facilitate the formation of a trusting relationship.

Burdensome or dangerous aspects of the unrealistically affectionate patient's investment in his doctor can be controlled in various ways. Firm limit setting, as discussed earlier in the section on the angry, dependent patient, is helpful. Also useful is reliance on the use of tokens, symbolic representations of relationship. The patient can regard the prescription of a medication, and indeed the medicine itself, as a gratifying manifestation of the doctor's interest; this is the basis of the placebo effect of many benign prescriptions. Then, too, particularly in an inpatient setting, effective use can be made of ancillary personnel, who can be seen by the patient as the doctor's alter egos.

The physician should avoid the seductive temptation to react as if he actually is omnipotent and omniscient. In addition to the reasons previously mentioned is the fact that contradictory or seemingly incompatible feelings can exist side by side in a patient. The physician who falls into the trap of being a hero is likely to find that he will not be able to meet the fantasy-based, idealized wishes of the patient, in which case affection and praise can quickly turn to anger and vindictiveness.

The above devices are basically ways of reducing the potentially burdensome time demands made by the unrealistically affectionate patient. To deal with the more subtle difficulties that arise as a result of the doctor's response to the patient's investment in him requires both maturity and honesty. Both grandiosity and the temptation to use patients will be reduced as a function of healthy and satisfying peer relationships. The doctor in training, in particular, should share with peers his trials and successes as a physician in the making, while cultivating opportunities to create life and life satisfactions not bounded by the walls of the hospital or consulting rooms.

*   *   *   *

In this chapter, we have discussed the psychological and social factors which foster unrealistically affectionate feelings in patients. Whether these feelings impede or foster the treatment relationship will depend on the doctor's sensitivity to them, his understanding of their origin and meaning and his skill in managing them.

REFERENCES

1. KARDENER, S. H., FULLER, M., AND MENSH, I. A. A survey of physicians' attitudes and practices regarding erotic and nonerotic contact with patients. Am. J. Psychiatry 130:1077–1081, 1973.
2. PERRY, J. A. Physicians' erotic and non-erotic physical involvement with patients. Am. J. Psychiatry 133:838–840, 1976.

CHAPTER 7

THE RIGID, DENYING, OBSESSIVE PATIENT

CHARLES L. BOWDEN, M.D.

Among the common maladaptive responses to illness are those in which the patient is rigid, minimizes symptoms, withholds information or doubts the correctness of treatment. These responses can be classified into more specific characteristic patterns.

Aggressive, Pseudo-independent Patients

Some patients act aggressively as a means of dealing with their own anxieties or feelings of helplessness. To be sick, to be immobilized, to be obliged to submit to a hospital routine are especially upsetting to such persons. Behaviorally, such patients are restless and overactive even when quite ill. They are likely to minimize or deny symptoms and to dwell on past vigor.

Pseudo-independent patients usually attempt to control the treatment situation by such measures as proclaiming that they cannot enter the hospital just now because of important business or by taking charge. The physician who jumped off the recovery bed after his surgery and walked to his room, carrying his intravenous bottle elevated in one hand, is a too typical example. Affectively, these patients appear irritable and are easily provoked to anger.

The key to handling such a patient is to help him to regain the feeling of being in control of the situation. He should be assured that his active collaboration with you is most helpful and important. Treatment procedures should be fully explained and the results of diagnostic procedures shared. Providing direct emotional support should be attempted cautiously. In general, it is better to let the patient adopt the degree of emotional distance which he finds tolerable.

Withholding Patients

Some patients minimize, distort and deny symptoms. Such efforts can occur both deliberately and outside of awareness. However, even when consciously distorting, these patients are not fully aware of the amount they withhold or of their motivation. They may withhold or distort out of fear that if they tell the truth the physician will be angry, scornful or wish to hospitalize or commit them. Similarly, they may fear embarrassment if the truth is acknowledged. Others distort out of a wish to please the physician, to report what they believe he wants to hear, even if it does not reflect their experiences.

Behaviorally, this kind of patient is betrayed by the disparity between his condition and the way in which he reports it. These are the patients who dismiss all symptoms as "just gas," "a touch of rheumatism," "a little indigestion" or "just a virus."

In treating such patients it is important to keep returning gently but firmly to the symptom areas and to emphasize questions about the concrete circumstances of the problem. Functional limitation should be carefully assessed: whether, for example, the person has limited his life by not climbing stairs. It is essential to interview a reliable informant when treating such patients. For the hospitalized patient, daily notes by nurses and other staff who are able to observe him in a more casual, less threatening way are especially useful.

Rigid, Obsessive Patients

Obsessive Personality Predisposing to Psychosomatic Disorders. The obsessive personality predisposes to, or is a causal factor in, many psychosomatic disorders. Among them are ulcerative colitis, granulomatous enteritis, peptic ulcer, irritable colon syndrome, myocardial infarction, hyperthyroidism, urticaria and rheumatoid arthritis. All of these disorders are multifactorial in origin. The predisposing personality pattern is certainly not present in every case, and the term is not always used by the original researchers. Yet it is striking that one and only one basic personality structure seems to correlate with most psychophysiological disorders. What influences the organ system involved is unclear, but it appears to involve early life patterning, wherein, in response to the same stress, some persons respond as "gastric reactors," others as "cardiac reactors" and so on.

These persons are characterized by orderliness, obstinancy, parsimony, pedantry and meticulousness. They often have difficulty in opening up and sharing with others, both their possessions and information, on the one hand, and their physical affection on the other. They have significant dependency needs but cannot tolerate expression of them and even tend consciously to repudiate their existence. They seem to fear letting go of their emotional control, lest the underlying emotions overwhelm them. They deny their own anger, although it may be expressed in passive-aggressive behavior such as keeping an important person waiting.

The common defense mechanisms used by such persons include (in addition to passive aggression) hypochondriasis, intellectualization, repression and reaction formation.

The situations which precipitate illness or maladaptive behavior in a person with an obsessional personality make-up are *threats to the survival, security and dependency needs* of the individual, which he cannot acknowledge, either to himself or to others, primarily because he would view clinging to others as weak, shameful and unlovable. In other words, only through doggedly plodding on in his obsessive fashion can he ever hope to gain the gratification he desires. He does all of these things because *performance* is seen as the only means acceptable to his conscience for achieving approval, love and security. To do otherwise causes him anxiety.

Parents of these individuals are usually performance oriented, with high standards, and often couple with this an intellectual orientation. Mothers are seen as harsh, domineering and not having directly provided much affection or dependency gratification. They overemphasize the dictum that nothing is free, everything must be earned. Goodness is thus viewed as almost solely a means to an end.

Although these interactions can occur throughout development, they tend to occur most predictably, and with the most pathological consequences, in the age period of 2 to 4. At this age, parents first require the child to inhibit his impulses, setting up a struggle between conformity and independence. He is expected to gain control over his bowel and bladder functions, to eat without making too much of a mess and largely to dress himself. These tasks tend to bring about a reactionary aggression and negativism in the child. Parents who have expectations which the child is neither biologically nor psychosocially ready to meet thus sow the seeds for an obsessive overconcern with details, a fear of expressing angry feelings and a fear of loss of bodily and emotional controls in general. An example of a similar pathogenic childhood experience occurring at a later age is a boy whose father died suddenly when the boy was 13 years old. As the only child, he had new responsibilities thrust upon him. He had to work long hours to help out financially. He was in many ways the man of the house, a role which he could not adequately assume for both maturational and relational reasons. As a result, he developed an overseriousness and related characteristics which had not been a part of his previous personality.

Two general principles of child rearing can aid in preventing the later development of maladaptive, rigid, obsessional behavior. First, a child should not be expected to live in a world of controls until he is biologically ready to do so. It makes no sense to attempt bowel training until a child is maturationally able to control his bowels or to emphasize verbal controls until he is able to comprehend and verbally respond to word statements. Second, control should not be exclusively emphasized at any stage of development, whether for bowel, verbal, intellectual or other functions. The reason is that some release of controls, at least over one's feelings, is essential for pleasure.

Obsessive Personality Influencing "Nonpsychosomatic" Disease. Ingrained personality traits which may have previously facilitated adaptation may be seriously detrimental under changed circumstances.

A 36-year-old woman had maintained her self-esteem in her marriage by being a vigorous helpmate in her husband's business and stoically taking over many of his responsibilities around the home, while also caring for their six children. She developed hepatitis. In the hospital, she was overactive and unable to rest. She minimized reporting symptoms and avoided making appropriate demands of the nursing staff. After hospitalization, she continued her pattern of overworking herself and was unable to set personal limits. As she was not able to help with her husband's business, she felt she was not "earning her keep" and was frequently depressed. A particularly hectic, unnecessarily physically exhausting weekend was followed by a recrudescence of her symptoms.

This woman consciously denied angry feelings but continually expressed them by haranguing her family in a moralistic tone. She harbored considerable unconscious anger toward physicians and her husband for not meeting her needs. This was expressed only in cynical comments and negativistic behavior. She believed that when physicians told her to "ease up" on herself, both in terms of her harsh conscience and her physical activities, they were practicing "reverse psychology" and were actually trying to get her to be more orderly and self-disciplined. Because of the ingrained nature of such characteristics, psychotherapy should usually be involved in the treatment of such a patient who finds that his life is catching up with a bad character adaptation.

Illnesses Which Encourage Rigid, Perfectionistic Behavior. There are a number of disorders wherein successful management inclines the patient toward, or even necessitates the behavioral development of, rigid, perfectionistic behavior. These are, in general, chronic illnesses which require regular, fairly constant attention and responsibility on the part of the patient. Diabetes mellitus is a good example. The patient must learn about the procedures for self-injecting insulin and for checking urines. He must know about dietary equivalents and the effects of exercise, weather, irregular eating and intercurrent illnesses on his diabetes. He must know the importance of such small items as carefully drying between his toes. Little wonder that such behavior may generalize into hygiene-oriented life-styles, sometimes to the consternation of friends, relatives and physician. Other examples include obesity management, which often involves the development of elaborate and compulsive rituals about eating and avoiding food, and treatments of alcoholism in which the avoidance of liquor becomes a theme which dominates the patient's life. Frequently the successful management of the obese or alcoholic patient literally involves the induction of a benign or positive compulsion and/or obsession, a positive addiction to healthy diets and liquor avoidance.

The physician treating patients with such disorders should assess how prone they are, on the basis of their pre-existing personalities or their fears concerning their illness, to exceed his basic instructions for responsibly managing their illnesses. He can then modify his instructions and subsequent encouragement or criticism of the patient's actions accordingly. That is, patients with a basically rigid and perfectionistic orientation require reassurance about the acceptability of deviation from the minutiae of a schedule, whereas many other patients require the opposite kind of emphasis.

Treatment Approach

We have discussed some treatment approaches in the presentation of the various types of rigid, denying, obsessive patients. Some additional general instructions are in order.

These patients are not infrequently late for treatment. The physician may say, "Mr. Brown, if you continue to be this late for treatment, I'm not going to be able to give you as good care as I'd like, because I am rushed, knowing I am keeping the next patient waiting."

These patients also tend to be overly frugal. An explanation of the long term financial and physical gains to be realized from treatment often will prevent the patient's failing to follow through with treatment, out of fear that not to do so will be too expensive.

Certain kinds of real or feared disorders are special problems for the patient who denies dependency needs. Cardiac and emotional disturbances tend to be feared because they are considered to be catastrophic and sudden, often striking without warning. Cardiac disorders are viewed as taking away the patient's ability to function, thus making him dependent, which he fears. A "nervous breakdown" is viewed as a loss of emotional control which is also feared by the rigid, obsessive patient. Although public education about these disorders has been helpful, it gives some patients raw material for obsessive overconcern. A careful exploration of unrealistic fears of the patient can lead to clarifying, educational explanations which diminish the patient's anxiety and increase his security and trust in the treatment process.

Problems with such patients are easier to manage if they are not ingrained. Although early life experiences are often very important, the nonpsychiatric physician should restrict his work to the area of current stresses, as he generally has neither the time nor the training to explore the patient's past experiences therapeutically. In patients in whom rigid, perfectionistic, obsessive behavior is characterologically rooted in past experiences, psychiatric consultation should be obtained.

* * * *

Rigid, obsessive, doubting behaviors constitute a large group of patient responses to illness. Proper handling is predicated on an accurate assessment of the determinants of the response. What is useful with pseudo-independence or denial as a response to transient situational factors may be considerably different from the appropriate handling of characterologically obsessive patients. Appreciation of the various factors, at different phases of the life cycle, which can predispose to these responses can be especially helpful in preventive efforts.

REFERENCES

1. ADAMS, P. L. Family characteristics of obsessional children. *Am. J. Psychiatry 128:*1414, 1972. (A clear, preventively useful summary of the family, based on experiences of children with obsessional disorders.)
2. BLUM, R. H. *The Management of the Doctor-Patient Relationship.* McGraw-Hill, New York, 1960.

CHAPTER 8

PAIN, FEAR AND ANXIETY

CHARLES L. BOWDEN, M.D.

The frequency with which patients present with complaints of fearfulness or anxiety may be judged from the fact that anti-anxiety agents are the most commonly prescribed drugs in medical practice. Inappropriate use of such medications can be one of the least productive ways of dealing with such feelings, because it can reinforce the notion that anxiety as such is a disease and that the patient lacks the basic psychological capacities to deal with stress.

Not only can anxiety in patients be difficult for physicians to manage, but pain, especially when chronic and intractable, can also be problematic. Pain is a psychological state of suffering usually attributed to bodily damage. Fear can be defined as anticipation of pain or danger. Anxiety is sometimes thought of as more vague than fear, but this distinction is not always useful. Because of the natural links between pain, fear and anxiety and because of their amenability to behavioral control, they will be considered together in this chapter.

Origins of Pain

The neurological basis of pain is unclear. Some years ago pain was thought of as a fairly direct neurological response to tissue damage. In fact, the experience of pain was widely regarded as the psychological correlate of activation of special sensory nerve cells. Two lines of evidence have necessitated discarding this view. The first is the disappointing results of neurosurgical treatment of chronic pain. The second is the data which begins with the observation by Beecher of injured soldiers in World War II and culminates in studies such as those by Mersky, which clearly indicate that, although tissue pathology and pain are certainly related, the relationship is indirect and is mediated by many psychosocial factors.

Psychological Approaches to Pain Control

A striking application of psychological principles to pain control is the Lamaze approach to childbearing, known both as psychoprophylaxis in childbirth and childbirth without pain. The Lamaze approach is based on the principles of Pavlovian psychology and so-called classical conditioning. According to these principles, pain, an activity of lower or more primitive brain centers, is inhibited by activity of the higher brain centers. Psychoprophylaxis in childbirth stresses active, voluntary, cognitively focused participation by the mother in the birth process and minimal use of anesthesia. The mother is taught to visualize clearly the various stages of the birth process, and to control her breathing and diaphragmatic movements to influence the course of the fetus through the birth canal. Anxiety, which might be initiated by unfamiliar procedures and surroundings, is defused by early exposure of the woman to the equipment, procedures and setting of the expected delivery.

Another increasingly important psychological approach to pain control is the operant pain control ward or clinic such as that of Fordyce. These treatment units are largely based on Skinnerian principles of operant conditioning; they focus on clear specification of behaviors which are to be systematically reinforced and those which are to be extinguished. A great deal of attention is also given to careful sequencing or shaping of behaviors in the desired direction. For example, patients are not reinforced either socially or with medication for complaints or inability to perform. Praise and encouragement are offered for successful performance. Medication, when it is prescribed, is on a fixed time basis (e.g., every 4 hours). Slow progressive increases in levels of activity up to the point of physiological tolerance, without regard for expressions of pain, are rewarded with praise, rest periods or ward privileges. Successful operant control of pain requires careful study of the individual to determine which reinforcers will be effective for him and effective control of the environment so that desired behaviors are reinforced and undesirable ones are not.

Hypnosis as a means of pain control has a long and sometimes controversial history. Hilgard and Hilgard recently reviewed the solid basis for hypnotic phenomena and their application in the relief of clinical pain in cancer, obstetrics, surgery and dentistry. Specific techniques include inducing anesthesia, substitution of sensation and dissociation. The resultant effects are

highly specific and cannot be accounted for simply on the basis of reduced
fear and anxiety, although that clearly occurs as well.

Clinical Picture of Anxiety

Although anxiety is the most common symptom which patients experience,
it tends to be overlooked by the physician. One reason for this is that,
although most patients are anxious, they often do not explicitly reveal it,
feeling that it is a "childish" reaction that should be concealed. If the patient
does openly discuss his anxiety, the physician is often erroneously tempted to
calm him in ways that encourage the notion that anxiety is childish or sick.
In addition to its frequent occurrence, anxiety is important because it is the
basic emotion which brings repression and the other adaptational mechanisms into operation.

Anxiety may be defined as the *emotional reaction to perceived or anticipated
danger.* The ability to avoid a danger is increased if the danger can be
anticipated. Thus the signal, or anticipatory, quality of anxiety is central to
our understanding. Anxiety and fear are indistinguishable in terms of physiological response and motivational stimulus. For this reason, the terms are
best considered as interchangeable, as Rado has cogently argued. Because
anxiety is a universal occurrence, it is important to distinguish between
"normal" and pathological anxiety. In general, normal anxiety is propor-
tional to the threat, is consciously perceived and does not lead to behavioral
blocking. Pathological anxiety is disproportionate to the threat, often involves
putting certain thoughts or feelings out of awareness and leads to the
maladaptive invocation of defense mechanisms.

The usual manifestations of anxiety in the overtly anxious patient include
fears and apprehension, feelings of impending disaster or death, complaints
of chest pain, palpitations, faintness, dizziness and respiratory distress. The
patient may appear irritable and inattentive and may have rapid, shallow
respirations, cold and moist hands, sweaty axillae, a rapid pulse, small pupils,
restlessness and tremor.

In the general evaluation and treatment of patients, more subtle indicators
of anxiety are often more important to recognize. When, during an open-
ended interview, the physician finds that the patient's responses are becoming
briefer and less adequate and that he is being forced to ask more directive
questions, he should strongly suspect a rising amount of anxiety in the
patient. The patient may talk excessively or ramble about irrelevant material.
A nervous laugh, especially with a "teeth-bared" kind of tense smile, may be
present. The patient may ask innumerable questions. While acknowledging
no *personal* concern or anxiety, a patient may speak about a *third* person and
that person's fear of surgery, or the manner in which the doctors and nurses
treated him or the consequences of his medical treatment. Similarly, the

anxiety may be displaced to the patient's family: the patient states that he cannot come to the hospital because his children need him or he has work which "just can't wait." Although there is often a realistic issue in any of the above presentations, it is important to recognize that they predominantly reflect personal anxiety of which the person is either unaware or, if aware, is unable to express directly.

A useful distinction between trait and state anxiety has been introduced by Speilberger. Persons high on trait anxiety are characteristically anxious across situations. State anxiety, on the other hand, is situationally specific. Trait anxiety, which the person brings to the situation, and state anxiety, which the situation induces in the person, can be separately assessed.

Hyperventilation Syndrome. One symptom complex is so common and so often misunderstood by the patient that it merits specific discussion. Anxiety can set off overbreathing and a consequent chain of frightening symptoms. More often than not the person will be unaware of either the anxiety state or the hyperventilation. In fact, the person may subjectively have a sense of air hunger, a feeling that insufficient air is getting past the throat, which may feel blocked. Symptoms include faintness, visual disturbances, nausea, dizziness, headache, a sense of fullness in the head, neck and chest, breathlessness and palpitations. The person may have parasthesias, especially numbness and tingling in the tips of fingers and in the perioral area, difficulty swallowing and tetany. Vasomotor changes of either a hot, flushed sensation or cold and sweating may be present.

The physiological mechanism for the reaction is the lowered CO_2 concentration caused by the blowing off of CO_2. This results in the decreased caliber of cerebral blood vessels with consequent hypoxia and a change in acid-base balance leading to a respiratory alkalosis.

The experience can be a frightening one and can mimic a variety of acute problems, including myocardial infarction. Once the diagnosis is made, excessive testing should be avoided, as should medicating without explanation, because this may reinforce in the patient's mind the idea that something major is physically wrong. An explanation of the psychophysiological process in terms the patient can understand and application of crisis intervention techniques to deal with situational and emotional pressures are indicated. The patient can usually learn to recognize some premonitory symptoms and abort the syndrome, either through deliberately controlling breathing by taking measured, slow, deep breaths or breathing into a paper sack. This latter technique, which works because the person rebreathes CO_2, is limited in application because carrying and using a paper sack is often impractical or embarrassing.

Predisposing Circumstances

Factors inherent in many medical situations predispose to fear responses. The common feature in such situations is the sense of helplessness that is engendered, coupled with the expectation that experiences of pain may ensue. The prototypical experience is surgery, wherein the patient will be unconscious and totally at the mercy of a set of persons, some of whom he will never see, who will excise or repair his bodily tissue. Other representative examples include the experience of anesthesia, a proctoscopic examination, sitting with mouth agape and rubber dam in place in the dentist's chair or the simple procedure of blood drawing.

Cultural Variations

There are significant cultural variations in the expression of anxiety. Southern Chinese have a strong belief that proper function of the male genitals is essential to the preservation of life. Not surprisingly, then, over one-half of southern Chinese patients with anxiety complain of sexual symptoms. An unusual affliction among these Chinese is koro, for which the Chinese expression is "shook yang," or shrinking penis. It consists of an acute fear that the penis is shrinking into the abdomen, with potentially lethal consequences. The penis is grasped manually by the patient, his wife, a relative or a friend until the "crisis" is over.

A folk illness common throughout Latin America and among Mexican-Americans is "susto," or fright. The symptoms are dyspnea, indigestion, palpitations, loss of usual interests, irritability, insomnia, anorexia and fear of death. It appears to be a mixture of anxiety and depression and it is said to occur following a frightening experience or the death of a loved one. It is believed by folk healers to lead to heart trouble, ulcers or mental deficiency. In treating "susto," the curandero, or folk healer, uses a combination of activities. Magical rituals, such as brushing the body with a bundle of granada leaves or massaging with eggs, are used. Relatives and friends are urged to be tolerant and encouraging. To help the sufferer relax, vacations, listening to music and various diets are suggested. Extensive and central use is made of talking, of getting the patient to tell as much as he can about the circumstances which led to the development of the symptoms. The patient is encouraged to talk freely of his weaknesses and transgressions.

The point to be made by these examples is that anxiety must be understood in terms of the person's self-concept, personal values and culture.

Differential Considerations

Anxiety is a common feature of many psychiatric disorders, including affective disorders, obsessive disorders, organic delirium, schizophrenia, conversion symptoms, phobias and epilepsy. It may also accompany practically all nonpsychiatric illnesses, and it commonly occurs in otherwise nonsymptomatic people at times of "normal" crisis, such as before exams or a child's first trip to school. It is essential to differentially diagnose illnesses which may present with anxiety-like symptoms, especially because anxiety so frequently secondarily accompanies other illnesses. The patient with paroxysmal tachy-cardia usually has a heart rate of 140 to 220 per minute, whereas the rate is generally below 140 in the anxious patient. Thyrotoxicosis presents with a fine tremor and warm, pink palms rather than cold, clammy ones. The pulse remains elevated while the patient is asleep. The usual laboratory test abnormalities are present. Episodic hypoglycemia has an associated low blood sugar, and the symptoms are relieved by food. In the rare disorder of pheochromocytoma, all complaints are associated with high blood pressure, and the laboratory tests are abnormal.

Anxiety may stand alone as a syndrome. One syndrome in particular is, in fact, an anxiety state. This is the Da Costa syndrome, otherwise known as cardiac neurosis or neurocirculatory asthenia. The symptoms are essentially those of anxiety. In addition, feelings of fatigue are common, and a specific focus of anxiety on the heart is present. This syndrome is especially important to recognize and to know how to manage, as 10 to 15% of patients seen in cardiology practices have anxiety states only.

Physiological Processes

Compared with some of the detailed mechanisms of disordered norepi-nephrine metabolism and other biochemical parameters which have been discovered in depressive disorders, the detailed central nervous system phys-iology of anxiety remains unclear. The acute phase of anxiety is associated with vagal, parasympathetic hyperactivity. Clinically, the parasympathetic activation is usually overpowered by excessive secretion of epinephrine and, to a lesser degree, norepinephrine. Most of the visceral reactions associated with sustained anxiety are a function of this excessive adrenergic activity. An important point is that both trophotropic (primarily parasympathetic) and ergotropic (primarily sympathetic) systems are operative.

Fear, which is the source of conflict, is probably an inborn physiological response, with complex bodily responses that are mediated particularly by the autonomic nervous system, as classically described by Walter Cannon in *The Wisdom of the Body*. To these basic physiological responses have been added man's efficient distance receptors and his symbolizing processes. Thus, concepts and symbols within the sociocultural matrix can cause physiological fear responses. For example, man's awareness of his own risk of death can generate a fight-or-flight response, with increased blood sugar, heart rate, epinephrine and blood coagulability, which are not adaptive responses to the danger.

Treatment

In confronting the patient with his anxiety, it is usually best to make a remark such as "You look worried" or "You seem scared." It is often useful to make a comment such as "Of course, anyone in your shoes would be a little scared," when the physician knows from experience that fear is a usual concomitant to the illness, even if the patient has shown no evidence of anxiety.

Anxiety can be so great that the person is unable to comprehend or correctly respond to the physician's questions or instructions. Beyond that, it may set off maladaptive responses which make the patient even more difficult to treat. Thus, quick intervention is important. A fundamental fact is that talking about anxiety does not increase it. Do not depersonify the patient's plea by falling back on technological expertise. Too often, a prescription for a minor tranquilizer is written, but the person's fears are not discussed; or the patient who is anxious before surgery is given a technological explanation of the procedure and a reassurance of the surgeon's competence, rather than the concern and emotional support which he also needs. Physicians sometimes rationalize their behavior by stating that there is not sufficient time for such interaction. To a considerable degree, however, it is the *quality* of the concern, not the *quantity*, which is important. One famous surgeon was known for his ability to stride quickly into a patient's room before surgery and immediately perceive the patient's fears. Often an arm around the patient's shoulder or a similar physical contact produced a great release and relief of previously unresolved emotions. Seldom did his entire time with the patient take more than a few minutes.

Acknowledging and giving the patient an opportunity to talk about unexpressed or even unrecognized fears immediately reduces their harmful power. Ideas unspoken are threatening because they have no boundaries. Once put into words, they are to a great extent fixed within the limits of those words.

When anxiety is so severe as to disrupt the patient's functioning, minor tranquilizers can be quite useful as an adjunct to treatment. The physician should make clear what the rationale for the medication is. He may say, "Mr. Jones, this medicine should help relieve your tension. Of course, it won't totally remove it. As long as you're in this situation, you have a real source of concern, but, by reducing your tension, you should be better able to deal with the situation at hand and work through it to a more comfortable state of affairs." The important point is that the patient should not develop the incorrect idea that the medication is treating some specific bodily disease or that issues of how he understands and copes with the crisis are unimportant.

The above approaches should be coupled with a competent, confident attitude toward the patient and his problem. Efforts should be made to reduce ambiguity concerning the patient's understanding of his illness. Within suitable limits, the physician and others on the health-care team should make themselves real sources of support to the patient. The kind of reassurance and support will need to be tailored to the particular concerns of the patients. Nevertheless, several concerns are very common; standard responses to them can be gratifyingly effective. Patients with acute anxiety are often brought to emergency rooms, the patients and their families understandably concerned about some serious malady. The physician may say, "Mrs. Williams, I am 95% certain that you have had an anxiety attack. I am going to order several tests so that we can be fully certain that no other condition may be causing your symptoms. Although it may be little consolation to you, anxiety reactions such as yours are among the most frequent problems I see. Usually they are brought on by stresses which have piled up over time, plus a recent situation which has aggravated them." Such a statement provides straightforward information to the patient, provides a framework for him to begin to understand and modify his problem and helps avoid his misconstruing the nature of his disorder. It also helps to abort his using such a reaction in a hypochondriacal manner. Patients should be told that anxiety will not lead to their having a "nervous breakdown" or cause the development of heart disease, if there is any evidence that either of these common misconceptions is present. Similarly, many patients have been led to believe that they suffer from hypertension, when in fact they have shown only the moderate systolic elevation of blood pressure which often accompanies acute anxiety. It is easy to see the importance of avoiding a patient's learning an erroneous but plausible explanation for his anxiety, for, once fixed in his mind with the weight of respected medical opinion behind it, his conviction can be difficult to alter.

Reassurance should be emphatically given with the full authority of the physician backing it up. Not only is this necessary to help prevent rationalizations and misconceptions by the patient, as discussed above, but also to encourage the patient to make the kind of changes in his life circumstances that will improve his condition. Usually the patient will be tentative and uncertain, feelings that are almost intrinsic to the feeling of fear. The authority of the physician—who firmly but gently tells him to reassess what is happening in a part of his life, or to take a 15-minute break at work each day or to take a half-hour warm bath before bed—may be necessary to give him the courage to make the effort to overcome his anxiety.

The following guidelines will help to reduce pain, fear and anxiety.

1. Do not inflict unnecessary discomfort.

2. Do not say "This won't hurt" unless you are absolutely sure you are correct.

3. If there is a possibility of discomfort, warn the patient and explain.

4. Describe discomfort in as precise a way as possible. Avoid the general term "pain."

5. Explain new procedures as to content and function.

6. Promote the patient's active cognitive involvement with the procedures.

7. Reward desirable behaviors, use of less medication, increased activity and active participation.

8. Clearly indicate to a patient how he may ask you to stop a procedure and heed such requests.

9. Do not prescribe analgesics to be taken according to need.

10. Move slowly, talk slowly and give the patient a chance to talk and ask questions.

11. Humanize the environment.

*　　*　　*　*

Anxiety, the most common symptom, is almost always either present or being defended against. It is the basic factor which interferes with communication. However, when the physician understands its role in homeostasis, is attuned to its manifestations and knows a few straightforward principles of handling, it is among the more easily dealt with responses to illness.

REFERENCES

1. BLACHER, R. S. On awakening paralyzed during surgery. *J.A.M.A. 234:*67–68, 1975.
2. CANNON, W. B. *The Wisdom of the Body.* W. W. Norton, New York, 1939.
3. CURTIS, G. C. Psychosomatics and chronobiology: possible implications of neuroendocrine rhythms: a review. *Psychosom. Med. 34:*235, 1972.
4. HILGARD, E. R., AND HILGARD, J. R. *Hypnosis in the Relief of Pain.* W. Kaufmann, Los Altos, Calif., 1975.
5. HORNEY, K. *Neurosis and Human Growth.* W. W. Norton, New York, 1950.
6. RADO, S. Emergency Behavior: with an Introduction to the Dynamics of Conscience, in *Psychoanalysis of Behavior.* Grune & Stratton, New York, 1956.
7. WHITE, J. C., AND SWEET, W. H. *Pain and the Neurosurgeon.* Charles C Thomas, Springfield, Ill., 1969.

CHAPTER 9

THE TEARFUL, DEPRESSED PATIENT

ALVIN G. BURSTEIN, Ph.D.

The word depression has many meanings, and it is not always clear from the context which meaning is intended by the speaker or writer. We will discuss some different clinical usages of the term depression and, after so doing, consider treatment approaches. The diagnostic nomenclature for depressive disorders is confusing. Different authorities use different systems, in part because of recent discoveries about the nature of some of the more serious affective illnesses which are changing physicians' understanding of the basic mechanisms involved. Here we are using terms in a descriptive sense, rather than suggesting an official nomenclature.

Varieties of Depressive States

Depression as a Common Feeling State. When we allude to the feeling state we mean it as nearly synonymous with sadness, or being "blue." Such feelings are transiently common to most persons. The feeling state can have a bittersweet quality to it, whereas the subsequent forms of depression are without any pleasurable edge and often are quite intense.

Mourning. Mourning, or grief, is a healthy, normal reaction to loss. The loss may be of an *emotional tie,* such as the death of a loved one or the breakup of a friendship or love affair. The loss may be *physical,* such as loss of a limb or sustaining a crippling physical injury. The loss may be of a *source of* *gratification or self-esteem,* such as a serious business or professional failure. The loss may even be *symbolic,* such as the loss of one's sense of honor. The person experiencing such losses goes through a predictable series of psychological responses in resolving the stress. Symptomatically, there are feelings of sadness, and crying is frequent. The person has ruminations and acutely felt memories of the lost object. His usual interest in the world and his activity level are diminished. The first psychological response is one of *denial.* The person tries almost literally to shut his eyes to the event. Thoughts such as "This isn't real," "This can't be happening to me" and "This is like a nightmare" are common. Sometimes little emotion is experienced in this phase. The person speaks of being stunned, of being preoccupied with some irrelevant detail of the situation. A patient stated, "When they told me it was cancer, I couldn't seem to grasp it. All I could think of was that there was this fly in the room, and someone would have to get rid of it." This initial phase of denial probably constitutes an emergency shutdown of psychological processes in the face of overwhelming stress. It may last minutes, hours or, occasionally, days. Normally, it then gives way to the next phase of the process: anger.

In the *angry phase,* the person begins to express his reaction to the injustice of having to suffer pain and loss. Although this is often an illogical reaction, it is understandable and human to feel that someone or something has to be blamed for things that go wrong. In the eyes of patients struggling with painful illness, or of their families, that someone is frequently the doctor, the nurses or the hospital. It is important to recognize that anger is part of a natural response pattern, and that defensive replies to such accusations by patients are not usually constructive in that they tend to be interpreted as efforts to minimize the patient's loss. Rather, acknowledging the patient's anger and the magnitude of his loss or pain will facilitate the natural development of the process and the emergence of the next stage: grief.

In the *grief stage,* the full emotional impact of the loss begins to be perceived. Tearfulness, sadness, preoccupation with the loss and acute psychological pain are characteristic. The person feels and shows the hurt that has been suffered. The more complete and deep the grieving process, the more full will be the recovery. In fact, many pathological depressions are largely the result of normal grieving processes that have gotten "stuck"; that is, their resolution has been inhibited by environmental pressures or internal fears. Many cultures recognize the psychological necessity for deep grieving by providing socially sanctioned rituals to encourage full emotional expression on the occasion of the death of family members. Even in cultures in which full grieving following death is encouraged, a full, open response to psychological loss from causes other than death may be difficult. Our culture's stress on "bravery" and self-control may often have unfortunate psychological consequences in the response to any psychological loss.

The final phase of mourning involves *reintegration and reinvolvement:* a willingness to accept life on the terms that are available and an ability to enjoy the satisfactions that exist rather than to pursue those that are irretrievably lost. The course of mourning is usually measured in a few weeks to a few months, although, following major loss, diminished episodic experiences may recur for years, especially on the anniversary of the loss. Dramatic examples of the capacity to reintegrate are found among persons who, following crippling physical loss such as blindness or hemiplegia, are able to construct useful lives.

Secondary Depressive Illnesses. Here we are talking about depressions which occur as the result of, or concomitant to, some other emotional or physical illness or stress. Secondary depression is usually less severe than the primary depressive illnesses which are considered next. A roughly synomymous term for secondary depression is *reactive depression.* These patients have complaints of fatigue, anxiety, feelings of inadequacy, mild decrease in appetite, mild loss of weight and a decrease in their usual interests. Nevertheless, they usually continue to function in a minimally adequate way. These patients have a sense of worthlessness, guilt and hopelessness which is not present in an uncomplicated mourning reaction.

There are at least three common causes of this reaction. First, it may be seen as the result of an unresolved psychological response to loss. The term *pathological mourning* is often applied here. The patient has avoided, rather than expressed, his feelings of anger and grief. Common maladaptive modes of dealing with these submerged feelings include excessive use of alcohol; hypochondriacal complaints; reaction formation, wherein the patient may try to throw himself into activities with a fervor and enthusiasm which usually fools no one; and displacement, whereby the concerns are focused on the patient's job or on another person who does not cause such painful feelings as does the actual source of the loss.

Second, such reactions occur in response to situations which arouse hostility in patients who would feel guilty and anxious if the hostility were openly expressed. The patient may then direct the anger inward, through the defense mechanism of turning against the self. The patient then berates himself for real and imagined shortcomings and presents with the symptoms of secondary depression described earlier.

Third, secondary depression occurs as a response to illness. When the psychological test known as the Minnesota Multiphasic Personality Inventory is taken by physically ill patients, the scale most often elevated is the depression scale, not the scales which contain many items reflecting physical complaints. It is important to emphasize that depressive feelings as a concomitant of illness are normal and to be expected for two reasons. First, a number of diseases are intrinsically associated with severe symptoms such as lack of energy, tiredness and a depressed mood. These include congestive heart failure, hepatitis, mononucleosis, anemia and many types of cancer. Second, a patient is less able to cope while ill, and feelings of disappointment, futility and anger with one's self for being ill are normal. Even though it is illogical, when ill we all tend to regress to nonscientific notions of causality and ask the question, "Why me?" (In addition, the fact of being ill normally inclines most patients toward regressive behavior, increased self-centeredness and greater open dependency on others. Normally, then, depression as a psychological response proceeds in the physically ill patient in essentially the same sequence as that described for mourning.

Nevertheless, some patients, when physically ill, develop significant secondary depression. Their emotional reaction is more severe than the circumstances seem to warrant. The illness is mild, the prognosis is good, but the patient is morose and dejected. In such cases, the illness has activated the person's tendencies to use the mechanism of turning against the self and to maintain a pessimistic view of the future.

In all three of the above circumstances which result in secondary depression, a common psychological pattern is found. The person has a gap between the way he would *like* to function and the way he is *able* to function. The gap may be the result of an unrealistically inflated idealized self. For example, the patient who becomes ill may have fantasied himself omnipotent or invulnerable. On the other hand, the patient's expectations may be realistic, but his ability to perform is actually impaired. In most cases, interactions of the two factors occur. It is a useful concept to think of the *gap* between the person's *expectations* of his performance and his *perceptions* of his actual performance as a measure of the severity of depression.

The childhood experiences of patients with secondary depression predispose to this reaction pattern in response to stress. Such children were often treated as inadequate and incompetent by their overly critical parents. Memories of statements such as "you can't do anything right" are common. In addition, as children, these persons harbored much anger toward their parents but felt guilty and afraid of expressing it, and they developed the pattern of turning the anger and self-reproach inward.

Primary Depressive Illnesses. There is growing evidence that depression may occur as the result of lowered catecholamine production in the central nervous system, rather than as a response to loss. These are the so-called endogenous, or primary, depressions, which are among the most common of the major psychiatric disorders. The patient presents with a sad, depressed mood. He lacks energy, has markedly diminished interest in his usual activities, is unable to concentrate and appears slowed in his thinking and movement. Anorexia, weight loss and a sleep disturbance, wherein he awakens during the night or unreasonably early in the morning, are common symptoms. Agitation may be present, but anxiety seldom is. The patient may have a strong sense of guilt and may harbor suicidal thoughts. All of the symptoms tend to show a diurnal variation, wherein the patient feels worst in the morning and gradually feels better as the day progresses. The onset of this depressive disorder occurs most commonly in the mid-30's. There is often a positive family history of depressive illness.

When a primary depression is diagnosed, a variety of somatic treatments may be considered. Tricyclic antidepressants are effective. Lithium carbonate, first reported as helpful in manic states, now appears also to be helpful in bipolar depressions, which alternate with manic states. Finally, the convulsive therapies, such as electroshock therapy, are effective in some primary depressions which are not responsive to medications. The diagnosis of a biologically based depression should be carefully made. These somatic treatments are not benign and often involve significant risk for the patient.

All patients with primary depression should be referred for psychiatric care. Many other depressive states can and should be effectively dealt with by the nonpsychiatric physician.

Treatment Approaches to Depression and Suicidal Patients

Mourning. The person who is undergoing a normal response to loss may already be under the physician's care for a physical illness. Persons with this response following the loss of an emotional tie also come to the physician as the result of the urging of relatives. A key differential point that distinguishes this from other depressive states is that the patient understands the source of the feelings.

Knowledge of the psychological process of response to loss will help the physician to avoid the error of aborting such feelings. It is essential to be willing to spend time with such patients. Emphasis should be on recognizing the painful feelings that are expressed, rather than on attempts to distract the patient or to cheer him up. The doctor's continuing interest, even though the patient may not be able to acknowledge it at the time, can help toward reintegration of his feelings of self-worth. The short term use of medications for relief of anxiety or difficulties in getting to sleep is sometimes indicated. In addition to their pharmacological impact, medications can serve as a manifestation of the doctor's concern about the patient. They may thus exert considerable, desirable placebo effect, if they are not regarded as a total substitute for personal contact between the doctor and his patient. If the patient perceives the medication as the physician's way of avoiding him, an exacerbation of symptoms may occur.

Explaining to the patient and the family the elements of the theory of psychological response to loss will help them to focus their efforts appropriately. It is especially important to explain the need for catharsis.

The patient should be encouraged to lean temporarily on other people for support. An example of the involvement of family members was the situation of Anthony A. Mrs. A was 28, married, with three children 4, 3, and 6 months of age. One day while Mr. A was at work, his wife went berserk, attacking and inflicting knife wounds on the three children, killing the youngest before killing herself. Fortunately, physical injuries to the two older children were minor, but grave concern was expressed about psychological scarring that might occur as a result of their horrific experiences. One option was to involve the children in psychotherapy. The option chosen was to help the father to offer the children a continuing opportunity to discuss the events that had occurred as well as their emotional reaction to these events. In this particular case, Mr. A. required psychotherapeutic support to deal with his own reactions to the tragedy, but, interestingly, the enforced opportunity to deal with the events with his children facilitated his own recovery. The father's "therapeutic" interaction with his children had three major goals: the first was to avoid distortion and repression of the traumatic events; the second was to permit the children to express their feelings of fright, anger and sadness; and the third was to reinforce the children's trust in their father as a stable and helpful figure, rather than diluting that relationship with professional therapists. Mr. A. was urged not to have "sessions" with the children but, rather, to use the questions that would normally arise as opportunities for asking the children to share their feelings and for clarifying ambiguities in their memories of the event. This treatment really constituted a prophylactic effort to avoid a later depressive reaction. One of the first distortions with which the father had to deal was the children's view that their mother had been provoked by the naughtiness of the infant. This provides a dramatic demonstration of the way in which anger and fear can be transformed into blame and guilt.

A second clinical example of this type of depressive process is provided by the case of a mother whose infant was brought to the hospital for surgical reduction of a simple abdominal hernia. A routine preoperative electrocardiogram suggested a serious congenital heart defect, although not one that precluded the surgery. After the hernia surgery, the mother was told of the electrocardiographic findings by the cardiologist. Several hours later, the surgeon came to the infant's room to check on his condition. He found the infant sleeping and the mother staring out of the window. In the course of telling her about the surgical repair, he mentioned that he had heard about the electrocardiogram and wondered about her reaction. The mother said that she felt somehow to blame. The surgeon reassured her that guilt was a common reaction of parents in this situation and that he was glad that she was in touch with her feelings. In the ensuing 20 minutes, the mother was able to express many of her feelings of uncertainty and fear about her child's situation. She experienced a sense of relief and seemed better able to make the necessary decisions about the child's welfare.

Secondary Depressions. Many of the responses useful in dealing with the mourning patient are equally applicable in those secondary depressions in which the severity or duration of the response must be considered abnormal. An explanation of the depressive process is desirable. Because the precipitant in such cases may not be self-evident, the physician should especially explain how recent life stresses can cause depression. He should then carefully survey the person's recent history for evidence of stress in the areas of loss of emotional ties, loss of sources of gratification and situations which may have aroused hostility in the patient which he felt guilty about expressing.

The patient should be advised against making major life decisions during his illness. He should be encouraged to continue in activities which are sources of self-esteem. It is generally best not to point out anger. Many physicians make the mistake of encouraging such patients to "really get angry and let it all out." The patient already feels guilty about his feelings of anger and would only feel worse if he expressed them. Such expression often drives supportive persons further away. What the patient needs are different ways to cope with stresses which precipitate the feelings of anger. Generally, only in psychotherapy, after considerable rapport has been established, can patients usefully openly struggle with the issue of their anger.

The patient should not be treated as weak and helpless. Hospitalization, with its implications of stripping the patient of his sources of effective function and interpersonal gratification, is generally contraindicated. The depressed person suffers not so much from a loss of love and care as from loss of self-esteem. Any treatment approach which further undercuts self-esteem is thus generally unwise.

Some depressed patients tend to hold onto their symptoms and to use them to extract care and concern from others. Care-taking persons experience this as exploitative, which it is. Often the family members or physician feel anger toward the patient, which is difficult to express because the patient is already burdened with his depression. The best approach here is preventive: helping all patients to deal with loss and guilt-provoking anger so that it does not become maladaptively handled in such a manner.

Medications in this group of disorders are, at present, nonspecific. The statements made concerning medications for patients who are mourning apply here as well. Although specific antidepressant medications are often used here, the scientific rationale is much less clear-cut than it is in patients with primary depression.

All patients in this category should be carefully assessed to rule out occult physical diseases which can cause similar depressive symptoms. Among the possibilities are hypothyroidism, anemias, systemic carcinomas and brain tumors.

Referral for psychiatric consultation should be made for any patient who does not improve promptly. Those patients who use the depressive posture in an extractive, exploitative way should also be referred. Depressed adolescents are always best referred, because such illnesses portend significant emotional problems as an adult if they are not effectively dealt with and because suicide is the fifth most common cause of death among adolescents.

Crying. Crying may be a manifestation of mourning or a primary or secondary depression. It may communicate hopelessness, guilt, sadness, anger or frustration; hurt or a sense of personal injustice; or pain. Associated feelings are shame, humiliation and relief.

Generally, allow the patient time to cry. Offer a Kleenex tissue. Verbally encourage the patient to talk about what is troubling him. Ask about specific details, as facts are often easier to talk about than feeling states. If your own actions have contributed to the patient's crying, apologize. Do not reassure a patient that all will turn out well when you do not understand the full situation. Especially avoid false reassurance of the patient with primary depression who feels himself worthless and who may feel even more hopeless as a result of your optimistic statements which he cannot believe.

Patting the patient on the back or holding his hand can provide support and encourage composure. Such physical contacts are easier to have in locations such as the emergency room, where roles are clearly set. After the above has been done, actively encourage the patient to compose himself so that the interview or examination can proceed.

Evaluation of Suicidal Risk. Not only is the physician frequently called upon to care for the depressed person, he must also assess the risk of suicide and determine whether a depressed patient is sufficiently suicidal to require institutional commitment. Although exact provisions of mental health codes vary from state to state, all states provide for the involuntary hospitalization of an individual who is in imminent danger of suicide. The process is essentially a legal, rather than a medical, one and subject to legal review, but emergency 24-hour hospitalization providing an opportunity for fuller legal action is usually possible if a physician will complete a certificate indicating that he has examined the patient and found him acutely suicidal. Longer involuntary hospitalization usually involves a second physician's opinion and a court hearing at which the patient is entitled to legal representation and a jury.

The physician who works in an emergency room, treats a family member for a drug overdose or is approached by a family member concerned about suicidal threats made by a parent, spouse or child will be faced with the need to determine the desirability of involuntary hospitalization. In coming to an opinion, many factors must be weighed. Perhaps the most important single factor is the patient's social environment. Persons living in a setting which provides social interaction are at inherently less hazard. The ultimate in potentially lethal situations is the patient living alone in a sleeping room, hotel or YWCA.

In addition to the social environment, there are several demographic variables to be considered. Suicide rates peak in the fifth and sixth decades of life. Suicide is three times as frequent among men as among women, even though women make suicidal attempts three times as frequently as men. Patients whose history reveals a family member or a close friend who has committed suicide are at greater risk. Those who are self-accusatory are at greater risk than those who are self-pitying. Patients who have undergone a major loss in their sense of competency are at greater risk. The man who has suffered a myocardial infarction and feels that he will be unable to support his family or even be sexually active with his wife is an example.

Perhaps the most frequently misunderstood factor in assessing suicidal potential is the existence of previous attempts. Many professionals unwisely separate suicide attempters into two groups: those who "really mean it" and those who are "manipulative." The implication is that the manipulator makes threats and frequent superficial attempts but will not go to the point of taking his own life. Suicidal behavior frequently does have an element of interpersonal manipulation, but the fact remains that, actuarially, the larger the number of previous attempts the more lethal the next attempt is likely to be.

Change in usual behavioral patterns is one of the major clues to suicidal risk. Verbally, the patient may have made explicit statements such as, "You won't be seeing me around anymore." Behaviorally, he may have given away prized possessions or had marked change in patterns of eating, sex and interests.

When the judgment of suicidal potential is being made within the context of an active attempt, the nature of that attempt should be taken into account. Irreversible modes of attempting suicide (e.g., gunshot, jumping, etc.) are more ominous than modes such as taking pills or laceration of the wrist.

Eight of 10 persons who commit suicide have given recent definite warning of their intent. Three-fourths of all suicidal patients have seen physicians in the prior 4 months. Almost all suicidal persons are ambivalent and undecided about ending their life. Suicidal intent is practically always for a limited time period. These facts alone make a strong case for vigorous intervention by the physician and others.

Basic principles of management involve including hospitalization when indicated and siding with the value of continued life. Do not be afraid to explore the patient's suicidal thoughts; this is practically never hurtful and often cathartically, reassuringly beneficial. Pay particular attention to dyadic relationships, as perceived losses of loved ones are common precipitants of suicidal impulses.

Over-all, the assessment of risk in suicidal patients is complicated and fraught with serious consequences. That being the case, the use of expert consultation is highly desirable; when consultation is not available, errors should be in the conservative direction. A period of observation—giving experienced hospital staff members time to evaluate the patient in depth, providing the patient a respite from situational pressures and providing an opportunity to mobilize the patient's environmental resources—is often preferable to a hasty dismissal from the emergency room.

*   *   *   *

In this chapter we have reviewed the various meanings of the term depression and discussed the normal process of mourning. The distinction between primary and secondary depressive illness has been elaborated on. With respect to the latter, the treatment recommendations were discussed, with an emphasis on proper psychological management of the patient by his physician. Finally, the issues involved in the evaluation of suicidal risk were considered.

REFERENCES

1. GAYLIN, W. (ed.) *The Meaning of Despair: Psychoanalytic Contributions to the Understanding of Depression.* Science House, New York, 1968.
2. GRINKER, R. S., MILLER, J., SABSHIN, M., NUNN, R., AND NUNNALLY, J. *The Phenomena of Depressions.* Hoeber Medical Division. Harper & Row, New York, 1961.
3. KOVACS, M., AND BECK, A. T. Maladaptive cognitive structures in depression. *Am. J. Psychiatry 135:*525–533, 1978.
4. WEISMANN, M. M., KLERMAN, G. L., AND PAYKEL, E. S. Clinical evaluation of hostility in depression. *Am. J. Psychiatry 128:*261, 1971.

CHAPTER 10

THE HYPOCHONDRIACAL PATIENT

JAMES M. TURNBULL, M.D.

Hypochondriasis is a term with many meanings. The common feature in any condition for which the term is used is excessive preoccupation by the patient about his health and overconcern about illness. Hypochondriasis, as a common response to illness or other stressful situations, can be usefully grouped into two types. The first involves a common interpersonal dynamic in which the person's early life was perceived as relatively barren of gratification, with a consequent frustration of early, age-appropriate dependency needs. When the intense anger generated by this frustration cannot be openly experienced or expressed because of a simultaneous need to be approved of, somatic complaints as a way of unconsciously asking for dependency gratification and of unconsciously complaining about the shortcomings of parental surrogates may emerge. The unconscious anger involved in the somatic complaints sometimes generates an angry rejection response in the family or in the physician, leading to a vicious circle of complaining, rejection and intensified complaints.

Health professionals may be helpful in modulating their own anger toward such patients by reminding themselves that they are not malingering or conscious of their provocations; they are, in fact, among the victims of their self-defeating repetition of ungratifying childhood dependencies.

In other cases, the hypochrondriasis does not reflect these dynamics. It may involve a partial disintegration of ego functions and a developmentally primitive focus of bodily events, especially those which have some special symbolic meaning to the patient. Hypochrondriasis must also be distinguished from the sexual and exhibitionistic conversion reactions, with their elements of competitiveness and genital provocation, as well as from consciously manipulative malingering.

Whether the hypochrondriasis is an unconsciously motivated interpersonal maneuver or a regressive disintegration of ego function, it may emerge only under stress or appear as a chronic ingrained character pattern.

Temporary Hypochondriasis

Components and Causes of Temporary Hypochondriasis. Temporary hypochondriacal reactions are very common. At one time or another, some hypochondriasis can be found in everyone. In a difficult life situation, we use the mechanism of hypochondriasis to accomplish one motive or another. A boy facing a test at school may suddenly develop a stomachache or may exaggerate an existing but minor problem as a means of avoiding going to school. A husband's headache may be so incapacitating that he does not feel he can possibly go to a bridge party with friends of his wife whom he does not like. The same headache would hardly be a deterrent to a golf match he had been looking forward to all week. These responses are important because of their tendency to become fixed. Four major factors influence the course of these reactions. First, if the response occurs in a person with a healthy personality structure, it is less likely to become ingrained than if the person is one who utilizes mainly immature defenses to deal with distress. Second, if the current life stresses are transient, the prognosis is much more favorable than if the person is locked into a stress-producing situation from which he cannot escape. The man in his 50's, with no hope of advancement, involved in a physically exhausting, monotonous job, is thus at high risk for developing a plausible illness which would allow him to escape the situation. This is discussed further under "The Tired Housewife and The Tired Breadwinner" in Chapter 18. Third, the more *secondary gain* the symptoms provide, the more likely are they to be held onto. The patient who receives disability compensation, unusual attention or gratification of dependent longings is thus a greater risk. Fourth, the promptness and manner of treatment significantly influence the course.

Differential Considerations. Excessive concern about the body, as seen in both temporary and ingrained hypochondriacal conditions, can often reflect other basic pathological states. These include the following conditions. First are anxiety reactions in which the patient fears that the physiological concomitants of anxiety are signs of serious organic diseases; the Da Costa syndrome, or cardiac neurosis, is a classical example. This pattern is discussed at greater length in Chapter 8. Second are conversion symptoms. These are frequently precipitated by accidents for which compensation for disability is an issue. Common symptoms include pain, weakness and paralysis. The approach to the treatment of these patients is considered later in this chapter. Third are depressed patients who are preoccupied with some presumed bodily dysfunction. Here, it is important to recognize the basic disorder and to handle it accordingly, as discussed in Chapter 9. Fourth are obsessive illnesses in which the primary obsessional concerns are about bodily functions or fears of diseases. Treatment will often be facilitated by employing the guidelines in Chapter 7. Fifth is more bizarre preoccupation with bodily parts, as seen in disorders such as schizophrenia. In such conditions, a psychiatric referral is indicated.

Management of Temporary Hypochondriasis. Regarding treatment, the physician should assess the patient in terms of his personality make-up and characteristic responses to stresses. The stresses in the current life situation should be determined, as should evidence of secondary gains. Necessary diagnostic procedures should be done promptly and should be coupled with an adequate explanation of their purpose. If the person's disorder does, in fact, appear to be a hypochondriacal response, it should not be treated as if it were organic. In particular, the physician should avoid the still common practice of giving the person a "shot." Vitamin B_{12} used inappropriately as a "cure" for weakness, anxiety or vague bodily complaints is a notorious example. Such action solidifies the belief in the patient's mind that he really is ill, and it can be used by him as "proof" of the validity of his symptoms to doubting relatives. Suggestions for dealing with current stresses should be coupled with interpretations of the way in which these can lead to bodily complaints. An inexcusable response with such a patient is "There's not a thing wrong with you, Mr. Smith. Any problems you're having are just in your head." Similarly, it is inadvisable to use the words hysterical or hypochondriacal with such patients. Rather, the physician should acknowledge that the patient is indeed suffering from symptoms of physical distress, but that they have been brought on by emotional and life-circumstance stresses. The physician should endeavor to undercut any secondary gain. Certainly he should not provide secondary gratification through overtesting, overmedicating or treating the patient as "special," because these are patients who can become "infected" with the presumed disease for which they are being treated.

Handling Cases Involving Compensation and Disability. A special sensitivity to emotional issues is necessary for the physician who evaluates or treats patients involved in compensation or disability actions. In general, the above approach to the patient with temporary hypochondriasis is applicable. In addition, the physician who treats patients during the time they are seeking compensation or disability benefits needs to respond especially promptly and precisely. Delays in settlement of litigation or indecision concerning a disa-

bility evaluation often cause a patient's symptoms to become more severe
patient in simple, reassuring terms. Patients who feel that they are in the
hands of a "company doctor" should have the opportunity to obtain consultation with another physician. Such patients are often acutely sensitive to
any implications that they are undeservedly seeking money or that they are
malingering, and any such accusations tend to aggravate the symptoms. The
physician can make such remarks as "Mrs. Brown, I've seen a lot of patients'
medical problems following accidents. There's one aspect of these problems
I should mention to you. Sometimes a patient gets so involved and upset over
the financial matters and legal decision making that it slows down recovery.
Occasionally, I've seen patients get stuck in a rut of invalidism after such
injuries. I'm sure you can see how it could happen. Sometimes a person feels
that others believe he didn't deserve a disability rating, or wasn't really sick.
His holding onto his ailment is a way of trying to prove that he really was
injured. Or a man who had worked 20 years at a hard job may find it pretty
difficult to face the prospect of returning, and be willing to give in to his
symptoms and take the role of a semi-invalid. I don't mean that such a thing
is happening to you, but I've seen it often enough, to the best of persons, after
sickness and injuries where financial compensation was involved, that I think
it's important to discuss the subject."

Such statements are best made in the presence of the spouse. They open
up a topic about which the patient is often sensitive and guarded, thus laying
the groundwork for a preventive approach.

Ingrained Hypochondriasis

The second major category of hypochondriasis involves those persons in
whom the mechanism of hypochondriasis is a major, chronic, ingrained
aspect of their over-all personality function, which is thus intruded into all
aspects of the person's life.

Definition of the Syndrome. Hypochondriasis is not actually a disease
entity. It is a syndrome which consists of an anxious preoccupation with the
body, either as a whole or in parts. This concern is expressed as the belief
that the body or a specific organ is diseased or not functioning properly. The
physical symptoms have no basis in demonstrable organic illness. The hypochondriacal symptoms become, so to speak, the presenting aspect of the
person's personality. The syndrome appears in a number of conditions known
well to psychiatrists and may be symptomatic of a neurosis, a psychosis or a
personality disturbance.

Components of the Syndrome. There are three major components found
in the life-style of the hypochondriacal individual. First, the patient withdraws his interest from other people or objects about him and centers interest
on himself and his physical functioning. This development is seen poignantly
in those elderly persons who find few takers of their friendship and yet still
need to engage in conversation with, and relate to, others. Their attention

becomes self-focused and internalized. Bodily complaints also serve as keys to open the doors to the doctor's consulting room, providing a few moments of stimulation in an otherwise dreary existence.

② Second, the patient may use the discomfort produced by the hypochondriacal symptom as a punishment. He may unconsciously feel that he is partially making atonement for the unconscious, hostile, vengeful feelings he bears toward those close to him. A patient first developed stomach cramps—which had no organic basis—when his wife broke 80 in her golf game. He had tried for years to score less than 90 over 18 holes.

③ Third, occasionally the syndrome is created by a shift or displacement of anxiety from one area of concern to a less threatening concern with bodily disease. Thus, a man's concern over his failure to obtain a job (for which he might feel partially responsible) or his fear of being fired may present as a hypochondriacal concern about an ailment which he feels to be outside of his control. Somewhat later in the development of the hypochondriacal person's life-style, the spouse and friends become angry at the person's loss of interest in his job, his leisure activities, etc. The spouse starts to complain. The patient interprets these actions as meaning that the spouse no longer loves him, and he feels threatened and angry in return, controlling any guilt and rationalizing the anger by saying, "Why should I feel guilty? It's my illness which makes me this way!"

Predisposing Factors. Many of these patients, as children, had sickly or neurotic parents who used illness as a way of maintaining control. Others had sickly siblings who were always the center of attention and were given things the patients felt rightfully belonged to them. Others developed their symptoms as a way of communicating otherwise unacceptable feelings of sadness, apathy and emptiness.

Management. Hypochondriacal patients can be difficult for the physician to deal with. They resist efforts to help them and seem to enjoy being ill, making excessive demands for time and attention from the doctor. Their symptoms are often used as a means of expressing anger, which is frequently directed toward the physician. This is often apparent during the initial interview. A question such as "Have you been to a doctor before about this problem?" is followed by horror stories about the care the patient has received throughout his life. Because such patients have little insight into the way they affect others, it is hard to help them see that they bring out the worst in those who try to help them.

Management of these patients requires some skill and patience. Because it can be time consuming, irritating and frustrating, any physician has a right to choose not to treat such a patient. Nevertheless, there are steps which can lead to successful management of these patients. Busse and his associates at Duke University developed an outpatient clinic to treat "crocks and complainers," in accordance with the following guidelines.

1. Make a correct diagnosis. Even hypochondriacal patients suffer from

genuine disease. Do not dismiss a complaint as hypochondriacal until you are certain that there is no underlying organic disease.

2. Be accepting. The statement used by Busse, when a patient asks about his illness, is "I do not feel certain what is at the root of your trouble but I will be glad to do whatever I can to help you."

3. Prescribe medication cautiously. Do not obscure the clinical picture by palliative treatments. Be careful to use a medication which the patient has not had before. To do this requires obtaining an extensive history of all drugs which the patient has taken for everything he has suffered from in the past several years.

4. Set time limits. Probably the most important lesson to be learned from Busse's experience is the value of being able to cut off the visit after a set period of time. Twenty minutes is probably sufficient. If you are warm, empathic and a good listener, these individuals can be helped enormously in those minutes. The remarks in Chapter 3 more fully cover the techniques of bringing the visit to a close.

5. Be alert for conflict areas which may be exacerbating the symptoms. However, rather than suggest that these conflicts are the "real" basis of the patient's symptoms, simply suggest appropriate alterations in his pattern of living. As with all interpretations and confrontations, if these are to be made, they should be stated when the patient appears to be almost ready to be aware of the point by himself. For example, a physician who has good rapport with a patient who seems vaguely aware that his behavior is driving persons away may say, "You know, Mr. Smith, people sometimes get annoyed or distracted when others talk about their troubles. I just wonder if your wife may not feel that way sometimes?" Such a statement is minimally threatening, presents the physician as a continued ally and suggests that the doctor and patient consider some interpersonal approaches which have fewer negative consequences.

6. Avoid filling out forms for compensation from welfare and other agencies which compensate such patients for their illnesses. Nothing is more difficult than the therapy of someone who is being rewarded for being sick.

In addition to some "do's" there are also some "don'ts" which are common errors to avoid in the management of the hypochondriacal patient.

1. Do not try to explain the lack of findings of organic illness and then tell the person that he is well, and that you expect an early return to work. This simply increases the number of complaints or causes the patient to seek another physician. As we have discussed previously, hypochondriacal behavior represents an unconscious solution to conflicts and is rarely given up as a result of straightforward confrontation.

2. Another pitfall is a complex explanation of the mind and the body working together to produce disease. Theoretical analysis will help the physician but alienates patients who are not intellectually oriented toward, or who do not share, the physician's scientific assumptions.

3. Do not treat such patients for unknown diseases on a hit-or-miss basis. The treatment will almost invariably be ineffective, and the patient will often develop a panoply of new complaints.

4. Avoid falling into the traps which the patient sets, particularly with regard to diagnosis and prognosis. Be ready for questions such as "And when do you think you're going to get me better, doctor?" A promise of "cure in 6 months" will inevitably be used by the patient against the physician.

5. Avoid criticism of other physicians who have treated the patient. Neither is it helpful to defend them, because this communicates to the patient that you feel he is deliberately lying or exaggerating.

6. Do not treat such patients unenthusiastically or carelessly. Hypochondriacal patients, more than any others, are highly open to negative suggestion and can react strongly to a pessimistic tone of voice or other evidence of lack of enthusiasm on the part of the physician. The patient who feels that medications are being prescribed in a hit-or-miss fashion as a way of avoiding real involvement not only will be unlikely to improve, but he may develop new, more pressing symptoms in an unconscious effort to gain the attention he feels he needs.

*   *   *   *

Hypochondriasis, a difficult condition to deal with, at least becomes comprehensible and oftentimes is successfully managed if the physician understands the mechanisms of the condition, the purposes it serves and the principles of intervention. To recapitulate, the major defensive mechanisms are hypochondriasis and passive-aggressive behavior. The purposes served include delimiting the conflicts, legitimizing the patient's problems, justifying visits to and care by a physician, avoidance of responsibility, making the problem susceptible to ritual controls, such as medications, and providing a means of indirectly expressing aggression. Division of hypochondriasis into temporary and ingrained categories is useful clinically. The patient with temporary hypochondriasis requires prompt treatment, minimization of secondary gain and cautious avoidance of any treatments which would entrench symptomatology. Current life stresses should be relieved when possible. In contrast, intervention with the ingrained hypochondriacal patient emphasizes avoiding a host of pitfalls and strictly limiting the time spent with the patient, but, within that time, making oneself fully available to him.

REFERENCES

1. Busse, E. W. The treatment of the chronic complainer. *Med. Rec. Ann.* *50:*196–220, 1956.
2. Kenyon, F. E. Hypochondriacal states. *Br. J. Psychiatry 129:*1–14, 1976.
3. Lesse, S. Masked depression—a diagnostic and therapeutic problem. *Dis. Nerv. Syst.* 29: 169–173, 1968.

CHAPTER 11

THE DYING PATIENT

ALVIN G. BURSTEIN, Ph.D.

Birth and death, the twin doorways of life, are universal experiences. Paradoxically, they are experiences that our culture treats in a very gingerly fashion. In contrast with societies in which birth and death are events of high social visibility and in which ample opportunities exist for family members to learn how to react to these events, in our society these events have increasingly been relegated to specialized social compartments beyond the ken of family members. Especially, as the technology for maintaining life in extremis has been elaborated, terminal patients have tended to be maintained as long as possible in a hospital setting, dying isolated from their families.

Isolating these crucial events from their family contexts has important psychological consequences. The patient, denied knowledge of his impending death, may fail to make appropriate decisions relevant to the future of his family; the spouse, denied an opportunity to make a final contact and say the necessary goodbyes, may struggle with guilt that interferes with resuming life and investing in new relationships.

Current Practices

Fortunately, there are important countercurrents to the general trend of isolating these events. Psychoprophylaxis in childbirth stresses the importance of active, conscious involvement of the husband and wife in the birth process, and medical schools are increasingly making curricular time available for teaching about the psychology of the dying patient. Certainly, whatever the general cultural tendency toward dealing with death by evasion and isolation, the physician does not have the prerogative of avoidance; he meets with death too frequently and engages with it too intimately. The purpose of this chapter is to offer the physician guidance in dealing with the dying patient and his family.

Young physicians frequently emulate their older colleagues in matters of practice. It is therefore important to know what the standard practices are, what most doctors do in handling the dying patient. Specifically, do most doctors tell terminal patients the facts of their situation? Although individual practices vary widely, a number of surveys show that more than three out of four doctors make a policy of avoiding full disclosure of the terminal patient's situation. Is this preponderance of practice a reflection of a wish by patients to be kept in the dark, to avoid clear knowledge of their situation? The facts suggest otherwise. Once again, while individuals vary widely, field studies are quite consistent in indicating that at least three out of four patients would like to be told the full facts of a terminal condition.

Quite aside from the question of what most doctors do, or what most patients want, is the more taxing question of what is to be done at a specific moment by a specific doctor with respect to a particular patient. The answer to this question cannot be found in polls and surveys, but only in the knowledge of the patient's situation, viewed in the light of relevant theory. For that reason we next explore, in theoretical terms, the psychology of the dying patient.

Psychology of the Dying Patient

Initial Awareness. There is a point in the treatment of a terminally ill patient when he becomes aware of the seriousness of his condition. This is rarely the result of his being told directly that his illness is fatal; rather, it is more often the result of "detective" work on his part. He interprets what he gleans from a glance, or from the behavior of his caretakers. To illustrate, consider this excerpt from an interview with a 34-year-old migrant worker dying of bone cancer. This man was interviewed 8 days before his death, and his comments, which illustrate many of the points we will be discussing, are referred to throughout this chapter. The patient is recounting the events which followed his hospitalization.

> *Interviewer:* Um-hmm. It wasn't just an ordinary break.
> *Patient:* Yeah. And I started going over here and over there, and x-ray here and x-ray there, and I said, you know that's just too much x-rays, you know, for just an ordinary break, and. . . .
> *Interviewer:* Nobody told you, but you sort of figured out that something was going on.
> *Patient:* Yeah.

This detective work, the painstaking analysis of what is said and how it is said, is an almost universal characteristic of patients in this man's situation and is a reflection of feelings of being isolated and cut off, without knowledge of or the power to control his situation. Too often, the feeling of helpless isolation on the patient's part is fed by the hospital staff or by the family's tendency to resort to empty and platitudinous reassurance in dealing with the patient. The patient described above reveals his feelings of isolation from the staff when he describes an occasion when, after being x-rayed, several members of the house staff examined the films:

> *Patient:* This one day was when they radiated this leg and then they x-rayed it . . . and they received the x-rays there right in front of me. I was laying down and one looked at the other guy, and you know, he looked at the other one. One doctor looked at it (the film) this way and this way, and then this way and this way, and the other doctor says, "Well, what do you think?," and the first one said, "I don't know, here, let me see." And then they called another doctor and they said, "Look, look," and he said, "Yeah, oh yeah," and "That's nice, that's nice," you know, and then, you know, took me out of the room and they didn't come out before 30 or 40 minutes.
> *Interviewer:* So they had a conference, you mean?
> *Patient:* Yes, and I thought, that's strange, too. If I didn't have nothing wrong, why didn't they come right out when I did?

A little later in the same interview, the interviewer asks, "Have you talked to the doctors and nurses about this?"

> *Patient:* No (clears throat). They just don't, right now they just don't, you know, want to bother with me, or, you know, talk in them ways with me. They just say, "Paul, you're going to be fine."
> *Interviewer:* Um-hmm.
> *Patient:* That's it.
> *Interviewer:* Why do you think they tell you that?
> *Patient:* I don't know, maybe . . . they x-rayed me and all of that and then they say, "We can't find nothing on you, Paul," but they don't show me; well if they did show me the x-rays, I wouldn't know, and that's why . . . and even if I asked them they would say, "Well, why do you want to see them for; you won't understand them anyway."

It is the essence of the proper management of the dying patient to minimize this sense of alienation and isolation, and to short-circuit the tendency of the care-givers to evade psychological contact with the dying patient by such means as physical isolation or the more subtle form of psychological isolation that takes the form of responding in terms of clichés.

Assimilation. Preventing isolation is the most important general element in handling the dying patient. The specifics of that activity depend on an understanding of the psychology of patients who are terminally ill. Studies of the psychological processes involved are doubly important, in that they are generally similar to the psychological process by which patients respond to any information which drastically alters their self-concept. The main point, and one that is crucial to grasp, is that such information is not directly assimilated by the patient. It is not absorbed on a single occasion. Rather, the input must be redigested, gone over again and again, most often within the context of an interpersonal exchange.

To repeat, this process of digestion is required to assimilate all types of emotionally loaded or self-relevant information, and the awareness of one's impending death is no exception. The typical assimilative process can be regarded as proceeding stagewise. Although there is some danger in thinking of the stages as being too separate and discrete and the progress through them as irreversible, it is useful to conceptualize the process of a patient's coming to grips with his impending death as consisting of five steps: denial, anger, bargaining, depression and acceptance.

Stages of Awareness and Response

Denial. In this initial phase, the patient automatically and unconsciously attempts to minimize the impact of the information by excluding it from his consciousness. He may forget what he has been told directly or what he himself has said, or he may fail to draw "obvious" conclusions. Denial appears to act as a psychological safety valve, limiting the amount of "shocking" information that needs to be processed. Just as the mechanism of denial is automatic and unconscious in its operation, so is it self-limiting. It automatically recedes when the patient's psychological resources are again available for the assimilative process. It is not necessary or helpful to deal with denial by harsh confrontation; rather, the patient will indicate, for example, by asking a previously taboo question or by "recalling" something previously denied, his readiness to do further psychological work. One must also understand that denial is not irreversible—it waxes and wanes. What the patient "knows" clearly at one moment may moments later—or earlier— be inaccessible to him. For example, our patient, when asked whether he had ever thought that he might not go home from the hospital, says:

> *Patient:* . . . Yes, sir, sometime, maybe . . . in 2, maybe 5 years.
> *Interviewer:* Um-hmm.
> *Patient:* Maybe that'll be it.
> *Interviewer:* Um-hmm, couple of years?
> *Patient:* Yes. . . .

But, a few minutes later, he says:

> *Patient:* (voice tremulous) I've been feeling . . . (crying) I've been feeling, um, kind of bad this week; this week they, when they told me I (that he had to return to the hospital) . . . I felt that, you know, that this could

be it, you know, or, uh, stah, uh, you know, a long, long time here in the hospital or something like that. . . .

Anger. Subsequent to the state of denial is the stage of angry emotional release. In this stage the patient makes contact with the feelings of bitter unfairness and defeat that fatal illness elicits. The targets for this anger vary from patient to patient: his religion, his family, his doctor—all can come under biting and critical attack. This phase can be most difficult to handle, particularly when—as is frequently the case—it takes the form of ceaseless, whining complaints directed against the nursing staff. One of the most pernicious aspects of this kind of behavior is that it drives the staff away, motivating them to avoid the patient. This in turn increases the patient's sense of isolation and of being unfairly treated, and it lessens his ability to complete the process of coming to terms with his impending death. When a patient is in this phase of his response, the staff must be encouraged to resist the tendency to avoid him. The physician can do this by giving other staff members an understanding of the meaning and function of the patient's behavior and by giving legitimacy to the staff's own feelings in response to the unwarranted attacks. In terms of direct handling of the patient, interpretation is not called for. Empathic acceptance and clarification via reflection of the patient's reactions, and the persistent offer of interpersonal contact, will afford the patient the means of continuing the assimilative process.

Bargaining. This is the third stage in the process. In this phase, the patient manifests a token acceptance of his situation, but he makes it contingent upon certain conditions. For example, the patient may plead for sufficient time for farewells or to meet certain obligations, or he may request a guarantee of painlessness. The difficulty with such requests is they frequently imply divine omnipotence on the part of the physician or the hospital, and psychologically they represent an effort at ingratiation on the patient's part toward these powerful figures. If the physician tries to soothe the patient with promises, he may encounter anger at his efforts or bitterness at his lack of understanding. If, on the other hand, he denies the requests or points out their defensive nature, he be seen as cruel and lacking in feeling. The means of resolving this management dilemma for the staff and the physician is through a focus not on the content of the request, but, rather, on the patient's feelings about the issues involved. If, for example, the patient expresses an acceptance of his impending death, but on the condition that the end will be quick and painless, rather than reassuring him on that score, a sympathetic exploration of his thoughts about pain and death and of his experiences with others who died will facilitate his continuing efforts to come to terms with his condition.

Grief. The fourth stage of this process is most often called grief or depression. This stage is characterized by the open expression of the feelings of pain that are appropriate to the anticipated loss of contact with one's life, one's loved ones and oneself. The episodes of weeping and clearly recognized feelings of hurt and deep sadness which predominate in this phase can be difficult to handle in two ways: they can lead the staff or family to engage in the kind of avoidant behavior already described, or they can precipitate a more subtle kind of avoidance that takes the form of distracting the patient from these painful thoughts and reminding him of how rich his life has been, how much he has accomplished, etc. These manuevers, unfortunately, will leave the patient feeling even more alienated and are far less human than a recognition of his grief and the solace of a handclasp. Just as the patient's earlier anger can stir up a corresponding anger in those relating to him at an earlier phase, so can his grief at this stage bring tears to the eyes of his helpers. The family, of course, has the sanction to cry in response to their own loss; the hospital staff may feel weak and "neurotic" when their professional aplomb is threatened by their emotional reactions to the patient's pain. Honest expression of their feelings to one another and to the patient is mutually therapeutic.

Acceptance. The final stage of coming to grips with impending death is reached by traversing the previous stages. It involves a letting go, a denunciation of investment in the objects and activities that are to be left behind. The patient feels little psychological pain and appears to be peaceful and calm. He may ask for some solitude or for an opportunity to lie quietly with someone present, but without conversation. He is psychologically ready to die.

The Principles of Management

Having summarized the process of psychologically accommodating to impending death, it is time to recall why facilitating this accommodation is so important. There are three reasons: it promotes realistic planning on the part of the patient and his family, it minimizes psychological scarring in the family and it eases the patient's pain and maximizes his dignity. Patients who are locked in the denial phase, for example, will defer taking business or personal steps that may be crucial in making adequate provisions for those who will survive them; similarly, family members who are inhibited in openly exploring and exchanging feelings with the dying family member may forego the opportunity for saying goodbye and may develop guilt that makes it difficult for them to form new emotional attachments. It is a valuable form of psychiatric prophylaxis for the physician and the hospital staff to do all in their power to foster open communication and close contact between the dying patient and his family.

No discussion of the management of the dying patient is complete without some discussion of the ethical implications of euthanasia. Euthanasia is a topic which is usually avoided. Where it is discussed it is often discussed from a morally simplistic point of view or from a view preoccupied with legalisms that seem irrelevant to real life. It may be helpful to consider euthanasia as active or passive and voluntary or involuntary. Voluntary euthanasia is that to which the patient gives his full consent; involuntary is that which is visited on the patient without his consent. Active euthanasia is killing by some active means (e.g., an overdose of morphine or the creation of an air embolism); passive euthanasia is the withholding of a potentially life-prolonging treatment.

Passive voluntary euthanasia may be morally unacceptable to some physicians, but others see it as a simple extension of the physician's responsibility to limit pain where cure is impossible and to take into account the patient's right to refuse treatment. In fact several states, including California and Texas, have enacted "living will" legislation providing a means by which individuals may record, before the event, their wish to have treatment limited to the palliation of pain in the case of hopeless illness or injury.

Active involuntary euthanasia, in which active steps are taken to end the life of someone who has not or cannot consent to the procedure, is unacceptable by any standard. The most active controversies involve active voluntary euthanasia, which is essentially participating in a suicide, and passive involuntary euthanasia, deciding not to treat a hopeless case.

The recent advances in understanding the psychology of dying patients and the increased sensitivity to bioethical issues is finding expression in the hospice movement. Hospitals, which are designed to cure, often have difficulty in responding to the needs of patients who cannot be cured and are in fact dying. St. Christopher's Hospice in England is the pioneer institution tailored to the needs of the person facing imminent death. Two promises are made to the patient who enters. One is that he will feel no more pain than he wishes to. The second is that he will not be alone when he wants company. The only medications prescribed are analgesics and tranquilizers.

Institutions modeled on St. Christopher's are being developed in the United States. They typically stress maintaining the patient in the home as long as possible, interdisciplinary teams working with the patient and his family, adequate analgesia, and avoidance of life-maintaining heroics.

*   *   *   *

In summary, there is a series of clinical guideposts to the management of the dying patient which the physician should keep in mind:

—When you go into the patient's room, be prepared to sit down and talk.

—Start where the patient is. Begin by asking the patient for his understanding of his situation.

—Listen for the patient's feelings. Do not make the natural mistake of assuming that what you fear about death is what the patient fears.

—Promote involvement by the family. Do all that you can to keep the patient and his family talking honestly together.

—Avoid the twin dangers of saccharine reassurance and brutal confrontation. Let the patient proceed at his own pace and expect momentary reversals and inconsistencies in the process.

REFERENCES

1. CRAVEN, J., AND WALD, F. S. Hospice care for dying patients. *Am. J. Nurs.* 75:1816–1822, 1975.
2. GLASER, B. G. *Awareness of Dying.* Aldine Press, Chicago, 1965.
3. GLASER, B. G. *Time for Dying.* Aldine Press, Chicago, 1968.
4. KUBLER-ROSS, E. *On Death and Dying.* Macmillan, New York, 1969.
5. SCHOENBERG, B. C., CARR, A. C., PERETZ, D., AND KUTSCHER, A. H. (eds.). *Loss and Grief: Psychological Management in Medical Practice.* Columbia University Press, New York, 1970.

PART 2

THE LIFE CYCLE: ADAPTA-
TION AND CHANGE

CHAPTER 12

THE HUMAN ENDOWMENT
CHARLES L. BOWDEN, M.D.

Whether one regards it as an expression of divine planning or as the blind thrust of Darwinian coincidence, it is clear that biological success in the evolutionary game requires the organism's ability to adapt to new circumstances. The ability to meet environmental challenge flexibly can exist on the species level, with high birth rates, short life-spans and high mutation rates. It can also exist on the level of the individual organism's developing the ability to change responses and to respond in new and adaptive ways to the environment. Central to human potential is this plasticity of individual behavior, an ability to learn and change unequalled in any other species, one strongly mediated by the psychological factors of language and learning.

In this chapter, we will review in summary form the basic factors most central to an understanding of the plasticity of human behavior. We will consider genetic variation, perception, affect, stress, motivation, learning, language and intelligence.

Genetic Variation

Our hereditary make-up is mediated by genes which are molecules of deoxyribonucleic acid (DNA). DNA is a large molecule consisting of a double helix with a complementary sequence of purine bases—adenine and guanine—and pyrimidine bases—cytosine and thymine—joined together by deoxyribosephosphate chains. There are many different forms of DNA, each responsible for directing some characteristic chemical process in an organism. The differing sequence of nucleotide bases in a molecule of DNA determines the sequence of 20 amino acids in proteins.

This is a simple hierarchy: the four bases are the four letters of the alphabet; any combination of the four letters makes up a word known as a triplet. Each word or triplet codes for one *specific* amino acid. The order or sequence of these words (triplets) makes up a sentence that tells the machinery of the cell the sequence in which to assemble the amino acids to make various proteins. Genetic mutation can thus now be described in chemical terms. It consists of the alteration of a triplet base sequence by the addition, deletion or substitution of nucleotide bases.

Some characteristics are *genetic polymorphisms*; that is, they are totally under genetic control. An example is the A-B-O blood types. Some other characteristics, such as skin color, are primarily genetically determined. But skin color is also influenced by the intensity of the sun, the length of exposure and the psychological willingness of the person to be in the sun. Most behavioral characteristics are *polygenic*. Using intelligence as an example, there are many genes which contribute to what we know as intelligence. What we measure as intelligence is many steps removed from genotype, and involves complex gene-environment interactions.

Added to this are several important principles of genetic variation, which apply to the study of intelligence as well as other genetically influenced characteristics. First, the extent of variation within any population generally far exceeds the average difference between populations. Second, differences between populations and races are primarily measured by the relative frequencies of a given set of genes, rather than by a qualitative difference; that is, any genetic combination may be found within any race, but the frequency varies. Sickle cell anemia and amaurotic familial idiocy are examples. Third, differences are neither totally stable nor continuous because of hybridization.

Genetics and reproduction are, of course, inseparably interlinked. The genetic recombination which occurs with the conception of a new individual is, in effect, a reshuffling of the same deck of genetic cards, a reshuffling that takes place anew with each generation. It has far-reaching psychosocial consequences. There is on the average about a 50% regression toward the mean in I.Q. from generation to generation. I.Q. varies directly with social class. Based on Burt's studies, at least 22% of the offspring must change class in each generation to maintain the I.Q. differences in social class levels. The evidence is strong that this occurs. Thus intelligence itself is a major determinant of socioeconomic class.

As another example, schizophrenia, a disease with a genetic diathesis, has an increased prevalence among persons of lower socioeconomic status. A recent ingenious study by Wender et al. supported the hypothesis that the lower socioeconomic status was a *consequence* of the individual's psychopathology. There was no support for the hypothesis that factors associated with lower socioeconomic status, for example, nutrition, contributed to the development of schizophrenia.

No biological processes work with certainty. Life involves two separate processes. The first is accurate copying. The second is change. A cell makes proteins over and over again from the same blueprint and replicates the blueprint when it divides into two cells. Occasionally there is an error in producing a molecule, which is relatively unimportant because the next molecule can be expected to be normal. But when the abnormal molecule is one which plays a basic part in the productive function of the cell and acts as a template to help make copies of other proteins, it will cause errors in subsequent production which will be cumulative. It may well be that these cumulative errors are the cause of cells breaking down and dying. But these very errors that destroy the individual are also the origin of change. Without these errors there would be no raw material of genetic mutants for natural selection to work on. Thus, we come to the conclusion that the machinery of life ensures the death of individuals.

Perception

Perception is the process of organizing and interpreting sensory data by combining them with the results of previous experiences. Accurate awareness of the outer and inner worlds is not the result of the passive registration of data. Even simple perceptions require active structuring and organization.

Perception does not correspond in any point-to-point way in the brain, nor is localization of neural activity in particular parts of the brain a full explanation of sensory capability. Sensory perceptions as diverse as touch, cold, warmth, movement, pain and pressure may arise from stimulation of the same cortical area. An explanation of sensory capability probably lies in patterns of activity involving large areas of the brain in a systematic way.

Objects are not transmitted whole, as it were, from the external world into the brain. A pencil does not inherently register in the brain as a pencil. What is perceived is a set of sensations having to do with dimension, form, color and similar attributes of the object. Through experience, an individual learns that a particular set of sensations is called a pencil.

Sensory data which are experienced together tend to be re-experienced together. The child who experiences pain from medical procedures performed by a white-coated physician is prone subsequently to associate white coats with the anticipation of pain. Similar elements are readily associated perceptually. Thus, a person with a history of angina pectoris may perceive chest pain and assume that it is of cardiac origin, when, in fact, it stems from a hiatus hernia. Another mode of perceptual organization occurs when the individual perceives *part* of an object and *fills in* the rest of the object from memory or by symbolical processes. We see only the profile of a friend's face, yet we know that it is the friend. The physician performing a pelvic examination obtains only a limited amount of tactile and proprioceptive information, but from this he is able to form a visual and symbolically meaningful percept of the pelvic structures.

Perceptual Styles. Perceptual styles vary in a basic, enduring way among individuals. They correlate with, and may causally account for, a host of psychological variables: the tendency to make judgements independent of contextual clues, the tolerance for ambiguity and the tendency to accept as equally valid apparently contradictory experiences. Perceptual style demonstrates the interrelatedness of intellectual function and personality variables. A series of important studies on perceptual style has been carried out using a luminous rod inside a luminous frame, both against a dark background. The spatial orientation of each was manipulated separately. Subjects then estimated the rod's deviation from vertical. Those who tended to rely on the position of the frame were judged field-dependent; those who more accurately estimated the rod's position regardless of the tilt of the frame were judged field-independent. Field-dependent subjects, who make the greater errors in their estimations of verticality, tend to be more dependent as people, to lack insight, to be more suggestible and to have poorer self-concepts. The work in this area is a good example of the way in which personality can be understood through the study of perception.

Neurophysiology of Perception. The reticular activating system plays a major role in perception through its function in determining levels of arousal and attention. Not only do processes in the reticular activating system fundamentally influence arousal levels, but they also help to sort out relevant from irrelevant stimuli. Recent studies suggest that a disorder in the reticular system's function is a basic component of the disease schizophrenia. Patients with schizophrenia are unable to attend selectively to stimuli in a normal way. "Noise" from the perceptual field intrudes upon that to which the person is trying to attend, and irrelevant stimuli from other perceptual fields may also intrude. Thus a schizophrenic person who is trying to listen to a lecturer in class may be abnormally distracted by noises in the class, bright colors in the professor's dress or irrelevant physiological states such as tension and sexual impulses.

The nervous system operates at another level to reduce stimuli. The so-called gate theory of neural transmission postulates that large nerve bundles within the spinal cord maintain a tonic electrical input which effectively eliminates many incoming stimuli before they reach the brain. Some scientists have postulated that the effect of acupuncture may be through direct influence on this system. Even now, for the treatment of some types of chronic pain, there are experimental electronic devices which supply a continuous electrical current to discrete nerve fibers, thus blocking out or "closing the gate" to painful impulses arising in body parts.

Affect and the Nervous System

The nervous system involves only four basic operations: (1) the conduction of a wave of excitation over the undifferentiated protoplasm of the cell; (2) the more rapid conduction of a wholly similar wave of excitation over the axons of nerve cells; (3) the secretion of humoral or chemical agents that serve to excite or inhibit other cells, including nerve cells; and (4) transmission across the synaptic junction between nerve cells. The nervous system acquires its complexity by combining these four basic operations into an elaborate network of communication extending to all parts of the body, and coordinating it by a "central nervous system." But in all of the evolution of the nervous system, which reaches its greatest development in the cerebral hemispheres of man, no new functional features have been added to the four listed. Rather, behavior has evolved in complexity by grafting new structures onto old ones. Man's brain—cerebral cortex, limbic system, brain stem and spinal cord—is essentially a hierarchical system which works as well as it does because, at least in most instances, the new is able to dominate the old.

Implicit in the above is that the capacity to learn was acquired early in the course of evolution. Thus it is not the fact of learning but what is learned that differentiates animals along the evolutionary scales. And, in man, learning is importantly concerned with abstractions and symbols, specifically with language.

Neurophysiology of Affect. Most primary drives and affective responses appear to involve the limbic system. In this regard, MacLean's description of the "three brains" of man deserves quoting:

> Speaking allegorically of these three brains within a brain, we might imagine that when the psychiatrist bids the patient to lie on the couch, he is asking him to stretch out alongside a horse and a crocodile. The crocodile may be willing to shed a tear and the horse to neigh and whinny, but when they are encouraged to express their troubles in words,

it soon becomes evident that their inability is beyond the help of language training. Little wonder that the person who has responsibility for these animals and who must serve as their mouthpiece is sometimes accused of being full of resistance and reluctant to talk, or that the psychiatrist's interpretations and diagnosis suggest a certain lack of training in veterinary neuropsychiatry.

MacLean's "crocodile" is, of course, the limbic system. The anatomical description of the structures constituting this system will be found in any neuroanatomy text.

The frontotemporal portion of the limbic system, in particular the amygdala, appears to be concerned with eating behavior and the concomitant behaviors, such as searching and fighting, which are involved in the effort to obtain food. The adjacent septal region, including the septum and medial portion on the dorsal medial nucleus, is involved in sexual functions. The hippocampus appears to modify the excitability of the areas involved in penile erections and to induce tranquil, placid behavior. MacLean suggests that excitation in one region may spill over into the contiguous region. Thus, oral mechanisms are closely tied anatomically and neurophysiologically with genital functions, a finding that helps to explain the intimate interrelationship between oral and sexual functions.

A similar interplay occurs in those areas responsible for ejaculation, which is primarily a sympathetic event. The regions include the ventral lateral nucleus of the thalamus, the contiguous parts of the dorsal medial nucleus and the parafascicular-central median complex. Extremely close to this area are points which cause such visceromotor responses as salivation, vomiting, urination and defecation.

Heath has summarized the evidence, much of it based on his own work, that the septal region, the medial forebrain bundle and the interpeduncular nuclei constitute a *pleasure and alerting system*. Stimulation of the rostral septal region (defined to include the nucleus acumbens septi and the nucleus of the diagonal band of Broca) both electrically and with acetylcholine results in pleasurable, even orgastic responses. This same area is associated with distinctly abnormal electrical activity and dysphoria in patients who have signs and symptoms of schizophrenia. The descending outflow of the septal region is primarily through the medial forebrain bundle and, in particular, to the dentate nucleus in the cerebellum by way of large myelinated fibers. Other areas that appear to be involved in this system of pleasant feeling states are the lateral hypothalamus, the paraolfactory areas and the striatum. The neurohumors which appear to be primarily involved in this system are acetylcholine and norephinephrine.

Unpleasant emotions (fear and rage) are associated with increased electrical activity in the hippocampus and amygdala. This system for painful, unpleasant emotions has connections with the fastigial nucleus in the cerebellum; the medial lateral geniculate bodies, with possible implications for the auditory changes observed in schizophrenia; posterior hypothalamic and midline hypothalamic nuclei; tuberal and supraoptic nuclei; and dorsomedial and midline thalamic nuclei.

The evidence for the principal pathways involved in emotional expression comes from several lines of study. The classical study by Olds in 1962 involved monkeys' self-stimulation of electrodes implanted in different brain areas. Maximal stimulation, sometimes in excess of 8,000 responses per hour, occurred with electrodes in the medial forebrain bundle. Subsequent electrical self-stimulation and passive stimulation of the septal region in humans has resulted in feelings of profound pleasure. Ablation of the septal region in animals was followed by lowered levels of awareness and impairment of emotional expression. Fast electrical activity in the septal region has been demonstrated when subjects were in pleasurable emotional states during interviews and during observation of sexual films. Administration of acetylcholine has actually induced orgasm, along with fast electrical activity in the septal region.

Aversive or painful responses were observed when the periventricular hypothalamus was stimulated electrically. Similar distress responses occurred when stimuli were directed to the amygdala, the hippocampus and the midline mesencephalic tegmentum. Stimulation of these areas acts as a strong negative reinforcer; for example, an animal will learn a task to avoid stimulation.

Two important points concerning the principal known neurophysiological pathways of emotional expression need to be made. First, new data demonstrate that there are direct connections between sensory relay nuclei in the cerebellum (for position and movement), in the thalamus (for somatosensory stimuli) and in sites implicated in emotional expression (the rostral septal region and the portions of the brain generally referred to as the limbic system). Second, the neurophysiological area associated with emotion is more extensive than that described in the traditional Papez-MacLean theory of emotion. It may well be that the limbic system is involved more as a final common pathway.

It is not likely that singular, discrete localization for emotional responses or for any other subjective or abstract function will be discovered. What is known of brain function is much more suggestive that such capabilities reside more in diffuse, interacting neuronal networks. With that caveat in mind, it still seems probable that over the next decade the most significant discoveries regarding brain function will pertain to these areas of the brain.

Clinical Stress

The neurophysiological organization of affective centers has a major interaction with bodily stress responses. In this section we consider some of the ways in which psychological conflict causes physiological responses which, in turn, may be causally important in the development of organic diseases.

What is stress and how does it affect well-being and illness? Many physicians debate the proper terms to apply, using *stressor* for environmental and emotional stimuli and *stress* for a person's physical and emotional state in response to stressors. In vernacular terms, we tend to blur the distinction between the various definitions and terms. Emotional stress is a significant risk factor in a variety of illness conditions. An important point is that it is the subjective meaning of an experience to an individual which determines whether that experience will be stressful. This partly explains why efforts to quantify stressors for all persons or to determine specific stress diseases in response to specific stressors have not proved useful. Nevertheless, it is possible that we can identify certain characteristics of life situations, relationships and social conditions which regularly evoke neuroendocrine changes. The following is an effort to provide an organizing classification which clinicians may usefully recognize in their patients.

Losses. Loss may be interpersonal (the death of a loved one), of a tangible physical object (money, one's home) or symbolic (one's sense of honor or pride). Death of a wife in men over the age of 55 resulted in a death rate 40% over that expected for married men of the same age. Among those widowed men dying of cardiovascular diseases, the rate was 67% above that expected. Only 22% died of the same illness as their wives, thus it is unlikely that a jointly unfavorable environment caused their death.

Major Life Change. Holmes and Rahe have reported that a weighted index of life changes in the 2 years prior to the onset of illnesses was directly correlated with the severity and likelihood of illness. The 12 events most powerfully correlated with subsequent risk of illness, in descending order of importance, were death of a spouse, separation-divorce, jail term, death of close family member, personal injury or illness, marriage, being fired from work, marital reconciliation, retirement, change in health of a family member, pregnancy and sexual troubles.

Geographically and occupationally mobile men had incidences of coronary artery disease respectively two and three times those of stable men. Socioeconomic change is also associated with increased illness risk. Managers whose family backgrounds and educational experiences least well equipped them for their work tasks had higher disease rates than better prepared managers. The increased risk extended to major and minor, physical and mental and long term as well as short term illnesses. All the changes which increase illness risk do not appear to be socially undesirable. A new job, receiving an honor or the challenge of new and enlarged work responsibilities may all serve as stressors. Changes which lead to a sense of meaninglessness and lack of self-worth are also stressful.

Work Pressure. Friedman and Rosenman have initiated an active study of personality type and emotional stress as they affect cardiac disease. The so-called type A individual has an excessive sense of time urgency, high competitiveness and drive, decisiveness and confidence. He drives himself harder than the people who work under him. He has little time to waste with people and tends to appreciate things more than people. He tends to deny pain, delays seeking medical assistance and too often pays a fatal price for his autonomy. Recent results of a well designed study indicate that removal of this behavioral pattern would reduce the risk of coronary heart disease by over 30%.

Job Satisfaction. Tradesmen, craftsmen, technicians and managers have higher rates of myocardial infarction—as much as five- to six-fold in some series—than do engineers and scientists. The more people work for extrinsic rewards, such as pay and prestige, the higher the risk. This factor alone accounts for about 50% of the variance by occupation.

Sex. Myocardial infarction is five times more common among men than among premenopausal women. The rates of myocardial infarction have increased 15% since 1950 for men between the ages of 25 and 44. Although these and other unfavorable health outcomes for men are strongly influenced by endocrinological and other sex-related factors, it seems likely that health behaviors, life-styles, responsibilities and the other variables discussed here differentially affect men and women. In 1900, there was less than 1 year's difference in the expectable life-span of men and women. Today that difference has risen to over 4 years.

Interpersonal Factors. Social supports are strongly protective of normal development and good emotional and physical health. Social cohesiveness and warm emotional support reduce susceptibility to physiological stress responses, including lesser elevations of free fatty acids and 17-OH corticos- teriods, (17-OHCS) which are increased under stress.

Lack of emotional support has a profound effect on infant mortality and development, as first reported in the classic study of Spitz, described in Chapter 13. Subsequent studies indicate that maternal emotional and stimulus deprivation can lead to diminished growth, subnormal intellectual development and clinical and laboratory data of secondary hypopituitarism.

Emotional vulnerability to stressful events influences response. Most parents of a group of leukemic children studied had relatively stable 17-OHCS excretion, unrelated to the clinical condition of the sick child. Parents judged most vulnerable psychologically had the highest 17-OHCS elevations. The most effective defenses were neurotic denial, suppression and religious faith, wherein the fate of the child was delegated outside the self.

Responsibility for others is associated with emotional stress. On the day before a platoon's attack of the enemy, men in the ranks were able to share their fears and concerns with one another. The platoon leader, responsible for their attack plans and safety, was less able to fraternize with the men in the ranks and had a much higher elevation in 17-OHCS excretion. The ultimate job of responsibility of our times may be that of air traffic controller. The incidence of illness and early retirement among controllers is several times that of the general public.

Socioeconomic Class. Socioeconomic variables are considered in detail in Chapters 1 and 2. Lower class status is definitely and strongly associated with a greater illness susceptibility, morbidity and mortality.

Invisible Entrapment. Fight-or-flight physiological mechanisms once had survival value. Our endocrine and cardiovascular systems were designed to meet the dangers of the enemy and predators of hunting man on the savannahs of Africa. In response to such concrete stressors, the cardiovascular system could suddenly pump more blood, redistribute it throughout the body, increase heart rate and blood pressure and increase blood coaguability. By running or fighting, the effects of emotional stress on the cardiovascular system were promptly vitiated. We are now faced with pressures which are not so clear-cut. In a complex, often threatening urban environment, rarely are such cardiovascular responses adaptive. The long term consequences of this cardiovascular overstimulation appear harmful. The term invisible entrapment has been applied to this consequent hyperdynamic state, wherein the person feels boxed into a corner with no acceptable options.

Health Habits. This subject is addressed in greater detail in Chapter 2. Self-induced habits are among the greatest contributors to the over-all health burden of the U.S. Approximately 10% of the total health costs of the nation have been attributed to smoking. Other health-related disorders of habit include unsafe driving, casual sexual practices (venereal disease, high risk pregnancies) and excessive drinking. Modeling, guided practice reinforcement and media use, such as billboards and television announcements, can result in substantial decreases in self-destructive habits. Importantly, media plus personal attention achieve better results than a media approach alone.

Physiological Correlates of Stress. In addition to the elevated 17-OHCS production, several other chemical parameters change with stress. The cortisol and ACTH response to growth hormone is decreased. Catecholamines, triglycerides, free fatty acids and uric acids are elevated. Production of male and female sex hormones diminishes during stress and for at least 1 day following stress. There is a wide variability between individuals. Intraindividual specificity is high, however, especially during steady state situations.

We do not fully know what regulates this organized release of hormones or what specific aspects of stressful situations set them in motion. It appears that the stimulus itself is less important than the individual's response to it. In other words, what is *emotionally* experienced, as influenced by the symbolic meaning of the percept, the motivational state of the organism, maturational level and temporary physical status, is what is critical. What seems clear from these and other studies is that emotional responses set off mechanisms in the brain which, in turn, are capable of regulating patterns of physiological change, which are mediated by autonomical and hormonal outputs.

An important recent finding is that of DiCara and Miller. They showed that specific physiological responses (heart rate, systolic blood pressure, gastrointestinal motility) could be specifically modified by operant conditioning. *Only* the rewarded responses changed, and the type of learned response was specific to the type rewarded, *not* simply a general autonomical discharge. This, of course, has important treatment implications which are beginning to be explored in the field of psychophysiological biofeedback.

Caveats. This summary of correlates of environmental, interpersonal and individual personality stress responses has reported the more consensual data from this field of study. As such it should be useful in helping physicians be alert to problems in the patient's life predisposing to illnesses. Much of this research is unconfirmed, based on uncontrolled studies or reflects the interpretation which the authors wished to give it. It is primarily correlational and may be confusing causation with association. Lastly, the field of study is relatively new, largely present since the mid 1960's in its current form. Therefore, perhaps more than in most areas of scientific study, we suggest that the reader maintain a cautious attitude toward reports in this field, attending as much to the data as to the interpretation given to them.

Motivation

Motivation refers to the complex of factors which prompt a person to act in a certain way. Motivation involves both a present feeling or thought and an anticipated future state of the person. It involves the universal tendency to search for pleasure and avoid unpleasantness. Some motivational forces are inherent in our biological make-up. Hunger, sex, anger, pleasure and thirst are basically regulated by neural and hormonal processes centered anatomically in the hypothalamus. Non-central nervous system factors, especially hormonal ones, also influence motivation. Testosterone is associated with higher levels of aggressivity and wider ranging, more risk-taking play in boys. The other sex hormones also influence behavior. These biologically based drives are usually involved in complex homeostatic mechanisms, thirst and its association with water regulation being a prime example. Physiologically, several systems are involved in thirst. Water deprivation increases osmotic pressure, the change in which is picked up by neurons in the supraoptic nucleus of the hypothalamus. The cells then stimulate the production of antidiuretic hormone from the posterior pituitary gland. Antidiuretic hormone then acts in the kidneys, which reduce urine output and thus conserve water.

However, to present only the physiological aspects of motivation is to oversimplify the situation. *Environmental* and *psychological factors,* in addition to the person's state of biological need, influence motivation. To continue with the example of thirst, motivated behavior to obtain water will be influenced by the person's *previous experiences* in terms of where and how he obtained water. *Expectancy of probable success or failure* influences motivation. The person stranded in the desert with no knowledge of where water lies will search less purposefully than one who knows the approximate location of an oasis.

Studies in this area reveal the truth of the statement that "success breeds success." The *value* which a person attaches to a particular goal or behavior also influences its drive strength. Even at the level of values, neurophysiological processes are involved. Normative frontal lobe function seems essential for motivation in the area of abstract values such as truth, honor and fidelity.

This last statement about values, or *symbolical* motivational forces, leads to a consideration of *unconscious motivation.* One of Sigmund Freud's major contributions to medicine and psychology was his demonstration that, in certain circumstances, memories which lie outside of awareness and resist recall can modify thoughts and feelings and thus serve as unconscious motivating forces. Again, water drinking can illustrate the point. A middle-aged man was admitted to the hospital in a coma. Laboratory tests were inconclusive except that serum sodium and other electrolytes were abnormally low. He was later observed going surreptitiously to a water fountain, where he drank copiously. His coma had been caused by his self-induced water intoxication. Subsequent psychiatric consultation led to uncovering that his self-destructive habit, which went on outside of easy volitional control, was influenced by an unconscious equation of water drinking with a purifying ritual and was rooted in childhood pleasures. His symptom served to give him some pleasure and indirectly enabled him to express his anger toward his parents by indulging in excesses of which he knew they would not approve.

In understanding and assessing motivation, there are also some important caveats. First, some people erroneously believe that all drives are aimed at reducing tension and appetites. In fact, we inherently seek out stimulation and excitement in ways that suggest a genetic, physiological component to such drives. This stimulus-seeking tendency is a component of what we refer to as curiosity. Second, in discussing drives, there is no need to postulate that such forces have a physical reality (for example, that there is an actual build-up of electrical energy in the brain which must be dissipated). Concepts such as libido and cathexis are at best loose metaphors and at worst grossly misleading in terms of what is known of the functions of the brain. Third, there is a danger in equating motivation with instinct. To do so often stops further study and analysis of the particular behavior. More correctly, drives become organized in specific ways wherein the final conglomerate may be only vaguely related to the original goals because of *displacement* and other psychological responses.

Learning

The evolutionary trend toward increasing plasticity of behavior, the enhanced capacity to respond to shifting environmental factors, depends on learning. Humans learn by attaching old bits of behavior to new stimuli, by acquiring new bits of behavior and by acquiring attitudes and values.

Classical Conditioning. In classical conditioning, a dog may learn to salivate in response to the ringing of a bell. During the learning period, a bell is rung shortly before or during the time food is presented. Thus there is a temporal contiguity between the bell (conditioned stimulus) and the meat (unconditioned stimulus). This eventually results in the conditioned stimulus' being able to elicit the response in the absence of the unconditioned stimulus. In this simple type of learning, no new responses are being added. Rather a person is learning to extend to a different category a response already in his repertoire. Many fear responses of patients are based on this mechanism.

Responses are often automatically extended to similar situations. A person who has learned to avoid bees may extend this avoidance to similar insects, such as wasps. In addition, identical elements in a new situation may cause a reactivation of a previously learned response. This occurs in all types of learning and is especially important in neurophysiological processes. Innate physiological response patterns to stress, such as excretion of biogenic amines and corticosteroids, may be elicited by situations which only symbolically and partially represent a danger to the organism.

Operant Conditioning. In this learning paradigm, *new* responses can be acquired and refined. The rat in the Skinner box (an experimental cage in which lever pressing produces food pellets) is at first disorganized and presses the lever clumsily and by chance. With repeated experience, the rat acquires an efficient response and one that may not have previously been in his repertoire in other than very rudimentary form. The reward, or reinforcement, can be of several types. A primary reward is a drink of water, food or a smile—something which is biologically significant. Avoidance conditioning is the process by which the desired behavior allows the person to avoid an unpleasant experience.

Operant conditioning studies have clarified why some maladaptive behaviors persist in the face of punishment. These show that immediate rewards are much more effective than delayed ones. Thus the defensive but maladaptive behavior is reinforced because it provides immediate, short term reduction of fear. An example is the exhibitionist, who may be punished by others and by his own conscience, but he experiences the punishment in a delayed fashion, diffused over a longer period of time. In contradistinction, the gratification he gets from the startled response of the woman seeing him is immediate, thus relieving him of his anxiety and reassuring him of his masculine prowess.

In addition, sporadically rewarded responses are more difficult to extinguish than regularly rewarded ones. The rat who receives a food pellet 25% of the time in an unpredictable sequence will persist much longer in his lever-pressing behavior after the pellets have been cut off than will a rat who has been reinforced on a 100% schedule. By extension, parental discipline which is inconsistent may aggravate behavior problems.

Identification. One of the most powerful factors in the acquisition of behavior in humans is identification. Identification is the largely unconscious and automatic process of imitating and copying those who are loved and admired. Hence, adopted children come to look like one of the family, unconsciously acquiring habits of posture, speech and facial expressions, as well as attitudes and values, from their adoptive parents. Identification is a lifelong process, not one that occurs only in the young, as is indicated by the tendency of married couples to grow more and more alike. The importance of identification as a mode of learning underscores the importance of one-to-one relationships in educational establishments from elementary schools to medical residencies.

Language

Language is the most human of all human qualities. It is the means by which we internalize experience, remember the past and consider alternatives. The ability to acquire nearly all other instrumental skills depends on language skills. The primacy of language as a tool for learning was graphically demonstrated in an experiment by Warden. Subjects were asked to thread their way through a maze solely by tactile guidance, because the maze was hidden from view by a screen. At the end of the experiment, the subjects were asked whether they had memorized the maze by the feel of it, that is, by motor-kinesthetic imagery or by making a "visual map" or by a verbal formula, e.g., "first left, third right, second left," etc.

Of 60 subjects, the 17 who adopted the "motor" method required an average of 124 trials with a range of 72 to 195 trials among the subjects. Eighteen adopted the visual method. They averaged 68 trials, with a range of 41 to 104 trials. Twenty-five adopted the verbal method. They averaged 32 trials, with a range of 16 to 62 trials. Thus, those using language learned *twice* as fast as the visual learners and *four* times as fast as the motor learners.

Words are symbols for perceptual and cognitive events. Thus, although they are the tools for formulating and communicating thoughts, they can entrap us if we are not careful in our usage of them. Most parents know that it is preferable to say to a child who has erred, "You did something bad," rather than "You are bad." However, many people do not know that the structure and common usage in particular language can facilitate or hinder expression. To take the above example, the natural verb choice in German would be machen (*macht ein fehlen,* made a mistake) rather than sein (*du bist schlimm,* you are bad).

Sequence of Speech Development. The "naming explosion" which begins when a child is about 18 months old is the culmination of a process that begins shortly after birth. The first observable change is about the sixth to eighth week and consists of cooing, initially characterized by sounds resembling vowels and later by sounds resembling consonants. (Sound spectrograms show, however, that they differ functionally and acoustically from true speech.) Syllable-like babbling begins to replace cooing at about the sixth month. About the eighth month intonations such as those heard in questions and exclamations begin to appear. Around the twelfth month the first words of the child appear. These are in reality word sentences. "Daddy" may mean "Here comes Daddy!" or "Where is Daddy?" or "Daddy do this for me."

Intelligence

Intelligence may be defined as the general ability to meet new demands by the purposive use of thought. Most other definitions of intelligence similarly recognize its adaptive and biological functions. Hartmann has considered the role of intelligence as " . . . organizing rather than taking the place of all other functions. At a certain level of development, intelligence becomes aware of its own role as one function among others. . . . " Thus, intelligence can serve a synthetic function of keeping the other aspects of ego interrelating smoothly. The functioning of intelligence at this level can lead to a better mastery of the environment and, perhaps more importantly, to better control of one's person.

Intelligence is always tied to specific tasks and to the frame of reference of a particular species. It is not a discrete physical property. Some of the discussion in the section "Genetic Variation" is relevant to this issue. Although intelligence is a useful concept, it has limitations. For example, many intelligence tests assume that intelligence is a single factor, and that all forms of intelligence are positively correlated. It is more likely the case that the flexible adaptation to environmental demands is multimodal and that there is endless variation in the multiple capacities of individuals. Many intelligence tests are biased in that they attend to very limited types of environmental demand. The tendency to oversimplify the concept of intelligence is apparent whenever the question is asked, "How bright is this child?" Rather the question should be, "What are this child's areas of strength and weakness, and how do they relate to his environment?" Intelligence is not synonymous with I.Q. The intelligence quotient, or I.Q., compares the person's mental age—how the problems he answers correctly on a test match the median of an age—with his chronological age. The mental age divided by the chronological age and multiplied by 100 yields the I.Q. The 5-year-old with an I.Q. of 125 is more intelligent than most children his age. He is not more intelligent than a 10-year-old with an I.Q. of 100. This measure of problem-solving ability is relatively stable from the sixth year of life onward. The I.Q. correlates highly with the person's potential for learning and the ability to achieve in occupational categories.

It is firmly established that I.Q. is, to a large degree, an inherited characteristic, heredity accounting for about 50% of variation in intelligence in the strict sense of the term.

Nevertheless, a variety of environmental variables may positively or negatively influence intelligence. All of the factors have their major influence within the first 2 years of life. Thus, programs aimed at improving a child's I.Q. should begin well before the child is 3 years old. Programs which did not involve parents have uniformly shown meager and reversible results. The amount and clarity of verbal interaction within a family, and specifically with a child, are important. Stimulation in general, so long as it is not chaotic and allows the child to rest sufficiently and to be free of tension, positively influences intelligence. The quality of verbal interaction, especially in terms of invoking the reasoning process in a child, is likewise important. For example, two mothers may be sitting in a bus with their children. One mother may say to her child, "Sit down and shut up," whereas the second mother may say, "Why don't you sit so that when the bus moves you won't fall and get hurt." The second mother not only provides a model for sentence structure lacking in the first mother, but also generates a reasoning process in the child, encouraging him to consider actions in terms of their consequences.

Character traits interact with intelligence. In the Fels study of the I.Q. of children tested from the age of 3 until they were 12, two-thirds of the children varied more than 15 points, despite a mean I.Q. for the group which remained at 120. When tested at age 5, the children who showed I.Q. gains displayed traits of independence, competitiveness and self-initiative. Children scoring low on those measures subsequently showed I.Q. decline.

Language deficits, dyslexia and visual and hearing problems can all contribute to diminished ability to learn. Nutritional deficits, especially of protein, which is essential to the formation of myelin, can result in irreversible intellectual deficits.

The issue of I.Q. has been heatedly and at times intemperately and unscientifically argued in recent years, in part because of studies which suggest that the mean I.Q. of black Americans is 5 to 20 points lower than that of Anglo-Americans. This is not the place to assess the various arguments fully. Many of the previously discussed factors which influence intelligence similarly influence I.Q. scores. Disadvantaged circumstances may contribute to lowered I.Q. within a family. Homes in which there is little opportunity to hear and participate in the richness of verbal experience yield children with lower I.Q.'s. Families with poor social cohesiveness are not likely to appreciate the importance of education; thus they inadequately motivate the child to learn, both in and out of school. I.Q. tests have been criticized for cultural bias. Specific questions are often outside the experience of significant numbers of persons. In addition, some test responses probably become dated when, for example, new word usage occurs. It is probably impossible to structure a useful I.Q. test which is not rooted within the framework of a culture. The more important attitude to have is to realize that, insofar as any group is denied full access to the experiences and opportunities of the culture or is in some ways prejudicially dealt with, that group's performance on standard I.Q. tests will be diminished.

It is crucial to avoid reification of the concept of intelligence. It is not a real quality, but a hypothetical construct, and its measurement is inherently an artificial process. Reducing the intellectual characteristics of a person to a single number is a procedure of little merit in most situations; we would be better served by considering a profile of the person's intellectual strengths and weaknesses. Over-reliance on I.Q. scores is analogous to reducing ego strength to a single number on the basis of a simple test, overlooking the multifaceted adaptational and defensive activities comprised by the ego.

*   *   *   *

In this chapter, we have dealt with the special plasticity of individual behavior which is so marked in the human species. We have examined genetic variation, perception, affect, motivation, learning, language, and intelligence. Man goes through life with this remarkable biological and culturally influenced adaptational endowment. We now turn to the infant, to learn what happens biologically, psychologically and culturally, both in terms of normative development and minor adaptational difficulties, from birth until death.

REFERENCES

1. ARIETI, S. *The Intrapsychic Self.* Basic Books, New York, 1967.
2. BODNER, W. F., AND CAVALLI-SFORZA, L. L. Intelligence and race. *Sci. Am. 223:*19, 1970.
3. BOURNE, P. G., ROSE, R. M., AND MASON, J. W. 17-Hydroxycorticosteroids in combat. *Arch. Gen. Psychiatry 19:*135–140, 1968.
4. BRAND, R. J., ROSENMAN, R. H., SHOLTZ, R. I., AND FRIEDMAN, M. Multivariate prediction of coronary heart disease in the Western Collaborative Group Study compared to the findings of the Framingham study. *Circulation 53:*348–355, 1976.
5. CHOMSKY, N. The Formal Nature of Language, in *The Biological Foundations of Language,* Lenneberg, E., ed. John Wiley & Sons, New York, 1967, p. 397. (A good exposition of the views of the world's most important linguist.)
6. DiCARA, L. V., AND MILLER, N. E. Instrumental learning of systolic blood pressure responses by curarized rats: dissociation of cardiac and vascular changes. *Psychosom. Med. 30:*489, 1968.
7. DOBZHANSKY, T. The Pattern of Human Evolution, in *The Uniqueness of Man,* Roslandky, J. D., ed. North Holland Publishing Company, Amsterdam, 1969, pp. 41–70. (A superb clarification of the difference between *equality* as a political, ethical precept and *diversity* as a biological fact.)
8. ELIOT, R. S., AND FORKER, A. D. Emotional stress and cardiac disease. *J.A.M.A. 236:*2325–2326, 1976.
9. HARTMANN, H. *Ego Psychology and the Problem of Adaptation.* International Universities Press, New York, 1958.
10. HEATH, R. G. Physiologic basis of emotional expression: evoked potential and mirror focus studies in rhesus monkeys. *Biol. Psychiatry 5:*15–31, 1972.
11. KIRITZ, S., AND MOOS, R. H. Physiological effects of social environments. *Psychosom. Med. 36:*96–114, 1974.
12. LENNEBERG, E. *The Biological Foundations of Language.* John Wiley & Sons, New York, 1967. (This is a major work on this subject. The depth and breadth of scholarship and fairness are evident throughout. There is an excellent section on aphasia.)

13. Mac Carthy, D., and Booth, E. M. Parental rejection and stunting of growth. *J. Psychosom. Res. 14:*259–265, 1970.

14. MacLean, P. D. New findings relevant to psychosexual functions of the brain. *J. Nerv. Ment. Dis. 135:*289, 1962.

15. Mason, J. W. Organization of psychoendocrine mechanisms. *Psychosom. Med. 30:*565–808, 1968.

16. Napier, J. R. *The Roots of Mankind.* Smithsonian Institution Press, Washington, D. C., 1970.

17. Olds, J. Hypothalamic substrates of reward. *Physiol. Rev. 42:*554–604, 1962.

18. Pribram, K. H. Emotion: Steps toward a Neurophysiological Theory, in *Neurophysiology of Emotion,* Glass, D. C., ed. Rockefeller University Press, New York, 1967, pp. 3–40.

19. Silverman, J. Variations in cognitive control and psychophysiological defense in the schizophrenias. *Pscyhosom. Med. 29:*252, 1967.

20. Smith, H. *From Fish to Philosopher.* Little, Brown, and Co., Boston, 1953. (Smith's ability to present complex issues lucidly, such as evolution, genetic recombination and consciousness, is unexcelled.)

21. Washburn, S. L. The Evolution of Human Behavior, in *The Uniqueness of Man,* Roslansky, J. D., ed. North Holland Publishing Company, Amsterdam, 1969, pp. 16 –189. (Excellent anthropological overview of man and, particularly, the effect of genetic changes on alterations in human social behavior.)

22. Weiner, H. Presidential address: some comments on the transduction of experience by the brain: implications for our understanding of the relationship of mind to body. *Psychosom. Med. 34:*355–380, 1972.

23. Wordworth, R. S. *Experimental Psychology.* Holt, Rinehart and Winston, New York, 1938, p. 148 (quotation).

24. Wyler, R. A., Masuda, M., and Holmes, T. H. Magnitude of life events and seriousness of illness. *Psychosom. Med. 33:*115–122, 1971.

CHAPTER 13

INFANCY

ROBERT L. LEON, M.D.

To a significant degree, a child's fate in the world is determined before he is born. In a real sense, decisions and chance circumstances surrounding the time of birth also predetermine many aspects of a child's fate in life. It is one thing to consider the issue of genetic variation in terms of scientific precepts, another to realize that the genetic make-up of the individual child will be determined by his particular mother and father. Similarly, consider the way in which factors of choice and chance also predetermine some aspects of the child's environmental or cultural experience. A child born out of wedlock to a white mother and a black father will very likely be placed for adoption, in which case the culture of the adoptive parents will be paramount. On the other hand, a child born out of wedlock to a black mother and a white father will probably not be adopted but will be reared by the maternal grandmother in the same subculture as that of his mother.

Ordinal position among siblings is another chance factor which influences later development. Parents are less experienced with, and tend to protect,

121

first-borns and "only" children. These children receive more attention from their parents, and, growing up in adult-centered families, they have adults who serve more as models for learning, rather than the more peer-based learning of children who have older siblings. Oldest children tend to be less prone to fighting and displays of temper, to be performance oriented (they are over-represented in most measures of achievement, such as graduate school rosters and Who's Who lists) and to have a higher incidence of symptoms which bring them to child guidance clinics. Middle children seem to get things with less active striving and to be more socially gregarious. Youngest children may remain the baby because no one challenges the position. The youngest child tends to be more highly striving and defiant. Although such correlations are suggestive, they cannot substitute for diagnostic observation. The physician's intervention must be based on the case at hand, rather than on probabilities. Although cognizant that parents have a tendency to pamper the youngest child, he should not assume in advance that this is the case.

Another chance factor is whether a child is born into a one-parent family. Boys whose fathers were not present in the first year of life have more behavioral difficulties in later life. There is a clear relationship between the absence of a father in the home, especially during the first 6 years of life, and subsequent antisocial behavior in boys. A boy's need for a strong father-figure does not mean that the father should be harsh and punitive. In fact, more masculine boys tend to see their fathers as both more authoritative *and* more protective and loving.

Prenatal Factors in Development

Genetic and Cultural Factors

Genetic endowment of the infant is determined at conception. It is the substrate on which all else is built. Sex, physical characteristics and some aspects of intelligence and temperament are more or less determined at this point. In the past, there was little that could be done about the genetic complement except to provide the baby with a favorable environment. With the rapid strides being made in human genetics, this may change dramatically in the future, as indicated by Hirschorn. He states that the most commonly described syndromes found after birth are those due to abnormal numbers of chromosomes. The most important of these is Down's syndrome, or mongolism. This and other trisomies tend to increase in frequency with advanced maternal age. If there is a question because of family history or the mother's age, a genetic diagnosis can be made by obtaining a sample of amniotic fluid through a transabdominal needle aspiration. If indicated, and if the parents so desire, a therapeutic abortion can then be performed. This predictive capacity raises many bioethical issues. Who should bear the cost of amniocentesis? Should it be universally available? If the fetus is defective and will require institutional care, should abortion be mandatory? What are appropriate considerations for abortions? Do they include sex of child?

Factors during Pregnancy

Planned and Unplanned Children. Studies show that about one-third of last-born children are unplanned. But "unplanned" is not equatable with "unwanted." Whether or not a pregnancy is planned can have an important influence on parent-child relationships and on the developing personality of the child, but these influences are subtle and complicated. Two opposite extremes can be taken as examples. A child of a planned pregnancy can be in great psychological jeopardy if the father wants the child to prove his masculinity and the mother wants to become pregnant because she enjoys the dependency gratification she receives while pregnant. On the other hand, a mature couple may not have planned a pregnancy, but, when the child arrives, they may happily adjust to the new situation.

Maternal Nutrition and Birth Trauma. Maternal nutrition, which relates to culture and socioeconomic status, affects the developing fetus and the later development of the infant. It is influenced by a complex interaction of factors, including the cultural definition of what pregnant women should eat, the mother's mental and physical state, whether she has seen a doctor and received good advice and whether she can afford proper food.

For two decades Pasamanick has been studying children born to poor mothers who were undernourished and who had little or no prenatal care. He concludes that differences in neurological, psychological and intellectual status may derive from exposures to risks of maldevelopment in periods before, during and after birth.

Initially noting that pregnancy and birth complications were associated with fetal and neonatal death due to brain injury, Pasamanick hypothesized that the surviving infants must include other, less severely brain-injured children. Depending on the degree and location of trauma, these infants develop disorders ranging from cerebral palsy, epilepsy and mental deficiency to diffuse behavior and learning disabilities. Pasamanick found that reading disabilities and certain forms of schizophrenic behavior in children were more common in children whose mothers had had problems during pregnancy or the birth of the child and among children who had problems during the early period of infancy. Only tics, accidents and juvenile delinquency were not correlated with a higher number of abnormalities during pregnancy and the perinatal period. Brain damage at birth, obviously not the cause of all subsequent problems, can be a major contributing factor. A study of preschool children from impoverished black families in Memphis showed that 60% of the girls and 58% of the boys were shorter than normal. Ninety per cent of those under 3 were anemic, as were 75% of those over 3. Birch and Gussow have done an extensive review of the relationship of poverty, disadvantage and school failure, beginning with the effects of poverty and malnutrition on pregnant women and newborns. They conclude that higher socioeconomic status is associated with higher birth weight, fewer perinatal and infant deaths and better performance in school; the reverse is also true. There is a cycle of poverty, with its poor nutrition creating lower energy level on the part of parents, and inadequate nutrition in infants and young children which runs from one generation to the next.

Since 1975 information has begun to emerge that alcohol consumption during pregnancy can cause major developmental abnormalities. This fetal alcohol syndrome, occurring with even moderate alcoholism, is characterized by delayed and incomplete growth, microcephaly and shortened palpebral fissures. Consumption of as little as 2 ounces of liquor per day during the first trimester of pregnancy may be associated with a partial expression of the syndrome, such as slowed development and intellectual deficiency.

Maternal Illnesses. Certain illnesses which occur during pregnancy can have a profound effect on the fetus. German measles during the first trimester of pregnancy is an example. The congenital defects produced in the newborn child are so severe that abortion is to be considered if rubella is suspected. Mothers who are addicted to heroin give birth to children who are also addicted.

The Mother's Attitudes. A mother's attitudes and feelings from past relationships influence her attitude toward her pregnancy and, even more profoundly, her relationship with her newborn child. Of greatest importance is the mother's maturity. Maturity is a general term used to describe many attributes. Here we use it to refer to the capacity to give and receive love. An immature mother who has not had her own need for love satisfied will resent the pregnancy because it represents future sacrifices on her part and because, while pregnant, she no longer feels as pretty and attractive as she once did. While some feelings of this sort are common to all women, in immature mothers they are central and abiding, conscious or unconscious concerns. The same is true with other attitudes and fears about pregnancy. Every woman has her share of frightening feelings, such as fear of having an abnormal child, fear of what will happen during birth, etc., but a more mature woman can put these fears in proper perspective. When such feelings become the major focus of the pregnancy or when they are so denied that they are never spoken, they are likely to cause problems in the later mother-infant relationship.

The Father's Attitudes. The father also has a number of predetermined feelings and attitudes about the pregnancy. His emotional maturity will have much to do with his ability to relate constructively to his pregnant wife. Like the mother, the father will have many irrational fantasies and feelings. He may look with pride at the prospect of giving his parents the gift of a grandchild, while at the same time be oblivious to the real responsibilities of parenthood. He may resent his wife's turning inward into herself, as all women do during pregnancy. If he fears loss of his wife's love when the child comes, he will react to the pregnancy with hostility, causing his wife to become even more fearful and concerned with herself.

The Physician's Response. During pregnancy the physician can be of tremendous help to the family. The courts have recently ruled that a pregnant woman does not have to bear a child if she does not choose to do so. Many women thus must make a decision about whether or not to have an abortion if the pregnancy is unplanned. It is usually unmarried women who struggle with this decision, but some married women and their husbands may want to delay having their first child or may be faced with an unwanted pregnancy later in life. Although the physician should not dictate a choice, he can point out elements of reality and can encourage both parents to explore their feelings frankly if he is careful to be impartial in so doing.

As the pregnancy develops it is important for the physician to listen carefully to what his patient says or does not say about her feelings about being pregnant. If she can express her fears to the doctor, she will be less frightened, her relationship with her husband will improve and the husband can then offer more support, which will further reduce the wife's fears. Such things as classes for new parents, training in natural childbirth and planning to have the father present during delivery all help to orient the couple positively.

Problems during Delivery

The way the infant arrives in the world is dependent on myriad prenatal and preconceptual factors, some of which have been discussed. In addition, the circumstances of the birth can be quite influential to later life, particularly if the birth is traumatic to mother or child. Good prenatal care which anticipates difficulties at labor can prevent much of this. This includes education of the mother and anticipation of possible complications by the physician. Subtle psychological complications may also occur. For example, the mother who has a neurotic fear that she will have a defective child will need more reassurance from the physician at the time of labor and birth. The generally dependent, frightened mother may need special handling to overcome her incapacitating fear, or she may be so frightened that she will not want another pregnancy. Whatever the problem, the feelings the mother and father have toward their newborn child can be much influenced by the feeling tones that doctors and nurses engender about labor and birth.

The First Year of Life

Human infants are unable to sustain life without the aid of a mothering person. The infant can take in oxygen and food and can eliminate waste. Beyond this, he can do nothing for himself. He is a metabolizing, feeling, biological organism with great potential for socialization, but, at the time of birth and for some time after, he has only an ability to receive and almost no ability to get. The latter comes very slowly and is related to increasing maturity.

The Role of Nutrition and Feeding

The interaction of mother and child in meeting the dependency needs of the child is one of the most crucial factors in determining the entire future life of the child. Nutrition is, of course, important; without proper nutrition the child will not survive or will be retarded in aspects of his growth.

The last several decades have seen much controversy concerning the advantages of breast versus bottle feeding. Recent studies are consistent in showing several advantages to breast feeding. Breast feeding facilitates uterine contraction. Human milk is high in IgA immunoglobulin, an antibody-rich substance which contributes to the greater disease resistance of breast-fed babies. Allergies are more common in bottle-fed infants, including the problem of specific allergies which develop to formulas. Infants who bottle feed are likely to be encouraged to drink the entire bottle, whereas the breast-fed baby stops when full. The former may result in a greater number of fat cells, predisposing to later problems with obesity.

Bottle milk is low in iron, leading to increased frequency of nutritional anemia. Low lactose content in bottle milk contributes to a greater suscepti-bility to infantile diarrhea. The high sugar content predisposes to a later preference for high sugar content foods and increased dental caries. Bottle feeding can result in deviant development of the oropharynx, a syndrome referred to as bottle mouth, because of the different sucking pattern.

For most mothers, the recent heightened interest in breast feeding is more related to the sense of fulfillment of the bond between mother and child. Breast feeding can provide a sensual, erotic feeling for the mother which further increases her sense of close relationship with her child. Supportive organizations such as La Leche League have helped dispel myths about breast feeding. It is not breast feeding, but pregnancy, that causes breasts to lose some of their firmness. Women with small breasts are as able to nurse as those with larger breasts.

Rational reasons for not breast feeding may relate to the fact that the mother is working or, for other reasons, does not want, or cannot be tied to, the demanding schedule of breast feeding. Aversions or strong emotions against breast feeding are primarily unconsciously determined and may relate to the mother's feelings about her own body or feelings she had about her own mother. The physician should not bring great pressure to bear which runs counter to such unconscious feelings. If she feels forced to go against her wishes, the mother may express her resentment toward the child, whereas if she is supported in what she wants she is able to have a more open and satisfying relationship with her child.

Maternal Affection

No one knows how an infant thinks or feels, but we suppose that he comes from the warm, supportive environment of the womb into an alien, frightening world after having had a traumatic journey down the birth canal. Some of the early psychoanalysts attributed too much verbal content to an infant's thoughts and feelings, but we do know that the process of birth upsets the child's homeostasis at a physical and a primitive emotional level. In the early months of life, it is important that the mothering person restore this tranquility as much as possible. As life progresses, the child must learn to deal with frustration. However, he cannot learn before he is ready, and early infancy is not the time.

This early mother-child experience lays the groundwork for the emotional or psychosexual development of the child. Various theorists have classified this emotional development in different ways. According to Erikson, this early period of mother-child interaction determines the basic sense of trust or mistrust which is likely to stay with the child for the rest of his life. Although behavior and feelings can be changed later in life, it becomes increasingly more difficult as layer upon layer of maladaptive interaction is built up.

The regular feeding and satisfaction of basic biological needs by the mother helps the infant to establish a regular homeostatic rhythm adapted to the outside world. If the mother is consistent and predictable, the infant anticipates satisfaction at a deep biological level. This is what is meant by *basic trust*. To use the vernacular, we are speaking of a "gut feeling." Literally, the infant must have the needs of his alimentary tract satisfied on a regular and predictable basis if he is to survive and have a good feeling about the world as a place to live.

It takes much more than feeding, warmth and cleanliness to produce this sense of trust. These basic conditions must occur in combination with a loving mother who can communicate through holding, stroking, talking and her very presence. It is this communication from the mother and the mutuality between mother and child, along with the predictable satisfaction of biological needs, which contribute to this sense of trust.

The pioneering work on the life-sustaining importance of the mother-figure in a child's life was done by Spitz. In studying children in a foundling home, he found that their developmental quotient deteriorated markedly with age, even though they were fed regularly and were kept in hygienic surroundings. In contrast, a control group of children who were cared for by their mothers developed normally. The infants in the foundling home were unable to sit or to stand at the usual times. They failed to gain weight and would not respond to adults. Many of them died. Prior to the studies by Spitz and similar studies by others, infants were occasionally dying on pediatric wards from unexplained causes. A common sequence was that an infant would come into the hospital with severe diarrhea and would be isolated because of the infection. After the diarrhea had cleared, the infant would fail to thrive and would remain underweight. Sometimes the infant would be kept in the hospital while a search was made for organic causes for the condition. If during this time a mother or substitute mother was not present, the infant might die.

The discovery of the effects of maternal deprivation led to the closing of the large orphanages, which were then present all over the United States, and to the early placement of infants for adoption or in foster care before the irreversible effects of maternal deprivation set in.

In the early months of life, the socioeconomic situation may have an important bearing on the mother's capacity to give the kind of love and attention needed. A harried mother with too many children, not enough money and no husband may have little in the way of tender feelings to communicate. The situation can be so neglectful for the infant that the failure-to-thrive syndrome, known as marasmus, develops. Although it was first identified in hospitalized infants, it can occur at home as well.

Although it is important for a physician to be alert to pathology, he must always pay equal attention to the assets of a given family structure. Most parents are loving; they want to do a good job, and they can potentially achieve much pleasure from being parents. The family doctor or pediatrician can reinforce this by paying attention to parental needs. In order to alleviate a potentially dangerous situation, it may be necessary only to help the father to find better ways to support the mother. Many young fathers are so tied up in their developing careers that they fail to perceive the necessity for this. The physician can reinforce the mother's desire to do what pleases her most. He can help the parents of infants to understand that no one has the last word in child practices, and he can help them to understand that they need not devote their entire lives to their child but should seek satisfaction for themselves as well.

Ethological Studies. Since the 1940's an active study into normative, instinctual and acquired behavioral patterns in animals has influenced child developmental psychology, especially in relationship to early bonding and maternal affection. It is important to note that no conclusive inferences about human behavior can be drawn from cross-species studies, even from those of higher primates. Nonetheless, careful studies in animals, particularly those using the animal's natural environment, can suggest areas of investigation or clinical attention in humans. Conversely, questions about early development in humans may be usefully studied in animal models, where the environment can be controlled and the behavior quantitated.

One major group of ethological studies relevant to human development are those in which animals were reared in social isolation. Such animals display a range of behaviors which in humans we would call autistic: rocking, self-mutilation and inability to engage in social play. Sexual behavior is virtually absent, although there are differences by sex and species. Male monkeys usually remain completely inadequate sexually for life. Females, in the presence of a sexually active and patient male, sometimes perform in an appropriate sexual fashion, but as mothers they do not show normal affiliative concerns for their infants.

Separation of the mother from her young results in an initial period of agitation in the offspring followed by apparent depression. Social play is not engaged in even when elicited. Spontaneous movement and interest in the environment virtually ceases. Some infants fail to eat and drink, and they die if they are not given fluids. Return of the mother results in an intensification of bonding behavior and excessive dependency, wherein the young monkey is reluctant to venture away from the mother.

Harlow's work demonstrates the phenomenon of mothering in an experimental setting. Infant monkeys raised with a cold, hard wire mother-surrogate at which they were fed but who also had available a soft, terry cloth mother-surrogate, would flee to the terry cloth mother for contact comfort when frightened. Although this demonstrates the importance of tactile gratification for infant security, the absence of any social interaction with a real mother led to profound consequences. When grown, these deprived monkeys did not know how to mate, and, even after successful impregnation, the females were seriously lacking in maternal behavior, refusing to permit their babies to approach or to cuddle them.

As important as these observations on the consequences of early childhood experience for later physical and emotional development are, they should not be applied too literally. Studies in the 1970's have tended to soften the view of irreversible changes from developmental insults as an infant. A long term study of the Fels Institute found little relationship between any aspects of maternal treatment of the child during the first 3 years of life and adolescent and adulthood disposition. The weight of all such data suggests that the child has an enormous capacity for resilience and change, even after a severely troubled early life, if the environment changes to one supportive of psychological development.

Recent applications of the knowledge that early mother-child contact is important include the increasing prevalence of rooming-in facilities, where the new mother has basic responsibility for caring for the newborn, and arrangement of neonatal intensive care units to maximize mother-child contact. It is now clear that close contact between mother and child from the earliest moments of life promotes a close emotional bonding between them. The presence of this bonding is the basis for care-giving and psychological development in the child; its absence is correlated with child abuse and abandonment and failures by the child to thrive emotionally and physically.

Basic Temperament

Chess defines temperament as "the characteristic tempo, rhythmicity, adaptability, energy expenditure, mood, and attention-focus of a child, independent of the content of any specific behavior." From birth, children seem to display a characteristic temperament independent of their parents' handling or personality styles. These original characteristics tend to persist over the years, but they can be heightened or diminished by environmental circumstances. Of the children in a longitudinal study who developed behavioral disturbances, each instance could be traced to a maladaptive interaction between the particular temperament of the child and the particular aspects of the environment.

Chess and her co-workers describe three major characteristic patterns of temperament. First are the "easy children." They have a positive, pleasant mood, have low to moderately intense reactions, are readily adaptable and have a positive approach to new situations. They participate openly with others and are easy to handle. About 40% of all children are in this category. Second are the 10% who are the "difficult children." Irregular in body functions, intense in reactions, negative in mood, they withdraw in the face of new stimuli and are slow to adapt to change. Third are the "slow to warm up." Their activity level is low, they are somewhat negative in mood, respond to stress with low intensity reactions, withdraw on first exposure to new stimuli and are slow to adapt; 15% of all infants fall into this group. The other 35% are mixtures of the three types. In general, demands that conflict excessively with any temperamental characteristics are best avoided. For example, an adaptable child may readily accept a new food. A nonadaptable, intense child may need to have the same food consistently offered in a nonthreatening way in order to accept it. A difficult child who responds slowly and with much turbulence is more prone to develop problems and is more difficult for any parent to handle. If he is given support and is exposed slowly to new situations, he will usually do well. He may, unfortunately, be born to loving but temperamentally different parents who cannot easily empathize with his balky behavior. In such cases, they may not be able to give the kind of support the child needs.

Biological Development

Development and change occur at a gradually decelerating pace, starting at conception and continuing until maturity. The rate of development from conception to birth is phenomenally fast. The rate of development of sensorimotor and social skills from birth to 1 year is equally rapid. For this reason, it is important to promote an orderly developmental process.

Vision appears to undergo progressive development, from initial random eye movements and pupillary response to light, to pursuit movements at 15 days and to binocular fixation at about 7 or 8 weeks. Apparently, precise accommodation does not occur until about 1 year, when clear-cut images appear.

Although the newborn responds to gross sensations in the areas of hearing, olfaction and gustation, these senses are poorly developed and relatively undiscriminating at birth. Discrimination begins to develop within the first 2 weeks. The 12- to 21-day-old infant can imitate specific facial and manual gestures demonstrated by an adult. This suggests that even at this early age human neonates have the capability to equate their own unseen behavior with gestures they see others perform.

At 1 month, the infant in a prone position can lift his head. At 2 months, he can raise up on his elbows; at 3 to 4 months, he can sit for a moment with support and smile selectively in recognition of the mother; at 7 or 8 months, he can sit without support. He can stand at 8 months with help and, at 9 months, he can stand by holding onto furniture. By 12 months, he is pulling himself up; by 14 months, he is standing alone, and by 15 months, he is walking alone. These figures, of course, represent an average range. Some children will be earlier and some will be later than others.

Gesell and Amatruda also carefully studied the ability to use the hands. Newborn infants have a grasp reflex, a reflex that was once necessary to survival. It helps the infant to cling to a mobile mother. This disappears by the time the infant is 4 months old. By 20 weeks, the infant can reach for and grasp a cube with the entire hand. By 60 weeks, the child can grasp a cube with the thumb and forefinger in much the same way as an adult.

Language also proceeds in a maturational sequence. Cooing and babbling begin by the third month. The child's first word is spoken at about 11 months. Stimulation of speech by the mother and family and reward for spoken words are very important at this and later stages of development. Children raised in institutions, as opposed to those raised in families, are retarded in language development. Infants in middle-class homes tend to be more developed in their language than children from working-class homes.

Piaget describes early mental development under the heading of *sensorimotor intelligence* or *sensorimotor schemata*. This term is used in contrast to *conceptual intelligence*, which begins at age 2 and continues to maturity. During the *sensorimotor stage*, language symbols are little involved. The stage is further divided into six substages. The first stage goes to 1 month and involves reflex actions. In the second stage, that of primary circular reactions, repetitive actions such as sucking or opening and closing of the fists occur. In the remaining stages, there is more and more intentional activity. By the fourth stage of coordinated secondary reactions, 7 to 10 months, the child will knock down a pillow in order to find a toy behind it. In the sixth stage, at 18 months, the child shows the first sign of foresight. That is, he considers in advance what the effects of his actions would be, rather than being limited to overt trial and error. A child this age who wishes to put a block into a box with an opening too small for the block will look at the size of the block and the hole and abandon the effort without making an attempt. A younger child will try fruitlessly to push the block through the hole.

In the early sensorimotor period, Piaget postulates that an infant comprehends objects only in terms of his manipulation of them or how they impinge on the field of vision. For example, before the age of 8 months, an infant will show no interest in an object with which he has played and which is subsequently placed behind a pillow or enclosed in a hand. At about 8 months, however, he will begin to reach for the object, indicating that the objects are acquiring some visual permanence. Even so, he has as yet no objective identity of an object or knowledge of spatial relationships. At 8 months of age, a child will look for a ball *not* under the pillow where he last saw it put, but under the pillow where he last found it. Only at 12 to 16 months of age will he seek it under the pillow where he saw it disappear. Even then, full *object permanence* is not present. For example, if the child does not see the ball moved from pillow A to pillow B, he will not look for it under pillow B.

Visual permanency and object permanency are reflections of the child's beginning symbolic capacity. He can now mentally represent objects not physically present by means of symbols, and he can discriminate in a finer way various aspects of his environment. These beginning cognitive discriminations are involved in the "8-month stranger anxiety." An infant who at 5 or 6 months readily accords the doctor a social smile may respond with fear 2 months later. He is now able to differentiate between the doctor and his mother, whose presence has become a specific source of comfort.

*   *   *   *

Examination of Infants

Infants and young children are often difficult for the physician to approach, unless he is one of those unusual persons who can naturally calm a frightened child, and even this rare person will not be able to overcome the "stranger" anxiety. How does the average physician deal with the mother and infant who come to his office? First of all, he chooses personnel—receptionist and nurse—who enjoy children, who are calm and who want to listen to waiting mothers. When the mother brings the child to the examining room, she should be made to feel comfortable and as free of anxiety as possible. A mother's feelings are immediately picked up by her child. The mother should be allowed to undress and hold the baby. Much of the examination can take place on the mother's lap. If it is necessary to hold the baby, the physician should watch how the mother holds the baby and try to do the same. In general, babies seem to prefer to be held firmly upright, perhaps with the face on the doctor's shoulder. The physician should be deliberate and unhurried. He should be as unobtrusive as possible, and should neither stare at, laugh at or make sudden movements toward the child. He should not attempt to amuse the child by making faces, tickling, etc. Such behavior only frightens young children. During the first 6 months of life, a prone child who is crying will usually stop if he is raised to a sitting position. The physician's feeling tone and the mother's feeling tone will make the difference between a successful examination of a relatively quiet infant and an inadequate examination of a screaming infant.

REFERENCES

1. ALTUS, W. D. Birth order and its sequelae. *Science 151:*44, 1966.
2. BIRCH, H. G., AND GUSSOW, J. D. *Disadvantaged Children: Health, Nutrition and School Failure.* Grune & Stratton, New York, 1970.
3. BOWLBY, J. Separation anxiety: a critical review of the literature. *J. Child. Psychol. Psychiatry 1:*251, 1961.
4. CHASE, H. P., DORSEY, J., AND McRHANN, G. M. The effects of malnutrition on the synthesis of a myelin lipid. *Pediatrics 40:*551, 1967.
5. ELKIND, D. Perceptual development in children. *Am. Sci. 63:*533–541, 1975.
6. ERIKSON, E. H. *Identity and the Life Cycle: Psychological Issues.* International Universities Press, New York, 1959.
7. GUTELIUS, M. F., KIRSCH, A. D., MacDONALD, S., BROOKS, M. R., McERLEAN, T., AND NEWCOMB, C. Promising results from a cognitive stimulation program in infancy. *Clin. Pediatr. 11:*585, 1972.
8. HARLOW, H. F. The nature of love. *Am. Psychol. 13:*674, 1958.
9. KAGAN, J. Emergent themes in human development. *Am. Sci. 64:*186–195, 1976.
10. MELTZOFF, A. N., AND MOORE, M. K. Imitation of facial and manual gestures by human neonates. *Science 198:*75–78, 1977.
11. MUSSEN, P. H., CONGER, J. J., AND KAGAN, J. Biological Changes in Infancy, in *Child Development and Personality.* Harper & Row, New York, 1974.
12. PASAMANICK, B., KNOBLOCH, H., AND LIBIENFELD, A. M. Socioeconomic status and some precursors of neuropsychiatric disorder. *Am. J. Orthopsychiatry 26:*594, 1956.
13. PIAGET, J. *The Origins of Intelligence in Children.* International Universities Press, New York, 1953.
14. ROSENBLUM, L. Ethology: primate research and the evolutionary origins of human behavior, in *Understanding Human Behavior in Health and Illness,* Simons, R. C., and Pardes, H. (eds). Williams & Wilkins, Baltimore, 1977.
15. SEARS, R. R., MACCOBY, E. E., AND LEVIN, H. *Patterns of Child Rearing.* Harper, New York, 1957.
16. SPITZ, R. A. Hospitalism: an inquiry into the genesis of psychiatric conditions in early childhood. *Psychoanal. Study Child 1:*53, 1945.
17. THOMAS, A., CHESS, S., AND BIRCH, H. G. The origin of personality. *Sci. Am. 233:*102, 1970.
18. ZEE, P., WALTERS, T., AND MITCHELL, C. Nutrition and poverty in preschool children. *J.A.M.A. 213:*739, 1970.

CHAPTER 14

THE TODDLER: CHILDHOOD FROM AGES ONE TO THREE

ROBERT L. LEON, M.D.

From a developmental point of view, each stage is built upon the previous one, and the character traits rooted in each stage of development are represented throughout life. Resolution or lack of resolution at one stage will influence the child's ability to cope with the necessary tasks of the next, just as a child must learn to read numbers before being able to cope with multiplication. Developmental tasks at the previous level upon which the new level is dependent must be mastered at more or less the right time. Erikson calls this the epigenetic concept. He compares psychosexual growth and development with the embryological unfolding of organs and functions at the proper time and in the proper sequence.

Piaget's psychology is a developmental theory in which one stage is built upon the previous stage. Piaget begins with innate behavior patterns and reflexes and describes how, through the interactions of these patterns with the environment, more and more complex intellectual capacity is built up. This is much like Erikson's epigenetic principle, which postulates the unfolding of each developmental period upon the other. It is also the process by which biological development takes place, beginning with the single cell. In each case, the unfolding of a developmental sequence occurs in a dynamic interaction with the environment. Piaget's theories and observations deal with intellectual development. Erikson's concepts deal more with the development of the emotions and the development of relationships with significant persons in the child's life.

Tasks of the Period

The phase of infancy ends when locomotion is established and the ability to control the sphincters begins. The infant then views his mother as a separate person but one who is essential to satisfy his needs. With the newfound control of his body, he sets the stage for interaction with those around him. The outcome of this interaction, which many times becomes a battle, can either be a child who feels in control of himself in relation to the world or a fearful child full of obsessions and doubts about the validity and acceptability of his impulses. If the child still has much unresolved primitive rage because his oral needs were not met during the period of infancy, he and his parents will encounter even more difficulty in the 1- to 3-year-old age period.

Separation from the Mother. The child not only recognizes his dependency on his mother but feels a true love for her. For example, he watches for her return when she is gone from the room. When she comes in, his face lights up, and he welcomes her with a smile and outstretched arms. Because the child has recognized his mother as a separate and distinct individual, he feels keenly any enforced separation from her. Freud and Burlingham studied the reactions of children who were separated from their parents during the bombing of London in World War II. Of those who were separated, the children between 1 and 2 years of age reacted more violently than the others. Emotional upsets were reflected not only in anxiety and depression, but also in the physical health of the child.

An important aspect of this problem for physicians was studied by Bowlby. He and his group did classical studies on children who were hospitalized and separated from their mothers. The children usually reacted initially with protest, fretting or crying—showing symptoms much like temper tantrums. After this, the children reacted with despair. Although they accepted care from others, the children seemed indifferent and were likely to turn away from their mothers when they visited. Interestingly enough, when such children returned to their mothers, they acted as if they did not recognize their mothers for a period of time. Similar reactions occur when mothers are hospitalized and separated from the child. This reaction in children is distressing to the mother because it increases her guilt. A small group of children do not show the typical reaction. These are either children whose attachment to the mother is much less intense or ones who have previously had a large variety of care-taking individuals in their lives. As a result of the work of Bowlby and others, practices in many hospitals have been changed to allow parents to remain with infants and young children.

At times the presence of the mother has been upsetting to the nursing staff because, with his mother present, a child is much more expressive and protests painful procedures by crying and by aggressive behavior. The nursing staff may feel that the parents are spoiling the child. Actually, it is much better for the child to express his feelings rather than to repress them. David Levy discovered that children hospitalized between the ages of 1 and 3 later developed phobias, for example, fear of entering any large building. The phobias disappeared when the child was able to express his feelings through play therapy linking the phobia of the large building to the child's conception of the hospital that he had entered for a traumatic procedure earlier in life.

Control of Anger. The second major developmental task during this period is the control of anger. The child moves from crude displays to the expression of anger in controlled and appropriate ways. Two dangers are that the anger will not become socialized and thus will be continued in the form of tantrums, or that anger will be so severely curtailed that it is repressed and turned inward. When an emotion is repressed, it generally becomes unavailable to modifications that can occur in the later developmental process and thus remains smoldering at a more primitive level than one would expect from the individual's age. One of the tasks of psychotherapy later in life is to help the individual to restore to consciousness some of these repressed early life feelings, enabling the development of age-appropriate ways of expressing and dealing with them.

Children in this age group react with outbursts of anger when they do not get what they want, when they are interfered with in doing something they want to do or when they are forced to do something that may be unpleasant or that they simply do not want to do at the time. This is the age at which negativistic behavior occurs; the child's first response to any request is likely to be "no." If the youngster is made to feel that all anger is extremely dangerous, he may repress it. Thus, in situations where he would ordinarily be expected to show angry feelings, he will not. Rather, he may be anxious and attempt to be overconciliatory. The repressed anger is still there and remains buried. The conciliatory behavior persists as the child grows. Moreover, the angry feelings persist at the primitive 3-year-old level because, as the individual has grown, he has not had the opportunity to express and modify these feelings in more mature, age-appropriate ways. The retention of the unconscious feeling and the style of response is an example of the mechanism of fixation.

Whereas loving parents can usually handle the dependency of a child in a way that helps him toward a satisfactory outcome of this aspect of his emotional development, the handling of aggression and the negativism of the child in the 1- to 3-year-old age period is much more difficult. It requires patience, skill and a great deal of humor. Children in this age group need definite limits and controls and should not be left to the tyranny of their aggressive impulses. At the same time, the controls should not be too severe. The physician counseling the parents during this age period of their child's growth should not expect to be able to advise them specifically on how to handle each situation. He can give some general principles which can be tailored to the needs of the particular child. The parents should maintain a consistent firmness but remain cognizant of the effects of too much or too little control. Too much control can lead to overcompulsiveness, obsequiousness and a desire to please adults that is far beyond the norm for this age period.

Toilet Training. We have delayed the discussion of toilet training, which usually occurs during this period, until after the discussion of dependency and anger. Toilet training takes place within the context of the family relationship and is not, in itself, the crucial variable of this age period. It is fruitless and even harmful to begin toilet training before myelination of nerve fibers has given the child the ability to control his bowel and bladder and before he has the intellectual ability to understand what his parents want and to communicate with them. Toilet training is best started at about 18 months of age. Bowel training is usually completed by 3 years of age. Many children, particularly boys, wet the bed at night beyond 3 years of age. If toilet training is handled casually, it is usually accomplished easily. Most children, out of identification with and love for their parents, in the long run want to do what their parents desire. However, toilet training, like other activities at this age, can become a battleground. The child may choose to use resistance to bowel or bladder training as a way of expressing his autonomy or of expressing his anger toward his mother. In a study of California mothers and their offspring, Heinstein found that the older the children were when bowel training started, the faster they learned bowel control. Anxious, tense and compulsive mothers may start toilet training much earlier than relaxed mothers and yet achieve less satisfactory results. Sears found that warm, permissive mothers' children were dry at night at an earlier age. The mothers whose youngsters were most prolonged in their bed wetting were cold, undemonstrative and used severe toilet training procedures.

Play

Children of this age group are not capable of cooperative play. They may show curiosity about other youngsters and may play alongside, perhaps exchanging a toy from time to time. It is not until the preschool period, however, that they begin cooperative play and show interest in group activities.

Motor and Physical Development

Motor skills appear in sequence as the child's neuromuscular system matures. From ages 1 to 2 years the child grows 4 to 5 inches in height. The brain of the 2-year-old is three-fourths the size of that of the adult. By 14 months, the child can stand alone, and by 15 months, he is usually walking awkwardly. Within broad normal limits, the age of walking does not indicate superior or inferior ability in later life. At about 18 months of age, a child can throw a ball, seat himself in a small chair, turn pages in a book, build a tower of three blocks, identify a picture and pull a toy behind him around the room.

Language and Cognitive Development

By the age of 2, the average child can speak about 200 words, although there are marked differences among individual children. However, he is able to comprehend about 400 words. By 5 years of age, his vocabulary will have increased to well over 2,000 words. Language ability can be greatly increased by activity on the part of the parents. If the mother talks a great deal to the child, if there are others in the home who often talk with the child and if the child is read to and shown pictures in books, he will advance more rapidly. Television shows, such as "Sesame Street," have been developed for the purpose of stimulating intellectual development. It appears that the more stimuli which are appropriately given, the more the child's curiosity increases.

Given the heightened negativism of children of this age, and their curiosity, inadequate maternal supervision can lead to dangerous situations. Children, out of wishes to defy parents and out of their own curiosity, can ingest poisons, burn themselves or have other so-called accidents. When these occur in a child of this age group, the physician should carefully assess the mother-child relationship.

At about 18 months of age, the child reaches what Piaget refers to as the sixth and final stage of sensorimotor development. The child becomes capable of hunting for things which are hidden, and he remembers where he has put things. Although he shows some knowledge of cause and effect, his knowledge is private and not yet influenced by the experience of others. His internalized model of his actions allows him to perform mental experiments with a rudimentary use of foresight and planning. Such behavior necessarily involves the use of symbols. The ability to symbolize is closely related to the development of *signal anxiety* at about the age of 18 months. From this time forth, objects in the external environment can cause anxiety, not just because they are "nonmother," or otherwise strange, but because they symbolize real or imagined dangers.

Treatment Approaches

The physician's relationship to the toddler will be much like that in the infancy period, until the child is able to talk in a basically adequate way, sometime around the age of 2 years. Especially between the ages of 1 and 2, most children will view the physician as a fearsome individual who may hurt them. Therefore, a child should be approached gradually in a warm, matter-of-fact manner, rather than confronted abruptly. At times, even this may not suffice, especially if the child is in the negativistic period. If the child cries or is physically uncooperative, it is because he is scared or in pain. A child is a child, not a little adult, and, in crying, he is doing what is to be expected. The necessary procedures should then be carried out as quickly as possible.

Additional considerations apply to the child who can talk. Children of this age attach a peculiarly literal meaning to all words. Accordingly, there can be no such thing as an analogy, illustration or example: all is direct or concrete. In talking with the child, choose words which are simple and accurate and avoid the use of analogies. Explain what you are doing, regardless of the age of the child. There is much to gain by this and little to lose except time, even if the child is crying or frozenly unresponsive.

*   *   *   *

In this chapter we have made explicit a theme which will recur throughout the chapters on the life cycle. This is that *stage-specific tasks* are a primary concern of development. Problems must be assessed in terms of their interference with adaptation, both current and developmental. The majority of behavioral disorders in children do not reflect "individual psychopathology" so much as they reflect problems located in the patterns of relationship between the child and his family, school, neighborhood or subculture. Knowledge of the characteristics of health at various stages of development and of mild adaptive problems is thus basic to the clinical competence of the physician.

REFERENCES

1. ERIKSON, E. H. *Identity and The Life Cycle: Psychological Issues.* International Universities Press, New York, 1959.
2. FREUD, A., AND BURLINGHAM, D. *Infants without Families.* International Universities Press, New York, 1944.
3. HEINSTEIN, M. *Child Rearing in California.* California Bureau of Maternal and Child Health, State of California Department of Public Health, Sacramento, 1966.
4. LEWIS, M. *Clinical Aspects of Child Development.* Lea and Febiger, Philadelphia, 1971. (An especially thorough presentation of psychological concepts and the more common clinical problems seen in children through middle childhood.)
5. PIAGET, J. *The Child's Conception of the World.* Harcourt, Brace and World, New York, 1929.
6. RICHMOND, P. G. *An Introduction to Piaget.* Basic Books, New York, 1971.
7. SEARS, R. R., MACCOBY, E. E., AND LEVIN, H. *Patterns of Child Rearing.* Harper, New York, 1957.

CHAPTER 15

THE CHILD FROM AGES THREE TO SIX

ROBERT L. LEON, M.D.

By the age of 3, the child has developed a sense of trust, the ability to control aggressive impulses and a sense of autonomy. He then emerges into the oedipal period, where he must make key resolutions of his relationships with his mother and father. This accomplishment is intrinsically tied in with his developing a superego or conscience.

Erikson refers to this as the period of initiative versus guilt. Initiative adds to autonomy the qualities of undertaking, planning and attacking a task. In boys, it is most closely associated with assertiveness and aggressivity; in girls, it is associated with increased self-awareness of physical appearance, ingratiation and acquisitiveness. The danger of this period is that guilt may arise over these real or contemplated acts, stemming either from external chastising or from a more internally operative oedipal guilt.

Psychosocial Development

Sexual Identity. At the age of 4, 50% of all children cannot make a sexual distinction on the basis of genitalia. Many differentiate by the way they go to the bathroom. "Boys stand up, and it comes out the front; girls sit down, and it comes out the bottom." A differentiation on the basis of breasts is the last to develop, usually not occurring until about the age of 8.

We will briefly review the development of gender identity, as a comprehension of recent data is essential to understanding the oedipal conflict and the formation of the superego. Girls have more physical and visual contact with their mothers in the first months of life than do boys. Mothers generally feel more comfortable in being intimate with infant girls than with infant boys. Thus, girls are shaped in their femininity from the start. Fathers reinforce the feminine role in girls by positive role reinforcement with statements such as "My, you look nice in that dress!" Clear-cut femininity is seen at about 1 year of age. The boy's first love object is also his mother. A major task for the boy is early separation from the mother as an object for primary identification. The same intimacy which would endanger the boy's masculine gender identity poses no threat to the girl, because such closeness with the mother only reinforces her femininity. Some cross-parent identification occurs in both boys and girls. This is desirable in that girls can take on some of the more instrumental qualities of the father, and boys can develop some of the warmth and nurturant qualities of the mother. In middle-class families, these cross-identifications are accepted and even encouraged. In lower-class families, they tend to be discouraged by both parents and peer groups.

Slater has written an excellent paper concerning two different modes of identification in children. In what he terms *personal* identification, the child adopts the values, attitudes and personality attributes of the role model. The child is, in effect, saying, "I want to be like you. If I were you, I would have you (and your virtues) with me all the time, and I would love myself as much as I love you. To achieve this, I will incorporate your qualities and values and ideals. I will view and judge myself through your eyes." This kind of identification emphasizes the role of parental warmth and affection and the importance of identification with both parents for psychological health.

In what he calls *positional* identification, Slater says that the child is telling us, "I wish I were in your shoes. If I were, I would not be in the unpleasant position I am in now. If I wish hard enough and act like you do, I may after all achieve your more advantageous status." In this mode of identification, the child wishes to destroy and replace the model. It occurs more as a defensive reaction to frustrations and the lack of personal warmth.

Oedipal Conflict. Some persons doubt the existence of oedipal conflict, or state that it is peculiar only to certain cultures; but, as Stoller summarizes, " . . . there are no descriptions of cultures in which the growing child is not looking upward toward a large and powerful male who serves as a model for masculinity for boys and a model heterosexual object for girls or toward a female who mothers. What varies from family to family and culture to culture is how much conflict there is in the complex." Cultural artifact or not, the importance of sexual impulses in children of this age and the patterned way in which these are resolved in our culture is quite clear.

During this period of heightened sexuality, the child clashes with the parents of the same sex in an attempt to displace him or her. The 4-year-old boy may suggest that Daddy go back to work so that he can have Mommy all to himself. Similarly, the little girl of this age may suggest that Daddy come to her room when he comes home from work and not spend time with Mommy. The oedipal conflict is resolved when the child gives up the wish to preempt a parent's role and begins to occupy his or her time and energies in learning the coping skills which will eventually allow him or her to take a place in the world similar to that of the parent with whom he or she has identified.

The resolution of the oedipal conflict in the boy stems from at least four factors. First, the boy experiences anxiety because of his hostile feelings toward his father, inasmuch as he fears that his father will respond with retribution. Second, the boy is motivated to give up the erotically tinged nurturant relationship with his mother by the distance she increasingly places between herself and the child. In addition to the mother's consciously providing less care, younger children may take her time away. Third, the child's sense of omnipotence is diminished by several events. He begins to realize that his mother's love is divided between him and his father and among his siblings. It becomes clear that she has not taken seriously his wish to marry her. Similarly, it is evident that his father has prerogatives with his mother which he does not have; not only that, his father does not treat him as a serious rival. Fourth, the positive benefits of identifying with his father, discussed in the previous section, impel him to become a man like his father.

The resolution of the oedipal conflict in girls follows somewhat different lines. The positive aspect of identification with the mother as someone to be like as an adult occurs in this period as it does in the boy. The awareness of genital differences in boys and girls is a motivational force to this identification. In contradistinction to boys, there is no decisive influence which forces girls to give up their love for their fathers in the oedipal period. In fact, erotic fantasies about the father continue during latency. It is not until puberty, with the physical changes in her body and the pressure of sexual drives, that the erotic aspects of her love for her father force her to repress these feelings.

The best insurance for a satisfactory resolution of the oedipal conflict is to have parents who are happy, compatible and mature. The most obvious maladaptive resolution is when the boy fails to identify primarily with his father or the little girl fails to identify with her mother, thus laying the groundwork for later overt sexual problems. A boy may have experienced his mother as hostile and threatening and may never choose a woman as a sexual partner for that reason. A child may fail to modify his or her initial love for the parent of the opposite sex. For example, a girl may remain with her father and care for him as her mother had done, never seeking a mate or sexual partner for herself. Problems also ensue if the child has the feeling of having actually defeated the parent of the same sex, a resolution which can occur through circumstances such as the child's being especially attractive or productive in comparison with the parent. As adults, these persons often have a sense of guilt when they succeed in other life areas, because they feel that the success is undeserved. This unconscious guilt can prompt expiatory, self-destructive behavior in the face of successes. The illustrations here are only representative, but they do underscore the importance of this period to later emotional well-being.

Superego Formation. The development of a moral sense comes from the identifications the child makes with his parents. Its development is primarily associated with the oedipal period because the sense of guilt promotes self-punishment, which is eventually internalized. It results from both conscious and unconscious emulation of parents in an effort to be like them and, thereby, gain their continuing love. After the child has made these values a part of himself, he begins to judge his behavior from an internal point of view of right and wrong.

Superego development continues throughout life. It later includes the direct influences of teachers, relatives, peers and social mores. In all cases, it represents an internalized code of idealized behavior. When one fails to live up to this code, shame or guilt may be experienced.

Masturbation. This is a period of increased genital exploration and much curiosity about sexual matters. Masturbation, although it begins in the first year of life, reaches its peak in this period, at about the age of 3 or 4. Almost all children engage in some masturbatory activity because it is pleasurable. Manipulation of the genitalia with the hands is the most obvious form of masturbation, but less obvious forms of masturbation are also common. Girls frequently masturbate by rubbing their legs together, by riding play horses or by similar activity which can stimulate the genital region. In a normally developing child, there is no reason for parents to be particularly concerned with masturbation. Parents should understand that it is a normal phenomenon and that attempts to control it with threats, ridicule or punishment are unnecessary and can be harmful. Compulsive masturbation in social situations and an inability to limit the frequency of masturbation are generally reflections of anxiety and insecurity in the child. In such cases, the physician should evaluate the parent-child relationship and review the earlier developmental achievements of the child. The origin of parental attitudes concerning sex should be assessed. A stress specific to this stage is sexual overstimulation of the child by unwitting parents. In this period, some parents unconsciously tend to use the child to satisfy their own sexual needs or to act out their own sexual conflicts. A mother having difficulties in her relationship with her husband may unconsciously turn to her little boy for companionship. In wartime, the father's absence from the home for protracted periods can pose serious problems. During the period of absence, the child in his fantasy feels that he has replaced the father. When the father comes home the child may become angry and hostile and may feel a severe blow to his narcissism. Similarly, a child whose parent of the opposite sex dies while the child is in the oedipal stage can develop difficulties. Most frequently, such children become inhibited sexually and feel guilty because, unconsciously, the parent's death seems to them a result of their competitive wishes.

In families in which parents are secure and happy in their relationships with one another, the oedipal period need not be turbulent or pathogenic. In these homes, sexuality can be treated as a normal phenomenon, the children's curiosity is satisfied at a level they can understand and masturbation and other sexual activities are appropriately modulated. The child feels support and help in handling his feelings and sexuality, particularly through the mechanism of identification with the parent of the same sex.

Peer Relationship and Play. During this period, the child becomes more interested in playmates and will usually have a few special friends. Most preschool children attend kindergartens which facilitate the development of peer relationships. Play during this period is *cooperative*, rather than *parallel* as in the previous period. Play serves the important functions of achieving mastery, of assuming trial roles regarding possible future roles as an adult and as a mode of regression from more task-oriented pursuits. The functions of peers are especially important at this period. Peers serve to challenge a child's sense of omnipotence. Thus they are an indirect motivational force to resolution of the oedipal conflict. In peer play, the child learns the necessity of rules of fair play. He has the opportunity for sharing and helping others and, in turn, receiving help. Peer-based learning begins. This learning can help to reduce the intensity of the oedipal conflict as a result of the realization that others do not lead the same kind of life as the child.

Motor, Adaptational and Language Development

Motor development advances rapidly during this period. Myelination of nerve fibers has been completed by the age of 6. By age 4, the child can run smoothly, make standing broad jumps, skip and execute other athletic feats. He can manipulate a paper and pencil, button his shirt and swing. Adaptationally, he is able to copy a cross by age 3 and a square by age 5. By the age of 5, his vocabulary has increased to well over 2,000 words. During this period, social class differences become even more marked, with children from lower class families having lower vocabulary scores and much less advanced sentence structure. Preschool programs have been found to aid such children in developing language and intellectual skills. However, such programs appear to be effective only if remedial work is begun before the age of 3 and if parents are involved in the program to reinforce the learning process within the home. Otherwise, children may improve temporarily but subsequently drop back to their previous levels.

Cognitive Development

Piaget's stage of *conceptual intelligence* begins at age 2. The age period of 2 to 4 years is termed the *preconceptual phase*. The preconceptual phase represents a beginning of some symbolical activity for the child. In this period, the child begins to represent one thing by another, as he can use language to some extent to help to interpret what is going on around him. At this point, he is still unable to form concepts. At about 4 years of age, the more complex stage of intuitive thought begins. Many of the child's thoughts are still based on irrelevant physical details. For example, if he sees the identical amount of water poured into each of two jars, one being thinner than another, he will say that the thinner jar contains more water because it is at a higher level than the other jar. It is not until somewhere between the ages of 5 and 7 that he develops the notion of the conservation of quantity and becomes aware that the jars contain identical amounts of water.

A child's intellectual ability during this age period is quite limited. He does not yet have a system for measuring time and space. He still thinks animistically and egocentrically. He explains things from his own narrow view and does not realize that others may not have the same view. Thus, a child of this age may say that the sun went behind the clouds because it wanted to. By centering interest on a single aspect of an object or an issue, to the neglect of other aspects, the child's reasoning and judgment are distorted. The above example of the liquid in the jars is characteristic.

Treatment Approach

A major issue in treatment of the 4- or 5-year-old child centers around his fear of bodily harm. There are four primary sources to this fear. First is oedipal guilt, the fear of punishment for erotic competitive feelings, which is especially common in boys. Second is the increased pride in bodily skills and functions. Third is the greater cognitive ability to conceptualize and to anticipate the future and, therefore, imagined dangers. Fourth, the child's cognitive abilities are still very limited, so that he may not fully understand what is explained to him and may fill in the gaps with fantasies that are more frightening than reality.

The child frequently extends his fear to doctors and medical procedures. The physician should encourage expression of this fear. He should not be misled by the reaction formation defense, stoicism, or further mislead the child by encouraging it. Even if the child does not openly express fear, it is better to let him know that you realize he is afraid and that it is all right. Fears can sometimes be allayed by explaining procedures to the child or by letting him see the needle which is to be used. Parents should be discouraged from promising what the doctor will or will not do. No child should be tricked, by a lie, into accepting treatment.

The child will often have a special fear of anesthesia, which represents a loss of voluntary control and even death. Because of the high value which the person places on his body and his fear of loss or mutilation at this period, elective surgery is best completed before age 4 or delayed until after age 7.

*   *   *   *

The physician should show interest in the child's healthy functions. With a background of healthy functions, he can afford to admit to a few symptoms.

Then the area of difficulty can be casually approached without arousing undue anxiety.

REFERENCES

1. LIDZ, T. *The Person.* Basic Books, New York, 1967. (In addition to a full discussion of the oedipal period, this major work has a wealth of psychosocial and psychoanalytical information concerning all stages of the life cycle.)
2. PIAGET, J. *The Language and Thought of the Child.* Harcourt, Brace and World, New York, 1926.
3. SALK, L. *What Every Child Would Like His Parents To Know.* David McKay, New York, 1972. (A most useful, soundly based reference for parents, concerning common emotional problems in children.)
4. SLATER, P. E. Toward a dualistic theory of identification. *Merrill-Palmer Q. 7:*113, 1961.
5. STOLLER, R. J. Overview: the impact of new advances in sex research on psychoanalytic theory. *Am. J. Psychiatry 130:*241, 1973.

CHAPTER 16

MIDDLE CHILDHOOD
ROBERT L. LEON, M.D.

Psychosocial Development

At 6 years of age, the child moves out of the home and into the world of school. In a sense, this is the first "moment of truth" for the child and his parents. The world of school is a world in which mothers are not allowed; the child must stand or fall on the basis of the character structure and ego strength that he has developed during his 6 years of life. If all has gone well, he will have a sense of trust in those about him and will be optimistic about being well received. He is confident in his ability to explore and manipulate the world about him. He firmly identifies with the parent of the same sex. He has a new sense of right and wrong which is appropriate, but not overpowering and punitive. With this solid emotional foundation, the child is equipped to begin to learn the skills necessary to allow him to take his proper place in the adult world. School can be a severe test of whether or not developmental tasks from earlier periods have been adequately met, as the tasks of the

147

school-age period bring to the surface problems which are the result of earlier, unresolved difficulties.

The child of 6 has his basic character structure formed. He has achieved over half the height he will have as an adult. All of the tracts of the nervous system are myelinated. He can carry out the majority of motor skills, albeit some still awkwardly, that he will be able to perform in his life. He reasons somewhat like an adult and is not totally dependent on immediate perceptions. Thus, the emotional task of middle childhood is not so much to wrestle with new problems as it is to strengthen the child's identification with the parent and others of the same sex and to get on with the lifelong process of learning how to relate to peers. Intellectually, the tasks involve the learning of important academic skills.

This period has been termed the *latency period* by psychoanalysts because sexual drives, sexual curiosity and masturbation seem to calm as the child turns his energies toward learning what his culture considers important. Erikson called it " . . . only a lull before the storm of puberty when all the earlier drives re-emerge in a new combination to be brought under the dominance of genitality." Although it is true that sexual interests do not play the dominant role which they had played in the oedipal period, they are still present and active. Biologically, for example, 17-hydroxycorticosteroids continue to rise gradually in both sexes during middle childhood. Culturally, overt sexual activity occurs throughout this period in societies which do not have sanctions against it, as Malinowski's study of the Trobriand Islanders indicated. In western European cultures then, latency can be viewed as a desirable cultural artifact which furthers development of relationships with parents and peers and physical, social and intellectual skills and acculturation. In this period, the elements of the oedipal conflict are repressed, and with the repression occurs the remarkable amnesia for the urges and events of the preoedipal period. Concomitantly, there is a shift from a fear-based, phobic orientation to a characteristically obsessional one, with feelings of shame and disgust being common.

Reputation. Important in addition to the above-mentioned tasks is the formation of *reputation*. By this we mean the idea of personal worth, of meeting one's self-concept, especially in terms of successfully learning the technological ethos of a culture. This important issue is often overlooked. This is the stage when the wider society becomes so important in initiating and admitting the child into its technology and economy. It is implied by Erikson, in his consideration of this, as the stage of industry versus inferiority. Of it he writes, "The child's danger, at this stage, lies in a sense of inadequacy and inferiority. If he despairs of his tools and his skills or his status among his tool partners, he may be discouraged from identification with them and with a section of the tool world . . . [the danger is that] the schoolchild begins to feel that the color of his skin, the background of his parents, or the fashion of his clothes rather than his wish and his will to learn will decide his worth as an apprentice, and thus his sense of identity."

Physical, motor, intellectual, social and economic factors can markedly influence the child's developing sense of personal worth. A well coordinated, muscular boy will gain more respect from his peers than will a slight, poorly coordinated child, even though he has successfully completed earlier developmental tasks. Difficulties caused by unidentified physical defects are often attributed to personality or intellectual deficits. The child who is hard of hearing may appear to be retarded. The child with visual problems may be unable to read a teacher's instruction on the blackboard correctly. It is such problems which make routine medical screening of the school-age child so important.

In the intellectual sphere, the child who is slow to mature, especially in the area of language skills, may be labeled a slow learner and become so identified in his own and his parent's minds. If nothing is done to correct this, he may continue to underachieve and never fulfill his potential for development in the world. This has been a particular problem for some children from lower socioeconomic groups and from black and Spanish-speaking families, wherein the child's English language ability is poor. Either the teacher may have the preconceived notion that such students cannot perform at the level of middle-class students or the students may, in fact, be unable to perform well initially, due to either language problems or a lack of stimulation. Study after study has demonstrated that children so identified either assume the deficient characteristic or continue it well beyond the time necessary in terms of their actual ability. One approach to what is too often a personal and social tragedy is the concept of teaching English as a second language. Accordingly, the child who is reasonably proficient in Spanish or "black English" might receive some of his initial instruction in that language mode, while at the same time he is being taught English as, in effect, a foreign language.

School Adaptation. Many of the changes of this period are *school based*. The teacher is a major model for superego modification, and, in contradistinction to the parents, evaluates the child on merit. With classmates, there is a turn toward peer competition, as opposed to the primarily sibling competition of earlier periods.

Numerous studies have demonstrated that girls outperform boys in all aspects of their school work until high school, when the situation becomes reversed. Girls in elementary school do better on all measures of achievement tests, even though some studies have demonstrated no differences in measurable intelligence quotient. A number of reasons have been postulated for this. Girls tend to be biologically more mature than boys of the same age. Girls tend to be more attentive to school material and to adjust better to the constrictions of the classroom.

Sex-linked expectations may also play a part in this; that is, girls are expected to do well and pay attention in school, but as they advance they are expected to be less interested in competitive academic pursuits and to be more interested in what society has described as the "feminine role." We do know that school children perform at a level that is expected by those important to them. Bardwick and others have hypothesized that the biologically based characteristics for which girls are rewarded in the early school years—greater compliance, less aggression and less restlessness—result in girls' undervaluing those aspects of personality function which are correlated with superior achievement as adolescents and adults. As the role of women changes in our society, this differential rate of performance in the later years of school may also change.

No one succeeds entirely on his own. It is true that motivation is an individual and internal matter, and, if one is not motivated, he cannot acquire the tools to cope with his society. However, for those who do succeed, there are always a number of persons along the way who have believed in them and have encouraged them, beginning with their parents, later their teachers and finally their peers and colleagues. If help and encouragement are not present all along the way, the child will fall victim to self-doubt and will lose all industry.

Peer Relationships. With the availability of classmates the child turns toward peer relationships and peer-based competition, as opposed to the sibling competition of earlier periods. Peer relationships in this period are almost entirely with those of the same sex. Boys have gangs with strict codes where "tough" behavior is valued and no "sissies" are allowed. At times a girl may be accepted into a boys' group, if she plays boys' games and is a "tomboy." It is much more unusual for a boy to play within a girls' group. Although girls are successfully identifying with feminine characteristics during this period, their group identification is much less cohesive than that of boys.

In both boys and girls an active unconscious fantasy life continues regarding sexuality. In both sexes, there are fantasies of finding the "right" boy or girl. The disillusionment about one's own parents which follows resolution of the oedipal conflict can result in fantasies of being someone else's child. Also common are the somewhat sexually related fantasies of daring, bravery and heroism. At about the age of 10, most children develop a special friend, someone of the same sex to whom they are quite close. This is an important relationship in the developmental process because it represents the first time a close, personal attachment has developed outside of the family.

Although it occurs more commonly in the adolescent, values which the child of 6 to 12 derives from his peer group can come into conflict with the values of the family. This may be a particular problem with children whose parents come from a different subculture or who were foreign-born. The parents may not understand and may disapprove of the values the child begins to acquire from his peer group. Because acceptance by both parents and peers is important to the child at this time, he is thrown into conflict. The conflict often remains unresolved until later, because the child will give up neither parents nor peers.

Reading. During the middle years, children derive both great companionship and learning through reading books. The models in books serve to develop further the child's personality and, especially, his superego and idealized self. Books naturally fit into the normative fantasy life of this period. Through books, a child has a sense of choosing his models, rather than being in real-life relationships with older persons where the sense of dependence threatens his autonomy and his efforts at active mastery.

Sociocultural Factors. The middle-class child usually leads a protected and happy life during this period. Through enclosed yards and separate homes, parents are able to establish more controls concerning when, where and with whom the child plays. In such playing, fights and difficulties are usually quickly resolved and forgotten. Parental intervention is relatively easy, if necessary. Children from economically marginal, disorganized families may not lead such happy lives. They are often lonesome and uncared for and take to the streets where the tyranny and support of the gang is unmodulated by a complementary family involvement. In addition to the above, minority group children still too often suffer from being different and discriminated against. These experiences, which are largely determined by culture and social class, profoundly influence one's feeling of worth and his ultimate social development.

Physical Growth

Physical growth, which proceeded at such a rapid pace in the early childhood years, now begins to slow down. Height between the ages of 6 and 12 will increase at about 5 to 6% per year, and weight will increase approximately 10% per year. The child loses his deciduous teeth and begins to get permanent teeth. Many girls begin to develop secondary sexual characteristics by the age of 9 or 10 when, by all other standards, they are in middle childhood, not adolescence. Physical size and ability are important in this period because they help to determine a child's relationship to his peers, the development of which, as has been discussed, is one of the important tasks of this period.

Cognitive Development

Piaget described the thinking of the child during the period from about 7 to 12 as the period of *concrete operations.* Several important aspects of the child's thinking are developed during this period. The first is *reversibility.* Prior to age 7, a child is able to add 6 plus 4 and say that this will equal 10, but, if he is asked what 10 minus 4 is, he cannot tell and will fail to recognize the relationship of the two problems. After reversibility is acquired, he can reverse his thought process. Another aspect of the thought process during these years is *conservation*. A 5-year-old child who is shown two balls of clay of equal mass and is asked to judge whether they are the same or different will say that they are the same. If one is then flattened so that they no longer look the same, he will say that one or the other contains a greater amount of clay. At a later stage, after the age of 7 years, he can tell that they both contain the same amount of clay even though one is a different shape. The ability to use logical reasoning is acquired during this period. He will abstract from his knowledge of one situation to another. A 5-year-old, when given a number of objects such as a metal pin, a wooden ball, etc. and asked whether they will float on water, will indiscriminately say that one will float and one will sink. He may even change his mind several times. After age 7, he tries to arrive at some rule that will explain which one will float and which one will sink, and he can explain that lighter items such as wood will float.

Piaget's work is of great importance for educators because, as stated earlier, if the child is consistently given tasks for which he is maturationally unprepared, he may begin to feel inferior and to be burdened with a sense that he is unable to cope with the world.

Common Developmental Problems

Dyslexia. Because of the demands of school and socialization with peers, problems not apparent earlier begin to show up. One of these is dyslexia, or the inability to read. This reading difficulty is often part of a complex of developmental problems which include motor awkwardness and disordered spatial orienting ability. Family histories of delayed development of reading skills are common. Studies show that in such cases the problem is based on a delay in the development of lateralization. Lateralization seems to develop normally in a sequence from motor laterality through sensory laterality to language laterality. This disorder is sometimes self-correcting with time, the child of 10 or 12 suddenly beginning to make sense out of what he reads. However, the problem often requires special education. The danger is failure to recognize the syndrome, which can result in irreparable damage to the child's abilities and sense of self-worth.

Minimal Cerebral Dysfunction. Another problem of this age group is minimal cerebral dysfunction or minimal brain damage. Children with these disorders are also sometimes referred to as hyperkinetic. Children with this syndrome usually do not manifest gross neurological defects. These children have poor coordination and short attention spans, and are distractable, easily frustrated and subject to marked mood changes. They have difficulty in sitting quietly in a regular classroom, and their lack of attention makes it difficult for them to concentrate on the subject matter for as long as the normal child does. They, too, require special handling and are in danger of developing an impaired self-concept. Sometimes stimulants, such as methylphenidate, are helpful in this condition. Some children who seem to be hyperactive are primarily anxious due to tensions within the parent-child relationship or, occasionally, as a result of past events. In these cases, family therapy and/or play therapy for the child can be helpful in solving the problem. In other words, when a child with a school problem is brought to the physician, it behooves him to make a careful diagnostic assessment of the etiology of the problem and to call on the necessary specialists to help him.

A great deal of controversy surrounds the pharmacological treatment of such children. There is the scientific question of validity of the disease entity, and there are bioethical questions of informed consent. The treating physician should be aware that some parents and teachers will exert substantial pressure to obtain an organic explanation for behavioral difficulties.

School Phobia. Another problem encountered in this age group is that of school phobia. This may be an initial reaction to school or may occur after a reasonably good adjustment has taken place in the school. The main symptoms may be overt anxiety and refusal to go to school, or they may take the form of multiple physical complaints, such as nausea, abdominal aches, etc., when the child is getting ready to go to school. Sometimes school phobias are a reaction to a difficult situation in school—a frightening teacher or other problems which may be too difficult for the younger school-age child to handle. More often, they are a reflection of a more basic parent-child problem. In this case, the child often has a fear of separation from the mother. This may be expressed in the child's concern about what will happen to his mother while he is away at school. This situation is often promoted by an insecure mother who is trying to solve other problems by keeping her child close to her. The mode of treatment depends on an accurate diagnosis of the problem. Family, child and school must be involved in both the assessment and the treatment of the disorder. An essential component in treatment is to arrange rapidly and unequivocally for the child to be in school each day.

Enuresis. Enuresis is a common problem in the elementary school-age group. In the majority of cases, several features suggest an organic component. There is frequently a family history of enuresis. These children are reported to sleep deeply and be persistently hard to awaken. Most wetting periods occur in stage 4 sleep, wherein the electroencephalographic frequency is 2 to 4 Hertz. Other disorders of stage 4 sleep, such as night terrors and sleepwalking, are common in enuretic children. Imipramine has proved to be of significant value in such cases, although its mode of action is not yet determined. Not all enuretic children are in this group. Some have been inadequately trained or are inadequately motivated. In others, enuresis may occur as a temporary regressive response to stress, such as the birth of a sibling. In some few, enuresis is the expression of a more stable, internalized psychological conflict. A frequent constellation is a passive child, a strong mother and a weak father. The child has strong hostility which cannot be openly expressed. Such severe problems call for family treatment and, sometimes, individual psychotherapy with the child.

Sexual Disorders. There are sexual problems for which referral to a psychiatrist should be made. An important example is the boy who dresses in girls' clothing, prefers girls as playmates and plays more typically feminine games. Such behavior portends serious gender identity and sexual problems as an adult, but it can often be effectively treated at this age.

Other behaviors, such as masturbation and sexual exploration with same-sexed or cross-sexed peers can become problems, sometimes primarily because of parental overconcern. The physician and nurse can perform an invaluable function of providing parents with information about the normal prevalence of such behaviors and providing opportunities for emotional ventilation. The physician's reassurance can be a useful prophylactic agent in this situation if he is familiar and comfortable with the sexual information discussed in Chapter 18.

Stealing and Lying. Stealing and lying are common symptoms which can stem from many causes. Frequently the child has developed a distorted set of values, through observing either his parents' pilferage of goods from work or their satisfaction from having "put one over" on a person by selling a car with a hidden defect. Such parents often compound the error by responding to a theft by simply paying for the item without dealing with the moral issue or by implying that the "firm makes enough money as it is and can take the loss." Other common occurrences are children who steal to compensate for a real or fantasied shortcoming or who steal as a covert means of getting even with someone who has in some way dealt harshly or unfairly with them. Others steal to symbolically obtain parental love which has not been forthcoming. Still other children steal as a reflection of what has been called subcultural delinquency; that is, a youngster may become involved in such activities as a result of his inability to resist peer-group pressure to engage in such escapades.

Responses to Illness. The predominant reaction of children in this age group to an *acute illness* is the fear of being unable to cope. The sick child may struggle unwisely to continue to express his newly acquired skills. As at any developmental period, regression to more immature behavior is also common. The physician does not need to be so concerned about simple language choice in children of this age. A full explanation of procedures, responding to the questions of the child in a confident, optimistic manner, out of which the child is reassured of his ability to cope well eventually, are the keys to treatment approach.

The dangers of *chronic illnesses* are that enforced passivity can lead to later anxiety about all movement and action, coupled with fear of loss of control. Persons with chronic diseases can begin to use their illnesses for *secondary gain*; that is, the symptoms can be used to force others to meet one's needs or as a means of controlling and dominating others by making them give special advantage to the person because of his illness.

With chronic illnesses, the attitudes and concerns of the parents are of prime importance. A child with congenital esophageal atresia was fed through a surgically performed gastric fistula until a plastic anastomotic procedure could be performed when he was 14 years old. A more "abnormal" development can hardly be imagined. However, he was reared by parents who were warm, affectionate, encouraging and optimistic throughout. His psychological and social development were superior.

Functional Pain Syndrome. One of the most common reasons for the school-age child to see a physician is functional pain. Abdominal, limb and head pains are the usual locations. For diagnosis, negative evidence for organic disease and positive evidence for psychosocial stress are required. The organic conditions to be considered are appendicitis, mesenteric adenitis, abdominal epilepsy, pinworms and menstrual disorders.

Probably the most common organic etiology is urinary tract infection. The presence of an organic condition does not always mean a causal relationship. A common example is that with the complaint of head pain, evaluation may identify an unrelated refractive error. Misdiagnosis, with consequent ingraining of the response pattern, usually is associated with overly intensive assessment for an uncommon disorder such as lupus.

These children tend to be excitable, easily irritated and critical. They are also commonly apprehensive, withdrawn and timid. Pallor and vomiting are frequently associated with pain of emotional origin. The prevalence of major psychosocial stress and similar somatic symptoms among other family members is about 50%.

The objective of management is to reduce excessive attention directed toward the symptom—in effect, to reduce the secondary gain. Usually this involves instruction and counseling aimed more at the parents than the child. The parent who says "I brought him in for you to do a physical so you could get him out of gym" is a common problem to be dealt with in such cases. The importance of intervention is epitomized in the comment of Christenson and Mortensen in their review of the disorder: "Little bellyachers grow up to become big bellyachers."

Psychosocial History

There is no better place to mention the importance of the psychosocial history in children and discuss its focus than in relationship to the functional pain syndrome. A first objective is to determine what was occurring at the time of symptom development. Frequently a history of death, separation, parental illness or divorce will be obtained. A next objective in the psychosocial history is to determine the reaction of the parents to the symptom. Does the symptom result in relief from doing chores, getting to sleep with the parents or cessation of parental fighting? Determine who decided to come for treatment, and why at the present time. Be alert to the possibility that parents may have an inappropriate script for the child, whether to make up for their own childhood failings or as the scapegoat for the family. Sibling and parental rivalries need to be assessed.

* * * *

Sleeping arrangements, dreams or nightmares, eating habits, medications used and any specific fears need to be determined. Recreational and religious activities and, especially, school behavior and performance are explored. The health and work status of other family members are important to know. Ask about any specific fears of the child. Try to ascertain who sets limits. An extremely useful question to put to the parents is, "What do you think the problem really is?"

REFERENCES

1. CHRISTENSEN, M. F., AND MORTENSEN, O. Long term prognosis in children with recurrent abdominal pain. *Arch. Dis. Child. 50:*110–114, 1975.
2. CRITCHLEY, MacD. *Developmental Dyslexia.* Heinemann Medical Books, London, 1964.
3. ERIKSON, E. H. *Childhood and Society.* W. W. Norton, New York, 1950. (Chapter 7 is a classical presentation of Erikson's epigenetic developmental concept.)
4. ERIKSON, E. H. Identity and the life cycle. *Psychol. Issues 1:*65, 1959.
5. GREEN, R., NEWMAN, L. E., AND STOLLER, R. J. Treatment of boyhood "transexualism." *Arch. Gen. Psychiatry 26:*213, 1972.
6. INHELDER, B., AND PIAGET, J. *The Growth of Logical Thinking from Childhood to Adolescence.* Basic Books, New York, 1958.
7. PIAGET, J. *The Moral Judgment of the Child.* The Free Press, Glencoe, Ill., 1948.
8. SEMONES, J. Hemispheric specialization: a possible clue to mechanism. *Neuropsychologia 6:*11, 1968.
9. SPARROWS, S. S. Dyslexia and laterality: evidence for a developmental theory. *Semin. Psychiatry 1:*270, 1969.
10. STOLLER, R. J. Symbiosis anxiety and the development of masculinity. *Arch. Gen. Psychiatry 30:*164–172, 1974.
11. THOMPSON, L. J. Learning disabilities: an overview. *Am. J. Psychiatry 130:*393, 1973.
12. WALDRON, S., JR., SHRIER, D. K., STONE, B., AND TOBIN, E. School phobia and other childhood neuroses: a systematic study of the children and their families. *Am. J. Psychiatry 132:*802–808, 1975.

CHAPTER 17

ADOLESCENCE
CHARLES L. BOWDEN, M.D.

Adolescence is that phase of life which the person enters as a child and emerges from as an adult. It is the period in which the person is expected to observe and perpetuate responsibly the commonly accepted values of his culture. The adolescent is therefore impelled to question those values, his personal adherence to them and their relevance to our culture. Adolescence is a developmental period which is unique to man. This is related to man's delayed and protracted attainment of full physical growth, mental capability and sexual maturity. Even after these are attained, they are not immediately linked with full function but, rather, are inhibited on a social basis. These delays introduce major frustrations into this period, but they also seem to be essential to the richer intellectual and cultural development which are functions of man's greater reliance on individual experience and learning, as opposed to a more instinctual unfolding of life development.

This chapter will discuss biological, psychological and cultural factors in adolescence. Particular attention will be focused on studies of normal adolescents and the implications of these studies for assessing developmental abnormalities.

Puberty

Puberty is largely a function of hormonal activity which is under the influence of the central nervous system, especially the hypothalamus and pituitary gland. It is initiated by pituitary gonadotrophic activity, which stimulates gonadal development. The adrenal glands form small quantities of estrogen and androgen in both sexes during the preadolescent years. With the onset of puberty in the female, the additional production of estrogen by the ovaries causes a pronounced rise which increases until about 3 years after menarche. In the female, estrogen is responsible for the characteristic fat distribution on breasts, hips and legs, as well as the growth and development of the nipple and duct structures of the breasts and the labia minora, vulva, vagina, uterus and fallopian tubes.

In males, with the onset of testicular function, there is an additional increase in 17-ketosteroids which eventually makes their excretion 20 to 50% greater than it is in females. In males, androgens are responsible for changes in the penis, prostate gland and seminal vesicles, as well as the development of facial hair and deepening of the voice. Androgens are responsible for the changes in pubic and axillary hair in both sexes. In the female, androgens cause development of the labia majora and the clitoris, the analogues of the scrotum and penis.

The age of onset of puberty is primarily genetically determined. Additionally, cultural, economic, climatic, nutritional and emotional factors may influence the onset and sequence of pubertal changes.

Puberty in the Girl. Puberty in the girl begins with enlargement of the breasts at about the age of 9 to 12 years. The breast-bud stage, elevation of the breast and papilla as a small mound, is followed by further enlargement of the breast and areola. Straight pubic hair growth begins about the same time as breast-budding, and in some studies it has been reported to precede breast-budding slightly. Axillary hair growth and maximal physical growth with relative lengthening of the legs follow in sequence. Menstruation begins at about 11 to 14 years of age, almost always occurring after the maximum growth in height has been achieved. Periods are generally anovulatory for 1 or 2 years.

The menstrual cycle is of great importance to a girl's sense of womanhood. More needs to be known about the biological and physiological functions and consequences of the cycle. Women greatly increase their sensitivity to musk and other strong odors during ovulation. Frequency of copulation tends to be maximal at midcycle, and some women report maximal sexual desire at this time. Cognitive function is impaired the few days preceding each menstrual period. An array of behavioral and emotional disturbances are more frequent during the few days preceding, and the first part of, the menstrual period.

Puberty in the Boy. Puberty in the boy begins with enlargement of the testes at about age 12 to 16. Straight pubic hair growth is followed by enlargement of the penis, early voice changes, ejaculation, maximal growth in height, axillary hair and development of the beard. Rapid growth in height and increase in the size of the penis usually occurs about 1 year after the first testicular changes.

Psychological and Social Reactions to Puberty. The rapid change in physical stature, both in the sexual and nonsexual area, is of great importance to the adolescent's self-image. Boys generally show more overt concern than girls, in part because their primary sex organs are external and readily seen. Size of genitalia has nothing to do with virility and potency. Nevertheless, it is common for boys to believe that it does and to make comparisons anxiously between themselves and other males.

Secondary sex characteristics are important in developing an adequate body image. In one study, height, breadth of shoulders, amount of hair and athletic prowess were the most important factors in boys' self-esteem. The rate of development in relationship to others is extremely important. If one is out of step with the ordinary course, it can be a cause of considerable anxiety. Precocious physical development can result in a boy or girl prematurely and detrimentally being given adult responsibilities. Delayed development in the male is the course most associated with psychological difficulties. Such boys are more dependent, more talkative, engage in more attention-seeking activity and have poorer self-images. These self-esteem effects are not present in girls and, if anything, there is perhaps a slight advantage for late-maturing girls.

A boy or girl may develop, usually temporarily, one or more characteristics of the other sex. Breast development occurs in about one-third of all boys but is not indicative of any hormonal malfunction. It can stimulate troubling sexual fantasies and concerns. It can be reassuring to know that this nipple and areolar development, which usually occurs at about the time of the appearance of pubic and axillary hair, generally disappears in several months.

Girls pay less attention to their primary sex characteristics, but they do develop a strong concern with menstruation, their breasts and their general figure. The concern with menstruation is heightened both by the variability in the time of onset and by the cycle irregularity which is common during the first year or two. Most girls today are well prepared for their menarche, although myths linking it to disease and dirtiness still persist. Too much is sometimes made of the menarche as tantamount to being a woman, without appreciation or communication to the girl that this is so only in a biological sense. A patient remembered with bitterness and sadness her own mother's statement that "Now you are a woman." "I didn't want to be a woman," she said, "I wanted to be a little girl." The threat to her unresolved, intense oedipal feelings and the sense that she was being pushed into a maturity for which whe was not ready had serious pathological consequences to her social development during adolescence. Menarche also challenges the secret fantasies of some girls that they can remain tomboys. This is often tied to the wish to please their fathers, whom they feel would have preferred a boy or would like them to be like a boy. Such persons are often so conflicted over their feelings of physical deprivation that they do not learn normally about their own bodies, which influences them to have undue problems in sexual adjustment. Despite such pitfalls, menstruation is an important badge of womanhood and usually provides the major impetus toward full acceptance of femininity.

Pubescence is often accompanied by physical symptoms which are acutely discomforting to the body-conscious adolescent. Acne is the most common affliction. They are also often unduly conscious of the accompanying physical manifestations, such as odor of sweating or menstrual bleeding. Such overconcern can lead to intense preoccupation with grooming, cleanliness and experimentation with diets.

Masturbation is an almost universal activity for adolescent boys. Fewer girls, perhaps half, masturbate using their hands, and then with less frequency than boys. Among other possible reasons, girls have no source of physiological tension equivalent to pressure from the seminal vesicles. Many girls in effect masturbate, sometimes unconsciously, by pressing their thighs together, taking bumpy rides, riding horses or pulling bedclothes between their legs.

The folk tales concerning the harm that masturbation can cause are largely a thing of the past. The erroneous belief that masturbation causes decreased physical vigor and strength is, however, still common. In addition, many religions view masturbation as sinful. More important sources of guilt and concern over masturbation exist. During masturbation, an active fantasizing takes place. At some level this usually involves incestuous elements—imagining sexual activity with someone like the parent of the opposite sex, who, of course, was the first such person with whom the adolescent had an intimate heterosexual relationship. Other elements of fantasy may include the parent of the same sex, or the girl's brother or the boy's sister. In all cases, the sources of guilt are readily evident.

Masturbation is a decisive factor in the development of good mental health, precisely because it provides a way for the adolescent to check out his primitive fantasies with reality and to bring these two gradually into harmony. Similarly, he or she can gradually become comfortable with and have a sense of mastery over surging sexual drives. This helps the adolescent prepare for eventual heterosexual relationships. In boys, the tangible quality of the erection and the ejaculate may also foster acceptance of the masculine, aggressive role in heterosexual relationships.

In the boy, if castration or other fears are so strong that masturbation is given up, development is usually seriously impaired for the two reasons just stated. The one male whom the author has interviewed who never masturbated came to psychiatric attention at the age of 20, when he was picked up on a bus following his repeatedly and compulsively running his hands up the skirts of female passengers.

Cognitive Development in the Adolescent. The capacity for the highest level of abstract thought develops during puberty. This development begins with, or shortly before, puberty and is usually complete by age 14 or 15. This capacity does not unfold in a purely maturational way. Its development is highly dependent on level of education and probably does not occur, at least in the terms conceptualized by Piaget, among persons in preliterate societies. The ability to reason at an abstract level provides the adolescent with an important new adaptive technique. For the first time he can deal with problems in his mind's eye, considering a variety of trial solutions before taking action in reality. Not only is the capacity for objective problem solving enhanced, but the capacity to explore one's feelings and the feelings of others in metaphorical and poetical terms also expands. This monumental change in intellectual capability contributes to interests in the arts, sciences, humanities and philosophy. The adolescent can become motivated by issues which take him beyond the present moment. Conscious attention to societal values and his own ethical standards now becomes possible.

Psychological Changes of Adolescence

Early Adolescence. The major characteristics of early adolescence can be summarized as follows:

1. Withdrawal from, and rebellion against, adults, especially parents and their values. The withdrawal from parents is impelled by oedipal fantasies reawakened by the changes of puberty and by the need to establish one's independent identity. It is a move from being somebody's child to being somebody.

2. A strong preoccupation with one's own body and self.

3. Vital support from the peer group.

4. Expression of intense sexual urges, at first in fantasy, later in masturbation and, occasionally, in group homosexual behavior, as the adolescent moves toward early heterosexual relationships.

5. Increase in physical size, attractiveness and aggressive urges.

6. Development of the capacity for abstract thought.

7. Wide fluctuations in behavior and attitudes. In his efforts to overcome dependence on his family he may engage in remarkably mature, responsible behavior, only to swing back to sloppy dependence the next day.

Pubertal maturation stimulates repressed incestuous wishes and fantasies. These impulses are usually blocked before they become conscious, but they are manifest in the marked increase in modesty around parents and the viewing of parental tastes as drab and old-fashioned. Sometimes these reaction formation defenses are insufficient. The boy may see his mother nude and suddenly find himself sexually stimulated in troublesome ways.* These issues often affect girls in a different manner. A father may react to his daughter's burgeoning attractiveness with erotic arousal. To defend against such feelings, he withdraws himself physically from his daughter. The girl may misinterpret this as disapproval or distaste of her by her father, thus complicating her identity development. Such was the case of a woman in psychotherapy who painfully recalled an incident when her father, on finding her walking home in a short majorette costume, careened his car to a stop, ordered her inside and intemperately accused her of being lewd and lascivious. Only in the retrospective light of treatment did it become clear to her that he was attempting to cope with his arousal by her.

The distinctive characteristic of early adolescence is withdrawal from the parents as incestuous love objects. This necessary emotional move away from the parents means that the adolescent deprives himself of a measure of help just at the time when he needs a great deal of support. In need of supportive relationships to provide the stability previously largely determined by his relationship with his parents, he turns to others for limits, guidance and identification. This is the period of intense transient crushes on a variety of adults. The relationship may exist only in fantasy, as with a movie star, or it may exist with an adult, such as a teacher. In each such relationship, the person tries out ways of behaving and relating and a set of values. Partly through such trial identities, he gradually develops his own enduring identity. But all adults represent the same dangers as the parents: subordination of one's own shaky identity to, and excessive dependency on, the adult. This often results in precipitous withdrawal of interest from the person. Such behavior accounts for part of the difficulty of psychiatric treatment of adolescents, who find the therapeutic relationship threatening to their fragile identity development.

Investment in a peer group culture is another characteristic of early adolescence. The sense of belonging is important at this time of life. The need for it often results in overconformity in dress, leisure interests and attitudes. The peer group also serves to diminish anxiety over boy-girl relationships. Conversations, usually among one's own sex, often are explicitly sexual, and provide for the sharing of expectant fantasies and exaggerated tales of one's own or someone else's sexual exploits. At this time, group sexual experimenting is not uncommon and does not necessarily lead to adult sexual deviation. Homosexual behavior at this age primarily represents a defense

---

* An excellent example of this, as well as of the need to have a narrow view of one's parents, is found in J. G. Couzzens' story "Eyes to See" in *Children and Others*.

against the fears associated with the move toward full heterosexual relationships.

Beginning heterosexual contact is frightening to the adolescent who has not mastered his impulses. The anxiety-laden urges toward the opposite sex are often expressed in aggressive body contact and roughhousing. Many of the social structures of early adolescent interaction help to set limits against excessive sexual stimulation. The peer group provides a safety in numbers. Early dating is likely to be in groups or with other couples. The telephone is an ideal instrument for both allowing and limiting intimacy. A boy has the soft lips of a girl next to his ear and is able to whisper into her ear. Yet both are spared the consequences of premature loss of control or unreadiness to go further in the relationship. Additionally, the telephone provides a means of flight from parents to peers without even leaving home.

Late Adolescence. The close of adolescence is marked by:

1. The attainment of separation and independence from the parents.
2. The establishment of adult sexual identity.
3. The commitment to work.
4. The development of a personal moral value system.
5. The capacity for lasting relationships, with both tender and genital sexual components in heterosexual relationships.
6. A return to the parents based on a relative equality.

Separation from parents gradually becomes more real than psychological as the adolescent develops more meaningful and more mature relationships with his peers. The wide pendulum swings from independence to dependence, characteristic of early adolescence, narrow. The adolescent gradually realizes that independence really is available to him. Changes in work and love most influence this and impel him to a firm sense of ego identity.

A summer job for the youth in college, or the opportunity to be self-supporting for the person who begins work after completing high school, strongly helps to define a sense of independence and competence in caring for oneself. The factors which influence occupational choice are both conscious and unconscious. The decision to become a physician may include identification with a friend or relative who was a physician. Personal memories of a physician during a period of illness or memories of a physician's ministering to one's relatives may contribute. In many ways, the role of the doctor may appeal because it is active, vigorous and interventional. On the other hand, the opportunities to express maternal caring qualities may also be important, as may be the intellectual challenge of medicine and the social and financial rewards. Unresolved wishes from childhood to explore and learn all about the human body, to know intimate secrets and to deal with pain and suffering also may contribute. The issues influencing occupational choice are important, for it is one of the two most important decisions in a person's life; the other is choosing a mate.

In contrast to the intense, erotically centered heterosexual behavior of early adolescence, the maturing adolescent develops a deep concern for his or her beloved. Tender affection makes its appearance alongside sexual feelings.

The gradual diminution in intense self-preoccupation, development of the ability for abstract thinking and the loosening of ties to the parents result in greater concern with cultural values and ideologies. A serious interest in ethics and religion is common. In part, this concern is in the service of modifying one's ego ideal and restructuring one's sense of conscience.

Although the ardor of adolescent idealism is well known, zeal is not necessarily synonymous with good judgment. For example, more youths were committed to the Aryan supremacy concepts in Hitler's Germany than actively involved themselves in the civil rights activities in this country in the 1960's.

Once the conflicts discussed above are resolved, healthily or unhealthily, adolescence has come to its psychological end. Many of the conflicts may remain, but as life tasks for the person to solve or to implement in the external world. Adolescence has narrowed the wide open spaces that lay before the child's eyes. But, although one gives up several possible identities, others remain, to be lived out in permanent relationships with others. In developing a stable ego identity, the person finds a niche for himself in society which seems both firmly defined and yet uniquely made for him. In finding it, the person gains an inner sense of continuity to bridge what he was as a child with what he is about to become as an adult, and he reconciles his conception of himself and his community's recognition of him. With the development of a stable, mature, ego identity, the person is usually able to re-establish a close relationship with his parents, based on relative equality and not posing a threat to his sense of autonomy.

Cultural Problems in Adolescence

Man is a social animal. There is not now, never was and never will be an autonomous self apart from society. Rather than man's enemy, social structures are the necessary, natural context in which he lives. Yet some of these institutions, customs and attitudes hamper, rather than facilitate, the adolescent's passage into adulthood.

Status-Function Discrepancies. There are two sets of criteria for defining adulthood: function definitions (earning one's living, being able to procreate) and status definitions (getting a driver's license at age 16, voting at age 18, drinking at age 18 or 19). The function definitions relate to the responsible roles the person assumes. In our culture, these functions are complex and often confusing, in part because of the protracted educational process. A 24-year-old medical student may be married and have children while he is still unable to support himself, remaining financially dependent on his parents, his wife or private or governmental loans. Financial and psychological dependency on parents, teachers and supervisors into one's 20's and 30's may well promote adolescent quibbling over "house rules" and trivia, instead of genuine value conflict and individuation. The status definitions of adulthood tend to be awarded or withheld despite function. This often creates status-function discrepancies about conflict and life tasks, which can be largely independent of age.

Affluence. The changes wrought by our technological society account for several potential problems. In an affluent society there is a tendency to give to and to gratify the child without expecting him to produce or contribute much himself. He is thus deprived of the pleasure of achievement and sense of mastery which comes with coping well. The environment should interpose inhibitions, substitutions and delays. These socializing interventions create conflict leading to conflict resolution, which constitutes a triumph of the ego over infantile, impulsive needs.

Shangri-La Fantasies. Adolescents may too passively succumb to the fantasy of the beneficient environment, looking for the instant tension reduction which too many advertisements promote. Drug abuse is a part of this. In no small way, it reflects adolescents growing up in an environment of "good" drugs and seeing their parent use—and abuse—drugs, expecting a chemical solution for every discomfort.

Change. The complexity of society with rapid social change is a problem for adolescents and adults alike. Rapid technological change and disorganization of social structures may leave adults unsure of their values and vacillating and unconvincing in training, education and rewarding the young to participate in that society. Rapid obsolescence extends to occupations. A father may find himself an outmoded or simply a vague and ambiguous role model for his son. Few fathers were computer programmers, yet many of their sons and daughters will be. The father who commutes to a distant office to work as an accountant presents a dim occupational image as compared with the man who farms the land on which he lives. Rapid change also involves education, especially the advances in scientific knowledge. Adolescents are concerned that what they learn may soon be out of date. In a deluge of information, relevancy is extremely important. A felt lack of relevancy can turn adolescents to ideologies—political, astrological and religious—which, regardless of questionable or specious premises, speak to the issues which seem most relevant to them.

The complexity of so many positive interests may be confusing. Our society offers a range of educational, vocational and recreational choices unknown until technological changes freed so much of man's time from the daily tasks of surviving. Even now, they do not exist in many undeveloped countries and among disadvantaged groups within our own country, a disparity between realities and expectations which creates its own conflict and strife. The surfeit of choices may be confusing, with a person being unable to choose, or to commit himself to a choice, in terms of work, values, place of residence or spouse.

These negative aspects of social change and complexity are countered by the advantages which a richness of choice provides in terms of fulfillment of one's goals. In a society where the most certain thing is change itself, learning to live with and delimit change and uncertainty is a special adaptation required of youths and adults alike.

Skills Gap. A technological society widens the gap between skilled and nonskilled persons in terms of their importance, income and knowledge. The implications of this are not fully clear. Our society has primarily approached this issue by broadening the availability of education and increasing its length, with only mixed success.

Minority Group Status. Our society tends to restrict the opportunities of some groups, particularly the poor, the nonwhites and, to a lesser extent, women. Such restrictions discourage the development of self-esteem by limiting access to a gratifying, productive life, and they deprive the larger society of crucial human resources. For ghetto blacks, for example, the absence of the usual channels for social mobility and opportunities for social improvement means that success depends far more on accidental emotional and intellectual factors, relationships to authority and opportunities for identification. Thus, siblings from the same family often vary greatly in life achievements.

Intensification of Familial Conflict. Middle-class adolescence is organized almost exclusively around the nuclear family (the biological mother and father and their offspring), as opposed to the extended family of grandparents, aunts, uncles and cousins. This is largely a function of our geographical mobility. With the significance of relatives thus reduced, the child directs most of his conflict and aggression toward his parents, rather than dilute it among a number of parent-surrogates. Later, in adolescence, when other authority figures (and cultural values and institutions) come into his life, he perceives them and reacts to them more as extensions of his parents than as new and different persons and concepts.

Competitive Hypocrisy. A democratic society exists on the premise that the best men rule and that rule develops the best in men. Yet at many points in our society there is a cynical corruptness among men both in private business and public life. The emphasis is on ends, not means. Throughout childhood and early adolescence, the family has provided the organizing influence for children. It is not surprising that we see such a range of problems among late adolescents just at that point in their development when the institutions of society must offer continuity in terms of structure and organizing principles, if those societal institutions are themselves disorganized, irrelevant or brutalizing.

Characteristics of Normal Adolescents

A widespread view about adolescence has been that conflict, turmoil, crisis and rebellion are to be expected as regular aspects of growing up. Some have even implied that, if a teenager does not have an identity crisis bordering on psychopathology, he is somehow impaired and emotional maturity is not achieved. A mass of empirical data has put such theories to rest, even though they persist among many physicians. One source of these misconceptions is psychiatrists themselves, who have overgeneralized from their patients, who are not a representative sample of adolescents. The recent studies are the more remarkable both because of the consistency of their findings and because the results were often contradictory to what the researchers had expected. They can be summarized in six areas.

1. The identity crisis is not common. Symptoms which impair functioning are not found in relatively healthy adolescents. Mood swings are mild. When depression occurs, it is usually from something external rather than endogenous and does not last long. Healthy adolescents do not act out agression because they have learned that such antisocial behavior can have negative consequences, in terms of both external punishment and internal shame. They are anxious and fearful at times, but the anxiety is usually a prelude to constructive action and, therefore, is facilitative rather than inhibitory. In a good number of healthy persons, relatively more anxiety is seen as they mature, because they are more comfortable in allowing such feelings to surface. They are more tolerant of unpleasant and painful feelings.

2. Relationships with peers and adults are good. They have many friends and are able to share feelings with them. They view adolescence as a period of great social involvement, and they report many successful achievements. The majority feel that they are an integral part of the community in which they live. They view their private lives as more important than academic and intellectual satisfactions. They see getting close to people and achieving intimacy as of over-riding importance.

Especially in early adolescence, they feel uncomfortable about sexual impulses and uneasy with the opposite sex. They often comment that their curiosity about boys or girls helps them to overcome their uneasiness. They get little straightforward sexual information from parents or teachers. Most approve of premarital intercourse but not until after high school.

3. Their sense of competence and their self-esteem are high. They have a sense of satisfaction from their work and social activities. They are eager to share their pleasure with others. They view new experiences as challenging, exciting and something to be mastered. Their competence takes place in three areas: intellectual, academic and interpersonal. As they mature they show a stability and a deepening of interests already important to them, rather than a change in direction or new interests. They move away from absolute value positions toward life-syles that offer more personal freedom in moral decisions and fewer constraints from the social order.

4. Their coping capacity is high. They sublimate anger and other drives in physical activity, such as sports, and club activities. These are areas where they can be physically aggressive, energetic and achievement-oriented in controlled and socially approved ways.

When conflict or painful feelings arise they confront the feelings involved, discuss them with others and search for interpretations of their behavior. They are able to be self-critical and to change their behavior constructively without losing their self-esteem. They are not at the mercy of their moods but can alter them, often consciously, by turning to other activities or concerns. Displacement, suppression and anticipation are frequently used adaptational mechanisms. They use humor. Their self-criticism is easier because they are not afraid to laugh at themselves, and the humor reduces their guilt and anxiety. Humor also provides a sense of release not only of unpleasant feelings but also of satisfaction and enjoyment of life.

5. Their relationship with their parents is good. They are generally closer to one parent than the other, but the specific parent may change from time to time. They view their mothers as warm and understanding. In early adolescence, boys are more ambivalent about their mothers, but this declines as they begin dating more. Fathers are viewed more with respect, as being more concerned with strict discipline, although not harsh. Communication with parents is good, and they are not harshly critical of their parents. Basically they share their parents' values.

When rebellion shows up, it is characterized by chronic disagreements with parents and teachers over small issues which, however, the parents usually do not view as trivial. Breaking the rules of the home is a typical example. Almost never does the behavior involve major differences in values, nor is it flagrantly antisocial or illegal. It gradually disappears as the adolescent becomes more involved in social activities outside the home.

6. The families of these healthy adolescents are intact, by an overwhelming percentage. The parents recognize and talk about issues with their children that are emotionally important to the children. Withholding of love is not used as a means of discipline. The parents satisfy each other's needs and feel secure with one another. If the above are present, it seems not to matter if the parents have some psychopathology themselves. But when they project their difficulties onto their children, or displace their anger or anxieties onto them, the children suffer.

The balance of power between the parents seems important. Families with an equalitarian, indulgent system tend to be confused, irresponsible, unable to solve problems and to have low levels of sexual differentiation. The children tend to be inactive, to have poor peer relationships and to be apprehensive about engaging in physical activity. Families in which either parent is significantly dominant are tension-ridden and unstable and tend to have harsh, vacillating attitudes toward their children. The children tend to be unpopular and insensitive to the needs of others. The healthiest adolescents grow up in families in which no one is particularly dominant, although there is a tendency for the father to lead in the areas of discipline and major decisions. There is a balanced, clear-cut and sustained division of labor. Not surprisingly, it is these families in which the parents are more likely to have a vigorous and satisfying sexual relationship.

Clinical Implications

Delayed Growth. This common area of concern for both parents and adolescents is a major reason for the importance of understanding the pubertal sequence of growth and development. In addition to careful physical examination and history, x-ray of the hand and wrist is a valuable source of growth information. Based on fusion of epiphyses, the radiologist can give the clinician an accurate bone age. Using standard charts of skeletal growth, the physician can provide factual information, including expected height at the conclusion of puberty. How much more useful this is than a dismissal with the curt words, "Don't worry, son, you'll grow." Concommitantly, it is important to avoid unnecessary tests and x-rays, for both financial and health reasons. The patient should be scheduled for regular follow-up visits so that, in addition to following the patient's growth, reassurance and clarification can be given to both patients and parents. The wide range of what constitutes normal should be explained to patients and their families.

Emerging Habits. The habits of smoking and drinking are usually acquired during teenage years. They are not the results of single point decisions which the adolescent makes, but complex, socially reinforced habits which tend to develop over an "induction period" of a year or two. Antisocial, delinquent behavior is at a peak during this period. As with drug abuse, two of the factors influencing whether such behavior becomes ingrained are the degrees to which it enhances self-esteem and contributes to close relationships with peers. Almost certainly, early recognition of these gradually acquired habits offers a better chance of stopping the habit than does intervening after a complex behavior is established.

Sexual problems are among the most common occurring in adolescents. One-third of all abortions occur in teenagers. One-half of 13- to 19-year-olds have had intercourse, with 55% failing to use contraceptives the first time. Venereal disease is an additional complication of such sexual patterns. One of every 10 adolescent visits to doctors is concerned with contraception.

Emotional disturbance. When should parental denial about emotional problems be confronted and clarified? Conversely, when can parental over-concern be alleviated by reassurance that the problem with the adolescent is largely "just a phase?" All parents who raise questions about their adolescents' adjustment problem should be carefully assessed. Five areas should be explored: (1) Family relationships: this includes items such as how quickly arguments are resolved and how much support the adolescent feels from various family members. (2) Peer relationships: The adolescent should have solid, mutual friends, who when asked about, he is able to describe in detail so that the person comes vividly alive and has depth. A disturbed youth is more likely to provide a flat, monotonous, simplistic description of friends. (3) School performance: Grades, school conduct, rapport with teachers, extracurricular activities, sickness and truancy are areas to explore. (4) Extracurricular activities: In addition to extracurricular activities related to school, the adolescent should be productively and pleasantly socially involved

in athletics, volunteer organizations, church groups or hobbies. (5) Pathological indicators: Marginally adjusted adolescents have several common symptoms. Anxiety is so severe that it may interfere with sleep or study. Depression
interferes with their ability to cope well. Fluctuations or deterioration in
school performance, severe headaches, gastrointestinal disturbances, fatigue,
localized pain and accidental injuries are relatively frequent. These persons
are much more likely than healthy adolescents to show up in the student
health clinic or private physician's office. It is important to note the disproportionately higher number of boys among both the marginally adjusted and
the severely emotionally disturbed. The physician should be alert to the
frequent association of underlying emotional problems in adolescents with
overtly "medical" conditions and not overlook the effective psychiatric
intervention that can be made directly or achieved through referral. Alertness
to latent or overt symptoms of schizophrenia is essential, as this most serious
of the mutual illnesses usually has its onset in the late teens or 20's. Suicide
is the second most frequent cause of death among 15- through 19-year-old
males, an additional reason to treat emotional disturbances seriously.

History and Physical Examination. The history and physical examination
of adolescents will be colored by their mixed feelings about their maturing
bodies. Often a girl may be both proud and embarrassed by the growth of
her breasts and by menstruation. She can usually talk more easily with a
woman doctor. Remember that pain associated with early menstrual periods
is usually psychological, because they are anovulatory.

Obtain the history from the mother with her daughter present, rather than
out of the office. Next interview the adolescent alone, in part to reassure her
about the confidentiality of the examination. During the physical examination of a girl, if the physician is a man, have a nurse, not the mother, present.
The physical examination should be performed, not conveniently rationalized
away. For example, the physician should examine a girl's breasts, rather than
just look at them through her sweater. Unless there is a question of an
imperforate hymen, many authorities do not recommend a routine vaginal
examination in the presexually active teenager. Others view the examination
as important for inculcating the attitude that the pelvic examination is as
basic and routine a part of the physical examination as is taking the blood
pressure.

When possible, let questions about facial hair or other potentially embarrassing topics (acne, dysmenorrhea) arise from the patient. Less denial and
more candor will result.

Masturbation. For the reasons previously discussed, masturbation is a
crucial issue for both boys and girls. When advice concerning masturbation
is asked for directly or obliquely, it is best to determine what the person
already knows or believes about the subject. Understanding his need for
control, the physician would not want to tell an adolescent, "It's O.K., do it
as you want." The doctor can put the adolescent's fear into words for him,

commenting that all boys fear losing control of their sexual urges and assuring him that control will come in time. The doctor can also firmly discount any misconceptions that the boy has. Although it is helpful for the adolescent to know that others his own age have similar problems, it is not useful for the physician to say that he did the same thing when he was a boy. The adolescent will be more readily influenced by an idealized adult than one he sees as like himself. He is most afraid of becoming attached to, or dependent on, someone as weak as he sometimes feels himself to be, and he has good reasons to avoid thinking of parents and parent-substitutes in sexual terms.

*   *   *   *

The doctor's chances of saying and doing the right thing are improved if he understands the conflicting ideas and impulses the adolescent possesses, his vacillations between mature responsibility and child-like dependency, his many false beliefs, his concern over mastery of his bodily impulses and, especially, his fear that they may get out of control.

REFERENCES

1. BLOS, P. *On Adolescence.* The Free Press, New York, 1962. (An especially lucid account of adolescence from a psychoanalytical frame of reference.)
2. BLOTCKY, M. J. Adolescence: when isn't it "just a phase?" *J.A.M.A. 237:*2232–2233, 1977.
3. COHEN, S. Alternatives to adolescent drug abuse. *J.A.M.A. 238:*1561–1562. 1977.
4. GROUP FOR THE ADVANCEMENT OF PSYCHIATRY. *Normal Adolescence.* Vol. 6, Report 68. Charles Scribner's Sons, New York, 1968. (A comprehensive account of biological, psychological and cultural issues which has become a classic.)
5. KYSAR, J. E., et al. Range of psychological functioning in "normal" late adolescents. *Arch. Gen. Psychiatry 21:*515, 1969.
6. MASTERSON, J. F. *The Psychiatric Dilemma of Adolescence.* Little, Brown and Co., Boston, 1967.
7. OFFER, D., MARCUS, D., AND OFFER, J. L. A longitudinal study of normal adolescent boys. *Am. J. Psychiatry 126:*917, 1970.
8. TANNER, J. M. *Growth at Adolescence.* Charles C Thomas, Springfield, Ill., 1962.
9. WEINER, I. B. Perspectives on the modern adolescent. *Psychiatry 35:*21, 1972.
10. ZACHARIAS, L., WURTMAN, R. J., AND SCHATZOFF, M. Sexual maturation in contemporary american girls. *Am. J. Obstet. Gynecol. 108:*833–846, 1970.

CHAPTER 18

ADULTHOOD

ALVIN G. BURNSTEIN, PhD.,
GEORGE G. MEYER, M.D. AND
JAMES M. TURNBULL, M.D.

One of Freud's most quoted aphorisms defines mental health or maturity as the ability to work and love. In this chapter we expand the aphorism, reviewing sex, love, marriage, family building and work as age-specific tasks with which the adult in our society copes.

Sexuality

We begin here with a disclaimer. Sexual behavior begins early in life and persists into old age. However, it is appropriate to give the topic special weight in this chapter because partly as a matter of cultural convention, sexual gratifications and frustrations achieve special primacy at this time of life.

In every culture there are official and covert rules or taboos which govern sexual behavior. These prescribe proper conduct not only between the sexes but also between generations, relatives and even races. The roles which are correct for each sex are also "understood." These rules of sexual conduct are learned, not inborn preferences. In Japan, for example, kissing on the mouth is a private and personal expression of deeply felt sexual arousal; in the United States, among many people, it is public affirmation of liking and respect. On Baffin Island, among the Eskimos, the visitor may be expected to share the wife of his host; the same could hardly be expected in Iowa. Such rules are necessary to avoid chaos, but they can become unduly restrictive if we fail to recognize that laws need revision to reflect changes in the circumstances and mores of society which devised them.

Today's physicians are increasingly expected by their patients to have knowledge of recent developments in the field of human sexuality. The years since 1965 have seen publication of a plethora of books explicitly concerning sex which have made the national nonfiction best-seller lists. These include the two scientifically important works of Masters and Johnson. However, it would be a mistake to believe that the new knowledge about sexuality is reaching all sectors of the community. There is still widespread misunderstanding, and the existence of myths about male and female roles and capabilities should not be underestimated.

Sexual Development

Precursors of Sexual Behavior. The appearance of the external genitalia at birth determines the sex in which the child is reared. The sex chromosomes exert their influence only insofar as they program the differentiation of the gonad into a testis or ovary. The next phase of development is under the influence of the gonads. The secretion of androgen by the fetal testes at a critical period is essential to programing differentiation of the external genitalia and certain central nervous system activities into masculine structures and function. Estrogen has no influence on morphological differentiation, because no fetal gonadal hormones are necessary for differentiation of a female. A number of naturally occurring disorders—the adrenogenital syndrome, for example— can result in external genitalia which are the opposite of the genetic sex. In such cases, the *sex of assignment always takes precedence over genetic sex.*

Core *gender identity* becomes firmly fixed by approximately 2 years of age, primarily as a result of the unambivalent reinforcement by parents, who praise the behavior of the child when it conforms to their sexual expectations and by their use of language which is highly differentiated sexually. Names, pronouns and generic nouns such as brother, sister, mother and father are all sex-specific. *Identification* with the parent of the same sex is coupled with *complementation* with the parent of the opposite sex. The boy not only strives to behave like his father (identification) but to behave in a way that will provide him a special relationship with his mother, wherein she relates to him as female to male (complementary relationship). At the same time that the child is learning his gender identity, he also learns about love and the needs and wants involved in the giving and receiving of affection. Early traumatic events, separations and deaths are important inhibitors to full expression later of the potential to love another person.

Sexuality in Childhood. Children, even during infancy, respond with pleasure to stimulation of the genitals. In boys, erection is usually a daily occurrence. In girls, patterns of arousal and stimulation tend to be more subtle, partly because the heavily innervated clitoris is less anatomically salient than the glans penis. Physiological considerations aside, the behavior of both prepubertal boys and girls is much more age-specific than sex-specific. The quality of genital sexuality is largely missing. The primary motive in sex play which does occur is usually curiosity. Even after the child becomes knowledgeable about sex and reproduction, the view that such activity would be engaged in largely for pleasure is seen as unthinkable or absurd, probably because the implications of intimacy, penetration and loss of bodily control are still frightening. A man remembered his father's sharing an experience with him when he was 14 years old. Remarking on the effrontery of another man at a party, he said that the individual in question had asked another couple how often they had intercourse. The son, missing the point of the story, interpreted it to mean, "That's odd. He should have known they had intercourse five times, because they had five children."

Sexuality exists. It is highly pleasurable, and children are curious about it. Parents should acknowledge this through their words to the child and in their own warmth and affection with one another. This does not mean that parents should ritualistically and compulsively inform their children of every sexual fact, nor that they should discuss their own sexual activity with them. Such an approach is often an excuse for avoiding realistic discussion with their children about sex and failure to instill values about it.

It is only on the basis of factual information that a child can realistically begin to develop moral values on an issue. This reason alone is sufficient to encourage parents, physicians and schools to be more candid about sexuality. Too often a girl's first full awareness of her own sexual bodily function occurs at the time she begins to menstruate. Girls are often given double messages about being attractive. On the one hand, she is taught to look her best in order to attract boys; on the other, the full responsibility for limiting sexual activity rests with her, not with the boy. The boy is encouraged to go as far as he can sexually with a girl, with little concern for responsibly limiting his behavior. Usually his sexual information has come from other boys. It is implied that if he does not show an overt interest in girls, he must be homosexual. His sex education in the schools sometimes consists of no more than observing movies about venereal disease.

It is the parents' responsibility to see that a child's behavior is socially acceptable and appropriate for his age. The physician should, therefore, encourage parents to discuss issues of sexuality with their children. For example, at some point in adolescence the issue of responsibility for one's own and another person's sexuality should be explicitly discussed for the moral issue that it is. Children need to know that some persons exploit others sexually. Parents should have no qualms about suggesting and advising their child as to their own values.

Masturbation

Self-stimulation through masturbatory activity is one way in which the child learns to perceive his body as a source of pleasure. During adolescence, masturbation serves to relieve sexual tension and to acquaint the adolescent with his or her sex organs and the sensations they are capable of producing. Through such activity, physiological impulses and reactions which can be frightening in their intensity are gradually brought under the dominance of ego controls. Through the fantasies which accompany masturbation, the adolescent is, in a sense, preparing himself for the gradual transition into adult heterosexual behavior.

Masturbation is a regular phenomenon in adolescence. Kinsey reported that almost all males and about two-thirds of all females acknowledged masturbation at some time in their teens. The supposition that genital manipulation has adverse physical consequences can readily be corrected by education; however, the specter of possible psychological damage is more difficult to exorcize.

Although some guilt is probably healthy because it plays a role in socialization, a considerable number of youths harbor strong guilt and paralyzing fear over their masturbation, usually related to lack of knowledge or frank misinformation. A medical student taking a precourse test of sexual knowledge was initially amazed and subsequently much relieved to note that a multiple choice question about frequency of masturbation had no alternative for "none." Only then did he realize that virtually everyone masturbates.

Masturbation is ordinarily a private matter. Mutual masturbation, which can approach the act of intercourse in its interpersonal aspect, is sometimes the earliest example of shared sexual experience, particularly in males. It does not usually connote a preference for homosexual activity. Rather, it represents an expedient solution to the mounting sexual desires of early adolescence, coupled with the absence of sufficient social skills and opportunities to develop heterosexual relationships and the sharing, and thus dilution, of the sense of guilt which accompanies the act. For some, masturbation retains a place in the adult sexual repertoire, providing an alternate means of satisfaction when needed or desired.

Masturbation becomes a problem when it is used as an attempted means of relieving nonsexual tension in the adolescent who is frustrated, lonely, inadequate in social relationships, under intense scholastic pressures or tense as a result of schizophrenia or other severe psychopathology. In such cases the masturbation is only the symptom of the underlying disorder, which is what should be dealt with in treatment.

Although it is essential that the physician educate and correct misconceptions of an adolescent patient in whom the issue of masturbation has arisen and make clear its healthful role in growth and development, it is unwise to encourage the patient to masturbate. The first reason is that adolescents, especially boys, have an intrinsic anxiety about the intensity of these newly awakened sexual drives, and they are understandably concerned about the issue of control of such impulses which threaten to overwhelm. The jokes of adolescents are efforts to handle this anxiety with humor. Typical is the jingle "Keep a cool tool, you fool, you know the rule in school. I'm wise to that rise in your Levis." Second, the adolescent's awakening genital sexuality is still tied, geographically and in fantasy, to the adolescent's parents and, thus, generates both anxiety and guilt on this accord. Nowhere is this more lucidly or humorously portrayed than in Roth's book *Portnoy's Complaint*.

Male and Female Sexuality

The model of equal sexuality for boys and girls is probably inaccurate. The less frequent masturbation observed in girls is not solely the result of massive repression but may be explained on the basis of the relative insensitivity of the vagina, lack of early breast development and the small and relatively inaccessible clitoris. Whereas male sexuality is always penile-genital and is relatively linear in development from childhood on, genital sexuality for girls occurs primarily after puberty. Although prepubertal girls may be tactilely sensitive, affectionate and even sensual, they do not particularly perceive their genitals as a salient source of pleasure. This underscores the fact that girls evolve their concepts about sex and reproduction at a time when their genitals are neither particularly erotic nor pleasurable. Following puberty, several factors combine to produce a sexually arousable young woman. The major factors are the periodic increase in sexual tension premenstrually, the increased erotogenicity of the breasts and clitoris and the psychological awareness and acceptance of the prospect of genital sexuality. Characteristically, the adolescent girl views her genitalia ambivalently, with an admixture of their being precious and dirty. Her genitalia are also a source of danger in our double-standard society, because premarital coitus will lower her self-esteem in her own eyes and in the eyes of her suitor. Her sexual inhibition has several origins. She is afraid of personal and social rejection, has no strong independent sex drive and has some difficulty in perceiving vaginal sex as pleasurable. She relates coitus to blood, mutilation and pregnancy. Ultimately, women develop significant investment in their genitalia through the occurrence of the menses and later of pregnancy, both of which lead to an awareness of internal reproductive functions.

In most cultures, negative feelings about menstruation are evident. The menstruating woman described in the Old Testament book of Leviticus is considered unclean or taboo. We tend to deny the normal qualities of menstruation, pregnancy and lactation. Many girls learn that these topics are not to be discussed. This idea is reinforced in most high schools when the classes are divided by sexes when menses or childbirth are described. As a result, the young woman is given little opportunity to express her fears and to gain reassurance. Girls who have been unprepared for menstruation commonly express fear that their body interior has been damaged in some way. Shainess found that 75% of the girls who had advance information anticipated the onset of menstrual cycles with anxiety, fear or dread. These negative attitudes are reflected in the negative tone of the vernacular expressions used, such as "the curse." Bardwick, reporting on 240 women, found that all but one could recall the circumstances of her first menstrual period and how she felt about it. This alone attests to the importance of the event in a woman's life.

Studies of women during the time of their menses reveal an extraordinary change in affect. Changes in personality may be extreme during this interval. Reportedly, premenstrual depression, irritability, anxiety and lowered self-esteem occur in 25 to 100% of the female population, depending on the criteria used for measurement. Sutherland and Stewart studied 150 women and found that 69% of them experienced premenstrual irritability, 63% felt depressed and 45% experienced both. During the 4 to 5 premenstrual days and the menstrual period, 45% of the industrial time lost by women occurs, 46% of psychiatric admissions occur and 49% of crimes among the female population take place. During the high estrogen phase of ovulation, women experience high levels of self-esteem, with an almost complete lack of anxiety-related themes. During the period of premenstrual activity in the reproductive system, when the levels of both progesterone and estrogen are low, women experience helplessness, anxiety, hostility and a yearning to be cared for.

Sexual Foreplay. For most American girls, petting, or making out, is the most common form of sexual behavior in the late teens or early 20's. Especially among younger adolescents, petting is usually conducted in romantic situations which are emotionally heightened by the sense of doing something forbidden. Petting is partly a socially and culturally determined phenomenon, persons of higher social classes engaging in more petting and foreplay than those in lower social classes. Anthropologists such as Ford and Beach have observed that many societies have little or no petting. On the Irish island of Inis Beag, foreplay is limited to caressing one another's buttocks. Kissing on the mouth, almost universal in North American and European societies, is not practiced in some societies.

During foreplay, as a general rule, a woman enjoys being wooed. Her arousal pattern is not encouraged by her availability being taken as a right. There are times when she may wish to be made love to quickly, with a hint of roughness. Much more often she responds to gentleness, to kissing and caressing of her erogenous zones. Many areas of a woman's body may lead to sexual arousal: lips, breasts, neck, buttocks, thighs and vulva. Deep kissing, with the tongue inside the mouth, is sometimes thought of as being analogous to entry by the penis into the vagina. Mouth-genital contact (cunnilingus and fellatio) is often part of a couple's foreplay.

The man is often expected to be responsible for giving pleasure and satisfaction to both partners during petting behavior. The woman who does little apart from giving her own body does not help to satisfy or please her partner. It is true that to achieve orgasm little more may be needed than her being receptive, but this does not make for a full and rich experience. Her active participation and enthusiasm lead to fulfillment for both. The variation of the man's being made love to, being the relatively passive partner, is often enjoyable. A woman may wish to initiate sexual preliminaries with a look, a word or an inviting body movement. Similarly, she should communicate either verbally or nonverbally that her partner is a good lover, reassurance which is important to him. Much of the pleasure of foreplay comes from the joy one partner gives to the other.

Although a man's secondary erogenous zones are not as erotically sensitive as the female's, the earlobes, neck, shoulders and region between the anus and the base of the penis are erotogenic. Stimulating these by pressure or gentle stroking may lead to heightened arousal. The penis is so sensitive in some men that its precoital stimulation may lead to premature ejaculation.

Foreplay or petting, then, can be anything along a spectrum from simple hand-holding to oral-genital contact. Whatever increases pleasure for both partners may be used to stimulate and heighten sexual responsiveness.

Sexual Arousal

The phases of sexual arousal are (1) excitement, (2) plateau, (3) orgasm and (4) resolution. Changes in the female during sexual intercourse and arousal occur in both genital and extragenital sites. Most obvious of the extragenital changes are those in the breasts. During the initial, or *excitement,* phase, the nipples become erect. Frequently, one side will precede the other. The veins of the breast may become distended and extended. In the second phase, that of *plateau,* the areola around the nipple becomes so tumescent that it may cause the nipple to appear less erect. Next, a pink mottling takes place, the so-called sex flush. This remains during orgasm and then disappears in the resolution phase. Changes also occur in the rectum, the skin, the urinary tract and the cardiovascular system.

In the female genitalia, changes take place in each of the four phases. During *excitement,* the clitoris becomes engorged. In the *plateau* phase, the clitoris, located at the upper junction of the labia minora, retracts under its hood. During this phase, the clitoris is exquisitely sensitive and further stimulation may actually be painful. The plateau phase also produces a deep red coloration of the minor labia. It is in this period that the cervix pulls away from the vagina and fits into the false pelvis.

Orgasm produces rhythmic contractions in the uterus and the vagina. The vagina has expanded its size during the previous phase and the walls have secreted fluid to lubricate and make passage of the male organ easy and free. The vaginal wall contracts rhythmically 3 to 4 times during a mild orgasm and 10 to 12 times during an intense orgasm. The female is capable of multiple orgasms. To do this, however, she must remain in the plateau phase of arousal, which means that stimulation must be continued. During the final phase, that of *resolution*, the cervix drops down into the vagina again and is bathed in a pool of spermatozoa.

The man goes through exactly the same phases during sexual arousal as does the woman. They are less clearly demarcated and may often occur in very rapid succession. Loss of penile erection during arousal may occur by the introduction of a distracting stimulus, such as a loud noise, internal thoughts or music. During the *excitement* and *plateau phases*, the penis fills with venous blood and becomes erect. The glans often takes on a purplish appearance. During the phase of *orgasm*, the penis undergoes rhythmic muscular contractions. Seminal fluid and spermatozoa are ejected from the prostate and seminal vesicles as well as from the testes. Most commonly, a man will spend about 2 minutes intravaginally in coitus, during which time he will make about 30 to 40 thrusting movements of his penis. A man differs from a woman in that he is seldom capable, after adolescence, of more than one orgasm per contact. He requires the intervention of a resolution phase of 1 to several hours.

The time of detumescence in the resolution phase for the man depends on several factors: (1) the greater the time spent during the excitement and plateau phases, the longer the penis will remain somewhat erect; (2) keeping the penis in the vagina will prolong erect position; (3) lying close to his partner prolongs erection; and (4) talking about nonsexual matters, arising to urinate, turning on the stereo or similar distracting behavior shortens the period of erection.

Myths about Sexual Response

Anxieties about Responsiveness. Some common myths persist about sexual responses. First are anxieties about responsiveness. Many women are afraid of being carried away with the intensity of their feelings, of being too sexually responsive or of losing control. Some women feel tremendous guilt about this and even persuade their partners to beat, scratch or pummel them as a kind of expiation. On the other hand, men commonly worry that they will fail to respond or perform at all. The fear may be of impotence, premature ejaculation or failure to satisfy the partner. Some recent studies suggest that, with the current emphasis on sexual freedom, more young males may seek treatment for impotence because of their own fears about meeting the sexual expectations of their partners.

The Large Penis. A second myth dating back at least to the popular pornographic books of Victorian England is that of the superiority of the large penis. Penis size plays an insignificant role in sexual satisfaction. The wide variations in the size of the flaccid penis tend to disappear when the penis is erect, as the smaller flaccid penis expands more with erection than does a larger one. Because most vaginal nerve endings which respond to sexual stimuli are located in the outer third of the vagina, the physiological stimulus will be essentially the same regardless of penis size. A man is likely to view his penis by looking down at it, thereby having a foreshortened view which makes it appear smaller. If this is a source of anxiety, simple observation in a mirror will provide a realistic perspective.

The Vaginal Orgasm. Much useless debate has occurred about the superiority of the vaginal orgasm versus the clitoral one. Masters and Johnson have demonstrated that the physiological responses are identical in the two cases. In fact, the changes which occur in the genital organs also take place when orgasm is achieved through stimulation of the breasts alone.

Mutual Orgasm. Apart from the general tendency of women to require longer at attain the plateau stage, there are variations in rate of response from one sexual encounter to the next and in the desires of a couple. To try to pace oneself so that orgasm occurs at the "correct" time neither makes sense physiologically nor is necessary emotionally.

The Male Superior Position. The traditional American fashion of having the male superior and the woman supine during coitus is not intrinsically superior nor proof of superiority in any other sense. Variations in positions for coitus generally increase interest. In particular, most women achieve more stimulation of the clitoris in the woman superior position and thus obtain an orgasmic response more readily in that position.

Necessity for Orgasm in the Woman. It is not always necessary for the woman to achieve orgasm in order for her to enjoy sexual intercourse. Some women engage in coital behavior primarily so that they may experience the satisfaction of being held. A woman can become involved in sexual play and intercourse without feeling any real desire to do so. In contradistinction, males are unable to sustain an erection in the absence of desire and sexual arousal.

Intercourse during Menstruation. Coitus during menstruation is neither unclean nor harmful to either the man or woman.

Intercourse during Pregnancy. Couples often unnecessarily restrict their sexual activity during the woman's pregnancy and in the postpartum period. During pregnancy, intercourse can be safely engaged in until the woman is at or near term, in other words well into the third trimester. The reason for cessation later, based on the obstetrician's assessment of the stage of pregnancy, is that studies suggest that the uterine contractions of orgasm can precipitate labor. It is worth noting that the interdiction at this time also applies to masturbation, as the orgasmic response of the uterus is the same regardless of how it is achieved. Prohibition of intercourse based on fear of infection has no basis in fact, except that coitus should not take place after the amniotic sac has ruptured. Intercourse should be interdicted during any periods of uterine bleeding. Cunnilingus, ordinarily harmless, may be dangerous during pregnancy if air is blown into the vagina. Death from pulmonary air embolism has resulted from air which has gotten into the placenta. The only other significant consideration is that intercourse may be physically uncomfortable for the woman during the third trimester, simply because of her physical bulk, and, accordingly, varying coital positions or cessation of intercourse may become necessary.

Intercourse may be resumed after delivery as soon as bleeding has stopped and after any incisions or tears have healed, both assessments which the gynecologist can quickly make.

Arousal Techniques. The popularity of sex technique manuals over the past several years has secondarily created a problem of persons concerned that their techniques are lacking. Sexual athleticism is not necessary for a fully gratifying sexual relationship. A common way with which this distortion presents is a too literal interpretation of the erotogenicity of the nipples and the clitoris. Prolonged, vigorous direct stimulation of either area may be quite discomforting. Most clitoral stimulation leading to orgasm comes indirectly from the pull of the hood of the clitoris by deep penetration of the penis in the vagina. Another misconception is a too literal reading of the stages of arousal. Nipple erection, for example, is not a fail-safe indicator of stage and degree of arousal, as it varies with age (greater in younger women), parity (less in parous women, due to increase in venous drainage which carries away increased blood to the area) and individual physical differences (often less pronounced in larger nipples).

Sex in the Aged. Although the strength of the sexual response does diminish with age, there is no automatic stopping point of sexual desire or ability. Many couples maintain an active sexual life into their 70's and even beyond 80. The most important variable is that those couples who had a relatively high level of sexual activity in earlier years are the ones who maintain their regularity of intercourse in old age. The adage that "It doesn't wear out, but it can rust out," is thus generally true. As a general rule, the physician should encourage resumption of sexual activity in an elderly patient at the earliest time compatible with convalescence from a period of illness or surgery.

Men can be reassured that prostatectomy has little effect on sexual ability. Joint and cardiovascular diseases in the aged may require coital techniques which involve less muscular activity. Couples should be assured that a hysterectomy does not alter the woman's previous level of sexual responsiveness, nor her ability to have an orgasm. However, if, with the hysterectomy, removal of the ovaries is also necessary, the result is largely equivalent to that of menopause, and estrogen substitution is necessary to maintain premenopausal hormonal effects.

Despite contrary belief, women have no loss of sexual satisfaction after menopause. An authoritative, positive approach by the physician can prevent a woman from worrying over this prospect or using the event of menopause to escape an activity about which she is emotionally conflicted or negative. Sexual libido is primarily a function of androgens in the woman, just as it is in the man, and production of androgens, which come primarily from the adrenals, continues essentially unchanged by menopause. Estrogenic hormones can restore a thin, atrophied vaginal epithelium if this presents a difficulty to intercourse. In both men and women there is a slowing and lessening of vasocongestion with age. The man generally takes longer to achieve an erection and may maintain it longer before ejaculation. The woman is slower to develop vaginal lubrication, which is generally of lesser amount than at a younger age, and has a less full development of the orgasmic platform. Both men and women have a quicker resolution following orgasm.

Common Sexual Problems

Lack of Sexual Response in the Woman. Nonorgasmia, or frigidity, is the most frequent sexual complaint among women. The term frigidity, with its pejorative overtones, would seem best avoided. The nonorgasmic response of women includes a range of responses and thus differs from the unequivocal response of men. Although the reported frequency of orgasm in women includes emotionally satisfying responses that are not in fact orgasms, it is still far lower than for men. Kinsey found that almost 100% of the males in his study had achieved orgasm by age 17, but only 25% of the females had.

With the current awareness of sexuality, increasing numbers of women who are nonorgasmic seek medical help. In some women, inhibitory sexual training in childhood accounts for the failure to respond. Clitoral adhesions occasionally may result in pain and may prevent orgasmic responses. Also, more disturbed psychological conflict may result in nonorgasmia. Such women usually had developed intensely negative feelings toward males during childhood, occasionally as a result of real or attempted incestuous relationships by their fathers. The anger which results from their feeling that "men are only out for one thing" is displaced to their husbands and is justified on the basis of real or fantasied abuses.

Vaginismus and Dyspareunia. Vaginismus and dyspareunia are related problems. Vaginismus consists of involuntary vaginal spasms when the man attempts coitus. Dyspareunia consists of pain during some part of coitus. Both often are caused by the early life inhibitory experiences discussed previously. Additionally, conditioned reflex as a result of sexual assault or rape or of coitus repeatedly taking place in the presence of painful pelvic illness, such as endometriosis, can result in vaginismus and dyspareunia.

When treating a woman who has the problem of frigidity, vaginismus or dyspareunia, it is important to bear in mind that most often the husband contributes to the difficulty by not taking sufficient time to ensure that she is stimulated, by his emotional distance or by other, more subtle, ways. Because the ability to be aroused is slower to develop in the woman and is more easily disrupted, the excitement phase must be significantly longer than it is in the man if the woman is to achieve a high enough plateau level to reach a climax.

Impotence. The fear of failure to perform well sexually has generally been a male burden. In the original studies by Masters and Johnson, the most common and erroneous beliefs by their subjects concerning the area of male performance were (1) that primary impotence meant that something was wrong with the penis or hormonal glands, (2) that impotence resulted from having a homosexual orientation and (3) that too frequent ejaculation led to loss of physical strength or emotional illness or both.

The cultural demands on the male are not focused on the attainment of orgasm, as they are in the female, but on the maintenance of an erection long enough for the woman to achieve satisfaction. Kinsey found that 0.1% of males were impotent at age 20, but by age 33 this incidence had risen to 1% and by age 60 to 18% of the male sample studied. In the strict sense, the term impotence means the inability to achieve and maintain erection commensurate with the performance of coitus. There are two main types: premature ejaculation and failure to sustain an erection sufficient for intromission into the vagina.

There are many ways in which the problem of impotence may present. Because some men are embarrassed by their impotence, patients may present with an entirely different symptom (e.g., backache or dysuria). Some casually mention if after their annual physical examination; others are sent by or brought by their wives. Certain causes of impotence are systemic. These include chronic alcoholism, narcotic addiction, anemia, malignancy, use of phenothiazines, diabetes and the Leriche syndrome. Lack of sexual interest and ability is a very frequent finding in both male and female depression. When a patient complains of diminished sexual interest in the spouse, the possibility of depression should be investigated.

The three most frequently found psychological dynamics operating in cases of impotence are fear, guilt and hostility. The fear may be of women in general, often arising from a poor mother-son relationship early in life. As teenagers, these men may have had frightening or embarrassing experiences while on dates. They may also have fears of hurting the woman, of acquiring a venereal infection or of making the woman pregnant. Fear of, or experiences of, failure at work or at school can be displaced to fear of sexual failure. A man may fear that he will not be able to fully please or arouse his wife sexually. Guilt may result from premarital affairs, extramarital affairs or earlier homosexual relationships. Hostility is frequently found in those males who have great difficulty in handling their own angry wishes, feelings and thoughts. The passive male whose spouse constantly berates him as a partner will often have difficulty sustaining an erection.

Helping to make the patient more aware of his underlying feelings and conflicts in these areas is often directly beneficial. When straightforward educative and supportive techniques do not lead to reasonably prompt resolution of the problem, a psychiatric consultation is indicated.

A serious mistake in the treatment of impotence is to lead the patient to regard the symptoms as basically an organic problem. When examining a man who presents with the diagnosis of impotence, it is important to take a complete history, including such items as his job satisfaction, his family situation, his sleep habits and his appetite. Not only is this information valuable, but the patient is helped to understand that psychological factors may play a significant role. Extensive laboratory tests and examinations are contraindicated in most cases, because they tend to fixate the individual at a somatic level and to prevent his subsequent involvement in a program with a psychological base.

Extramarital Sex. In order to rationalize extramarital sexual impulses, people look for socially acceptable excuses: long separations due to illness or business, their mate's preoccupation with his or her own nonsexual affairs and emotional conflicts of all types. But marital dissatisfaction is not the only impetus to an extramarital relationship. Even partners in a happy marriage may become involved with a different mate. As time passes in the monogamous relationship, there may be a blunting of excitement and a dull sense of routine. In the majority of cases, the extramarital affair does not begin with a fascinating stranger but with some person near at hand: the secretary, the boss, the next door neighbor. For most people, the extramarital affair is not an uncomplicated weekend in the country. It is likely to involve much soul-searching, emotional agony. According to the work of Hunt, almost half of all affairs last more than 1 month but less than 1 year; few last more than 2 years.

Control of extramarital desire may be internal or external. The internal controls spring from a moral sense of wishing not to hurt the partner, disrupt the family or feel the guilt and from a wish to live up to one's idealized self-concept. The external controls are largely the social penalties which result from such a liaison and the belief in religious laws. In our culture, an affair is difficult to reconcile with the obligations to one's family. Seldom does an affair become known to the spouse without the esteem of both partners suffering. Some individuals benefit from the experience, and a couple may find that their marriage emerges strengthened as a result of what has been learned about themselves and their relationship.

A particular kind of person often involved in extramarital affairs is the

Don Juan, who measures his success and self-esteem in the number of sexual conquests he has had. The sexual behavior of such individuals is compulsive and arises out of basic feelings of inadequacy as a male. Such persons seek reassurance of their masculine prowess, sexual and otherwise, by each new, usually fleeting, sexual affair. Because the behavior does not resolve the underlying psychological conflict, the acting out must be repeated again and again to assuage anxiety. Although less common, this problem occurs in women, too, so that we might speak of the Doña Juanita.

Homosexuality. Some homosexual behavior is common in our society, despite strongly negative social sanctions. Kinsey reported in his first volume that 37% of all males had had at least one homosexual experience before the age of 30. The significance of the figure is modified by the fact that Kinsey included all transitory same-sex acts of adolescence, such as mutual masturbation. Homosexuality, as an exclusive orientation, occurs in less than 5% of all males and females. Parental overconcern about sexual aspects of their children's development is very common. The physician should be aware of the damage which can ensue from the overdiagnosis of sexual dysfunctions. If there seem to be grounds for concern, a psychiatric consultation is preferable to either overdiagnosis or a poorly founded reassurance that there is nothing to worry about.

Clinical Considerations

Sexual History and Physical Examination. Most sexual problems presented to physicians fall into one of three classes: (1) Normal sexuality, where the person's fears about normal sexual behavior need to be allayed by education of the patient. (2) Diseases with sexual aspects which are perceived as sexual problems. Impotence from diabetes, endometriosis and paraplegia are examples of diseases in which major complaints may be in the sexual area. The physician's task is to make a proper diagnosis and to treat the sexual aspect as a part of the total problem. (3) Actual problems in sexual adjustment. Included here are disturbances in potency, pleasure and sexual orientation.

The sexual history is important, but it should be placed within the total context of the person's environment, emotional and physical states and life history. The physician should learn where early sexual information was acquired. This area of the history will often provide an easy opportunity to correct misinformation and lack of information. Such an explicit discussion of the aspects of sexual behavior is in itself often therapeutic, in that it provides the patient with a model of a permissive authority for such behavior in his or her own life. Such discussions are of most value if, on at least some occasions, both husband and wife can be seen together.

The most complete reference in terms of content of sexual history is presented in Master's and Johnson's *Human Sexual Inadequacy*. They divide their inquiry into four areas. First are baseline data concerning the present functioning of the husband and wife. Second are statistical data about the marriage; included here are the duration of courtship, any periods of separation or extramarital sexual activity and the social and educational backgrounds of the couple. Third is a thorough assessment of the person in terms of period in the life cycle. Fourth is the self-perception of the individual. He or she is asked to rate himself or herself as attractive or nonattractive and to describe his or her positive attributes. The reference is not especially useful in terms of interview technique, but the considerations discussed in Chapter 3 of this book apply equally well in this area.

Taking a sexual history, for professionals who are not regularly engaged in sexual counseling, is not as straightforward as it is for specialists in the treatment of sexual dysfunction. The patients of specialists expect to be asked such questions; the patients of most family physicians do not. It behooves the physician to develop a relaxed style of interviewing, a way of ensuring that both partners are involved and personal comfort in asking what, to some people may be viewed as intrusive questions.

Much information about sex can usefully come from examination of other areas. During the routine examination of a woman's breasts, the physician can ask about childbearing experiences, whether the woman nursed her baby and whether any sexual feelings were experienced during nursing. Instructions in maintaining good vaginal tone can be given during the pelvic examination.* During the pelvic examination, especially if there is a discussion of sexual response and assessment of physical capability, as during the exercises described below, sexual arousal can result. The importance of a female nurse for reassurance is evident.

Contraception. A well documented study by Bakker and Dightman showed that only 3% of the women surveyed had obtained their most useful birth control information from a physician. The need for such counseling is clear; what the physician must have is skill both in facts and in an approach to the issue. Calderone has listed three important axioms about contraception: (1) any method of birth control is better than no method at all, (2) the most effective method is the one which the couple will use most consistently and (3) acceptability is the key factor influencing the effectiveness of a contraceptive method. Most patients' contraceptive interests are based on personal and family considerations, not on social goals or benefits.

Discussion with a patient should be aimed at overcoming motivational

---

* One simple exercise is to tighten the vaginal muscles for 3 seconds, relax and repeat 20 to 50 times per day. Another is to tighten and immediately relax the vaginal muscles in a flickering movement. To identify the muscles involved, have the woman pretend that she is urinating and attempting to stop the flow. The exercise may be done during the normal routine of urination, until the woman achieves adequate awareness and control of the muscular response. Tightening the vaginal vault can assist the woman in achieving the stage of plateau necessary of orgasm. An exercise to facilitate this is to have the woman bear down as if to push the examining finger out of the vagina, and immediately afterward to tighten the pubococcygeal muscle. The combined activity increases vasocongestion, which is associated with higher levels of sexual arousal. Performing the exercise four or five times before sexual activity often will enhance sexual arousal.

blocks, two of which are quite common. First, because acceptability is so important, the patient should be well informed about the effectiveness and limitations of a method, as well as its proper use. Second, because fears associated with contraception account for much discontinuance, the physician should be aware of frequent fears and move to correct them, sometimes even without the patient's having expressed his or her fears. A statement such as "Some women I treat worry about cancer as a result of these pills; have you ever had any concern along that line?" can be useful. Common fears are of cancer, blood clots, loss of male potency, diminished sexual satisfaction and unfaithfulness.

Other psychological conflicts occur at an unconscious level. A recurrent theme of conflict is observed in some unmarried, sexually active women. Participating in sexual intercourse and assuming the responsibility for avoiding pregnancy are important and conflict-ridden behaviors for most unmarried women. Too often girls who are sexually active do not use contraceptives because having them and using them represents forethought and the absence of an overwhelming spontaneous passion. It is clear that taking an oral contraceptive every day is a conscious, deliberate and repetitive act; therefore, it may become a source of anxiety because of the implication of anticipating sexual relations.

Premarital Examination. The physician can do much more at the time of a premarital examination than determine that both the man and the woman are free of syphilis. This is an excellent time for counseling. It is best to begin by determining the couple's level of sexual sophistication and experience. The man should be apprised of the premenstrual tension and depressive feelings which periodically are likely to affect his wife. He should be made basically knowledgeable about other aspects of female sexual physiology. He should know that women often gradually learn to enjoy sex and that erotic arousal is not likely to be as automatic in his wife as it is in himself. The woman should know that her husband is sexually much more physiologically driven than she is. For example, erections in the man occur with almost as much biologically based regularity as do menstrual periods in the woman.

Some couples will fail to respond to the suggestions and short term psychotherapeutic efforts of the physician who is not a specialist in treating sexual disorders. Two major modes of specialized treatment are the combined therapist approach and psychotherapy. The combined therapist approach was introduced by Masters and Johnson. In this technique, the couple is interviewed and taught by a male-female therapist pair. Masters and Johnson show movies, have discussions and interview the couple both individually and conjointly. They stress the enjoyment of sex not limited to orgasm. Therapist pairs trained by Masters and Johnson or couples practicing variations of this technique are now found in most larger metropolitan areas.

There are some couples in whom one or both partners have such severe psychological problems that they require intensive psychotherapy. The passive man with tremendous unconscious rage toward his partner for real or imagined misdoings is an example. The woman whose early sexual repression has led to the beliefs that all sex is dirty and that men are to be feared or despised will also require referral for psychotherapy.

In perhaps no other area of human behavior do facts and attitudes clash as strongly as in sexuality. We have here sketched some of the reasons for the position of avoidance of sexual education. Scientific research of the past few decades, as so well amplified by the work of Masters and Johnson, offers the possibility of grounding our knowledge in empirical data. Some fear that disbursement of sexual knowledge will lead to hedonism. But the scientist, although guarding against value judgments in his work, can and should take into account his own and society's values when it comes to working with patients, just as parents should not feel paralyzed about discussing moral issues with their children. Science, through determining cause and effect relationships, serves in a small but important way to clarify the consequences of a particular path of action. Thus, in the area of sexuality, as in others, science stands in the service of value-based decisions.

Marriage

Marriage is a particular form in which love is sometimes institutionalized, and, for that reason, we will next deal with marriage and its relationship to love.

Reasons People Marry

With or without the benefit of clergy, marriage is a formalized relationship, acknowledging unique and obligatory responsibilities in the areas of sex, intimacy and sharing. The decision to marry another person is a life decision which is rivaled in importance only by occupational choice. The reasons why people marry are complex and not mutually exclusive. They include the following.

Love. Many persons marry for love. Romantic love, which in varying degrees is a state of intense but often transient passion, can be a poor foundation on which to base a marriage. Marital love, as discussed later in the chapter, is a different kind of love. It lacks the intensities of feeling of romantic love, but it is deeper and more durable because it involves commitment. In it, the partners have a steady, reciprocal and mutual responsibility in the business of establishing a home with a family life and a social life.

Love is a diffuse term with varied, partially contradictory meanings. At the very least, it implies an intense psychological investment in someone or something. One can obviously have a love for money, power, fame or science, for example, but these investments lack the possibility for reciprocal return. It is our love for other persons that is uniquely capable of being returned. As one approaches adulthood, the reciprocal possibilities of love—as of sex—

become increasingly important. Love involves the emotional valuing of the uniqueness of another being. George Bernard Shaw tells us that love consists of overestimating the difference between one woman and another. Shaw's misogynistic cynicism can become a psychological truism by substituting "esteeming" for "overestimating."

Two comments about the relationship between love and sex are pertinent here. The first is that although all love has a sexual component (minimally, the wish to be physically near, to possess or be possessed), the reverse is not true. Some highly passionate sexual activities do not involve specific and unique emotional investment in other persons. Second, love and sex not only come in vivid and dramatic forms, but also in calmer varieties. Enjoyable and healthy sex can be tempestuous or gentle; love can be passionate or quiet.

Completion of One's Identity. In our society, a person's idealized self-concept generally includes a view of himself as married. A sense of completion and personal adequacy can be achieved through an intimate life with others. Marriage can serve not only to stabilize the person's sense of identity, but also to provide a basis for further growth as an individual.

Procreation. The wish for children is usually a significant, and, occasionally, a primary, reason for marriage. Here we have in mind not the wish for ready access to mutual sexual pleasure, but rather the wish to be parents in a psychosocial sense. One important aspect of adulthood is the achievement of sufficient internal psychological consistency to be a suitable and attractive object for identification by one's children. The role of being a new parent is pleasurable, and a unique delight can be felt as one experiences the shaping influence that one has on one's children. In an irrational but important sense, man's mortality is transcended by procreation.

Sexuality. Sexual attraction and the desire for an outlet for sexual impulses are positive factors in the wish to marry. As George Bernard Shaw said, "Marriage combines maximum temptation with maximum opportunity." Although many sexual needs can be satisfied outside marriage, such experiences rarely blend with various other needs for affection, security and children. The security of a marriage can provide opportunities for exploring the limits of gratification.

Security and Escape. The wish for economic security, social status or to be cared for by someone can be a legitimate factor in marital choice. When this is the primary motive of one person, the seeds of discord are present, because the spouse may feel or may actually be exploited and unappreciated in any other aspect of his person.

Unhappiness in one's immediate social environment can impel a person to view marriage as a way out. As with the security issues discussed above, this motivation can become problematical to the extent that it leads to exploitation rather than sharing.

Social and Parental Pressure. As was mentioned earlier, one's idealized self-concept usually includes marriage. By implication, this suggests placing high social value on the married state. In some subcultures, self-esteem, especially for a girl, may be related to how early a person marries. If a woman is single and over 25, she may be viewed as a spinster.

Historically, and even today in many countries, parents arrange marital contracts for their children. In the United States, parental influence on mate choice is relatively strong in extended families and among certain religious and ethnic groups. The relative stability of such marriages in part reflects their conservative matrix, but it also illustrates the relative unimportance of romantic love in marriage.

Unconscious Needs. By their nature, unconscious needs always play a role in human behavior; they become troublesome when they predominate, as when the individual is struggling with neurotic conflict. Examples include the seeking of dependency gratification, the wish to dominate, the wish to gain a protector or the wish to get revenge. Rescue fantasies can be unconscious components, as illustrated in the case of a woman who had grown up with an alcoholic father who, while sober, was gentle with her. She had resented her mother's attitude toward her father. As an adult, she was in her second unsatisfactory marriage to an alcoholic whom she pathetically believed could be redeemed to achieve his latent potential through her revitalizing relationship with him. She was living out a fantasied relationship with her father.

Pregnancy. In about one of five marriages the bride is pregnant. The ratio is even higher among younger persons and lower socioeconomic groups. Clearly, the need to legitimize offspring can be a significant motivator of marriage.

It should be evident that none of the reasons described above for marriage is inherently pathological. Marital discord can arise when the marital partners have mutually exclusive, rather than complementary, needs, particularly if an important component of those needs is unconscious.

Marital Adjustment

Functionally adequate and satisfactory marriages may be of very different make-up, depending on the particular needs of the partners. There is a general characteristic of "good marriage," but it is one that is difficult to describe without sounding either pedantic or crudely sentimental. A minimum of tension, certainty of the esteem of one's partner, a steady warmth of affection, the sense of mutual support in the face of inescapable life crises and, perhaps centrally, the sense of reciprocal gratification define the parameters of an intimate marriage. To achieve this degree of intimacy requires time and struggle, but the effectiveness and gratification of the psychological forces involved are reflected in the growing similarity of interests, attitudes and even appearance of stable couples. The psychological process of identification, or growth by the assimilation of aspects of the significant person in one's life, is not limited to childhood. It is a lifelong process, and couples who possess sufficient inner consistency not only provide their children with elements for personality growth, but perform the same function for each other.

Marital Problems

From the point of view we have been describing, most marital problems can be understood as failures to meet the needs of those involved. Such failure can occur in several ways.

One partner may be unaware of the other's need and/or of his instrumental value to the other. For example, a former priest married a woman who had known him as a priest. She continued to picture him as an epic figure, casting his decision to leave the church into the form of a great ethical struggle. The husband, of course, partly collaborated in this view, but, more centrally, hoped to use the marriage as an arena in which he could give up the pose of being highly moral and ethical. Both began to feel increasingly unreal and artificial in the relationship and finally sought professional help.

A second pattern is that goals are discrepant or mutually inconsistent. For example, a black psychiatrist felt a strong need to become involved in civil rights advocacy. Although his wife intellectually agreed with his values, his focus on matters outside the family and his increasing absences from home became more and more intolerable, and a divorce ensued.

Discrepancies are sometimes rooted in religious or cultural values. A Chicano-Anglo marriage seemed relatively stable in that the middle-class Anglo wife supported the husband in his "macho" drinking, gambling and fighting. However, when she became pregnant, tension developed when she insisted that the child's welfare demanded a change in her husband's behavior.

Management of Marital Difficulties

The physician is often in a unique position to ameliorate marital difficulties. In the first place, many marital difficulties surface around pregnancy, the fruitless effort at pregnancy or the arrival of the child, and at these times the couple has a high probability of being in active contact with a physician. Second, as outlined in Chapter 6 "Affection in Patients," the couple's need for the doctor's care and attention to physical problems will predispose them to attach a high value to his advice in other areas.

To help in the resolution of marital conflicts, the physician should attend to three practical principles. First, a need inventory is required. Successful marriages result from the mutual satisfaction of needs. By listening carefully to the marital partners and observing their interactions, it should be possible to elicit the needs which each brings to the marriage and to determine whether the conflict is due to ignorance of needs or incompatibility of needs.

Second, the partners should be encouraged, and in fact required, to participate in this need inventory. With the physician's support, frank mutual discussion of the needs of each partner becomes possible. The couple must be reassured that most needs have some legitimacy and that openly voiced needs are more easily met than implicit ones. Where mutually incompatible needs exist, flexibility, accommodation and bargaining are required. Giving up on a particular point should involve a quid pro quo. Although this approach to resolving marital difficulties may sound excessively mercantile, open discussion of one another's needs can result in very good communication. The current vogue of marriage contracts in open marriages suggests the utility of being explicit about what is expected from each partner in a marriage, particularly at a time when our society has moved so far in the direction of role diffusion.

Third, the couple should be taught that conflict is part of a healthy relationship. Many couples submerge their needs either because they feel that these needs lack legitimacy or because they feel that expressing them would lead to undesirable conflict. The ability to express one's needs openly, and to express the feelings inherent in conflict situations, is essential to a stable marriage. A very useful book exploring the tactics and strategy of fighting fairly and in close relationships is *The Intimate Enemy*, by George Bach and Peter Wyden.

Divorce

Rather than recognize the interpersonal work that is necessary to balance the needs which the respective partners bring to treatment and the effort that must be expended to achieve intimacy, many Americans return to a highly romanticized and idealized view of perfect marriages based more on the clichés of popular women's magazines and television serials than on life. Unrealistic expectations are thus engendered which, particularly in the current social climate of increased tolerance for divorce and the more widespread use of contraceptives, have tended to produce high divorce rates. Nearly half of today's marriages end in divorce and although divorce is sometimes the best solution to incompatible needs, the event usually involves considerable pain for those involved. That the self-images of most divorced persons include marriage is indicated by the fact that three-fourths of them remarry within 5 years. Very often the divorce implies to the persons concerned a failure on one or both sides.

The emotional currents of the divorce situation become even more stressful when children are involved, as they are in the majority of divorces. The half-million divorces granted in 1967 involved about 700,000 children.

Not only are both parents likely to feel guilt, but continued involvement with the children requires continued contact between the now divorced partners. This continued contact provides an opportunity for squabbling and for using the children as counters in a continuation of the predivorce disagreements. In any divorce situation, the children become caught in loyalty conflicts which are exaggerated by the parents' neurotic struggles.

As in similar situations, the nonpsychiatric physician can be helpful in several ways. Educationally, he can help his newly divorced patients to anticipate and to limit the inroads of the tempestuous emotions that will ensue. Particularly, he can encourage them to attenuate as much as possible the effects of the child's tendency to idealize the missing parent and to feel anger at the retained one. The missing parent's guilty overindulgence and the present parent's retaliatory anger, for example, should not be acted on. Second, he can provide them with the opportunity to share and explore their feelings in a sympathetic and nonjudgmental atmosphere. Third, he can help to minimize their guilt by reassuring them about the positive potentials in the situation. Fourth, when it seems indicated because of intractable difficulties, he can make a referral to an appropriate mental health professional.

Family

The importance of marriage as an institution is a function of the fact that it is the mechanism by which, in our society, the family is formed. The family is the basic unit of the social system: the environment in which basic interpersonal needs are met and the locus of the child's crucial early socialization experience. Successful treatment of many patients, particularly children, depends on understanding that they live in a social matrix which limits and shapes their behavior.

Functions

Nurturance. The family provides for the physical, emotional, affectionate and security needs of its members. It defines the boundaries of illness and the circumstances of care appropriate for ill family members.

Personality Integrations. The "parental coalition" is the unified, stable approach of both parents to issues of discipline, values and family rules. It serves a basic role in the socialization of the child, eventually leading to the child's adoption of values, rules and attitudes similar to those held by the parents. Within each family, sex- and age-specific behaviors are determined. The importance of close parent-child contact, from the earliest postnatal hours, to promote adequate bonding cannot be overemphasized.

Value System. This is first learned through family role assignment. The child asks, "How old will I be when . . . ?" He learns to set the table, to be a host or hostess, etc. Teaching is important for this, but even more important is the parents' model for the child to emulate consciously and to identify with unconsciously. For example, Sears' work indicates that the parents' aggressive behavior is more important than the parents' expressed values about aggressive behavior in determining the child's behavior.

Emancipative Functions. Ideally, the family should function to see that

members leaving it temporarily or permanently do so with optimal smooth-
ness. This is a frequent area of conflict, especially in late adolescents and
young adults. A father became depressed and hypochondrical when his 24-
year-old son began considering moving away. His inability to support his son
in his reasonable effort at independence and, contrariwise, his efforts to play
on the guilt of the son, eventually led to hostility and rejection on the part of
the son.

Role Division

Definition of sex-appropriate roles is an intrinsic familial function. In
general, fathers serve as the more instrumental role models regarding the
work functions of acquisition and survival. Usually, the father's education,
activities and productivity largely determine the family's social status. The
mother usually provides for most of the biological needs of the family in
health and illness. She helps the children to understand their feelings and is
usually more responsible for affective communication.

What is the man's work in one culture may be the woman's in another. In
general, however, the more physically taxing, income-producing and creative
jobs have been handled by men. The patriarchal family probably replaced
the matriarchal family about 11,000 years ago, when man's pattern of living
changed from that of nomadic food-gatherer and hunter to that of farmer
and animal breeder.

Modern technology has largely removed the strength of the male as a
factor in job assignment. Through household convenience gadgets and foods,
it has also diminished many of the traditionally essential functions of the
mother. Birth control devices have resulted in a woman's having more choice
over the time of conception, and usually a longer span of life from the time
she bears her last child. These developments are the backdrop for the equal
rights movement of women in the areas of legal status, education and jobs
which have profoundly altered, and, in some cases disorganized, intrafamilial
relationships.

The patriarchal family no longer quite serves its function. The role of the
father has been greatly diminished by the technological factors mentioned
and because his absence from the home while he is working makes him
unavailable as a role model. The effort to retain the form without the
substance of patriarchal prerogatives can result in family tensions. The
"machismo" of the predominantly lower class, Mexican-American males who
pride themselves on a double standard which extols heavy drinking, male
friendships exclusively, disparagement of women and an expectation of
submissive obedience from the wife partly reflects past traditions, but it is
also supported by the limited work roles available to many Mexican-American men. Heavy manual labor for which women are unsuited is one of the
few job opportunities readily available to these men in American society.

The term equality is problematical, because men and women, blacks and whites, Californians and New Yorkers are neither equal nor all inclusively superior to one another. As Galdston states, superiority among human beings can only be partial, fractional and particular. Socially, equality best refers to opportunity, wherein each person has an equal chance to become different.

In the contemporary United States, narrow conceptions of sex-appropriate roles can lead to difficulties in personal development, marital relationships and rearing of children. Large areas of feelings, thinking and behaving might more appropriately be considered human rather than strictly sex-bound. These cultural sets need to be modified more in accord with basic human needs and as they are actually found in men and women. Sex-appropriate roles should be flexible, because crises may necessitate reversal. However, general role reversal provides children with unsuitable models for development, even if the relationship is satisfactory to the parents.

Extended Families and Isolated Nuclear Families

The extended family is not specific to any society. It is more common in essentially nonmigratory populations. In such settings, the nuclear family is not clearly demarcated from surrounding relatives, with whom they may live in close interaction. Advice and help regarding family problems including child rearing, is available from many relatives. The husband and wife may spend more time in the company of relatives of the same sex than with each other, and thus tend to be less dependent on one another. Children growing up in such families often learn child rearing by caring for young siblings or other relatives. There tends to be security and clarity of role function for all members of the family. This orderly, comfortable transmission of traditional roles has some disadvantages in a dynamic technological society. Role rigidity can make participation difficult in a changing society which requires rapid adaptation and learning revolutionary operational modes.

The isolated nuclear family is largely a product of the educational, social, vocational and geographical mobility of our society. The potential for conflict is great. It is more likely that the couple will have divergent backgrounds. In the marriage, each must assume many divergent roles, blurring the clarity found in the extended family. The mother, if trained primarily for education and a career, may be ill prepared for rearing children and carrying out household activities. In such a marriage, the parents are much more interdependent. Their personalities are of greater importance in the children's personality development. Most such children will have no other adult models who can compensate for parental deficits.

Such children are less likely to grow up with the experience of closely observing or assisting in child rearing and, thus, are less comfortably prepared for the nurturant role of becoming a parent. Children reared in extended families are relatively more likely to have problems involving dependency;

those reared in nuclear families are more likely to have oedipal, intergenerational problems. The encapsulated nature of problems within the isolated nuclear family impels them to seek help outside it—help which might have come spontaneously in an extended family through the efforts or simple presence of another family member.

Family Therapy

Family therapy is a psychotherapeutic specialty which makes the assumption that many behavioral disorders—particularly of children—are a function of disordered communication within the family unit. The therapist meets with the family as a unit, observes the pattern of interaction and, by heightening the family members' awareness of distorted communication and providing models of more valid communication, helps to restore the family's balance.

Although effective family therapy requires specialized training, the general physician can often catalyze positive changes in family members by confronting them with the need to work at communication and with the results of familial disintegration and discord.

Work

In an informal experiment in which one student was asked to define work, he said, "Work is what you wouldn't do except for pay." Although this statement lacks elegance, it contains the core of clear understanding. As opposed to activities which are presumably pleasant or gratifying in and of themselves, work is *instrumental* activity, behavior which, whether or not it is pleasant in and of itself, is primarily entered into because of its deferred consequences. The rat pressing the lever in the Skinner box in order to obtain a food pellet is working as truly as is the typist pounding her keys to receive her weekly check. This definition, correct as far as it goes, does not convincingly relate work to adulthood as a stage-specific task. For example, is not a 3½-year-old child struggling to learn how to tie her shoes working? Or the 10-year-old boy laboriously practicing his violin scales in order to "earn" permission to play ball with the guys on the block? The children in these examples are struggling for a defined reward; hence, these activities might be regarded as work. However, they differ from adult work in that, typically, adult work is not an attempt to earn love or regard, not an attempt to win control over other persons, but rather an attempt to gain mastery over the physical world or to obtain tokens such as money that lead to such control. In the sense that children, limited physically, satisfy their physical needs largely by the manipulation of other people (passive mastery—"Mommy, I need a drink"), and in the sense that active mastery of the world (getting a drink for oneself) requires certain physical competence, age and work are clearly related. The boundaries of adult work have been changed, in our society, as a result of the expectation that more and more education be completed before beginning to work. Size, strength and the psychological ability to focus attention and to delay impulses are crucial variables in the ability to work.

Less theoretically, then, the development of a work identity involves integrating the adult realization that one's impact on the world—in fact, one's survival—must be a function of one's own efforts, rather than the efforts of one's parents, family or friends. Mastery of this lesson leads to the adult possibility of utilizing one's strength not only to survive or to succeed personally, but to achieve security and satisfactions for others.

Emotional conflict has the same potential for interfering with work as does physical injury. The literature abounds with examples of neurotic work blocks. Of interest is the study by Riess, in which he demonstrated that the salaries of all patients in psychotherapy showed substantial increases (approximately 30% in 1 year), presumably in part on the basis of working more effectively.

As the Riess study implies, inefficiencies in work performance are a common feature of neurotic difficulties. The form of work inhibition which is most likely to present to the general physician is that associated with the general apathy that accompanies secondary depression. The treatment of depression is discussed at some length in Chapter 9. Here it might be well to emphasize one aspect of such treatment. A temporary withdrawal from involvement with formerly important life activities, both interpersonal and work-related, is a natural stage in the grieving process which follows psychological loss. An error frequently made by the families and friends of grieving people is rushing the grieving process. It is far better to permit the painful feelings full expression and afford the grieving process time to run its natural course. A clear-cut example of such a situation was the case of the prominent Midwestern surgeon who suffered a cerebrovascular accident, with significant motor and aphasic sequelae. With his characteristic energy, the patient threw himself into a rehabilitation program. For 6 months there was significant but gradually plateauing improvement, at which point the patient had a left hemiparesis and mild residual word-finding difficulties. He did not return to practice, but continued to involve himself in rehabilitation programs for 1½ years in pursuit of total recovery. The family collaborated with the patient by exaggerating the importance of tiny fluctuations in performance. The combination of loss of income and the expense involved in the now fruitless rehabilitation efforts was at the point of creating a financial catastrophe, when the patient's physician confronted the surgeon with his unrealistic behavior and plans. This confrontation permitted the surgeon's depression to surface, rather than being warded off by a belief in an illusory total recovery. The depression was understandably acute, but it was managed basically by encouraging the patient to ventilate his feelings about his lost abilities, status, etc. In the course of about 2 months, the pain and anger gradually subsided, and the patient began making constructive and realistic plans for a reduced practice and a lowered living scale that permitted him to continue to support his wife and himself.

Psychological Stresses of Adulthood

The major psychological stress of this period is that one must come to terms with a limit to one's accomplishments and responsibilities. The passage of time causes other psychological confrontations. One must confront the meaning of one's own life and make plans for using the time remaining. For some, the problem is having a second and perhaps last chance. For others, the problem is finding new meanings to life. A young father, rearing young children, can see them as projections of his own omnipotence. But a middle-aged father must confront the fact that his children will live their own lives, that they have their own failings and that he must find meaning in his own life, rather than in theirs. A young mother can invest herself in her household and her children, but her children's departure may leave her unprepared and newly anxious about her own fulfillment and competence. Psychologically, stresses lead to an increased proneness to anxiety and depression along with gradually increasing attention to one's own body, which often takes the form of hypochondriacal ailments.

In general, this phase of life brings about less disorganizing psychiatric illnesses, and those which do occur are often recurrences of illnesses first experienced in adolescence and young adulthood. It is not until old age that organic illnesses precipitate major psychiatric problems. Anxiety and depression, with their physical concomitants, are the most common psychiatric illnesses of this phase of life. Because of the greater risk of suicide in this age group, the depressed, middle-aged patient must be carefully assessed.

Rosenthal has reported that there is no increased rate of depressive illness associated with the menopause, nor are there special features of depression in the involutional period as opposed to affective disorder at other phases of life. A current consensus is the affective disorders have only a chance association with middle age and menopause.

Maladaptive Solutions

The judgment of what is adaptive depends not only on the solution itself, but on its context, its timing and its outcome. Furthermore, what is normal in one cultural group may not be so in another. Value judgments are implicit in any description of what is "healthier." At the same time, what is maladaptive and what is adaptive are not mutually exclusive. Lidz has further discussed many of the ideas contained in this chapter in *The Person.*

Mechanisms of adaptation and defense are described earlier in this volume (Chapter 4). Such mechanisms are age-related attempts at solutions of conflict. For example, we can speak of *denial* as a somewhat primitive defense mechanism. At any phase of life, a severe illness may precipitate denial as a mechanism of defense if the patient is unable to face the consequences of his severe illness. A more age-specific example of denial related to middle adulthood is the denial of the passage of time, seen commonly in efforts to overcompensate for the fear of weaknesses. Thus, a man needs to prove that he is "as good as ever," and pays with disabling back pain for the need to show that he can still run with the best of the others. A heart patient advised to recuperate slowly may find that the stress of dependency and vulnerability is too great and may attempt to compensate by showing that he can still handle a snow shovel. Fear of dependency is a common precipitating stress which leads to denial in patients who demand to leave the hospital early, immediately return to work and show the younger people on the job that the recent illness has had no effect. The denial is both an attempt to recapture youth and to deny illness. Who among us has not seen a matronly woman in boots and miniskirt, looking more like a teeny-bopper than her own daughter? How much effort and money are spent in search of the fountain of youth, whether it be through hormone creams or implanted monkey gonads?

Some degree of denial appears to be almost universal at this phase. The opposite of denial, a hyperacute awareness of the passage of time, may also lead to maladaptive efforts. Fear of displacement by younger rivals, whether at work or in one of the many social organizations to which middle-aged adults increasingly belong, can lead not only to anxiety but also to extreme competitive urges which can cause much anguish. The competition of grandparents for the attention of their grandchildren is a common example, in which family problems are precipitated by the need of the grandparent to compete with the parent of the child. Similarly in the business world, more experienced workers often resent younger colleagues.

Alcoholism, in all its forms, is a common maladaptive attempted solution. Those who previously did not drink to excess may now begin to do so. Those who had earlier binges will now find more frequent need to overindulge. Increasingly common is the problem of the lonely middle-aged housewife, her husband busily involved in his own career, who drinks at home to blunt her anxiety and frustration.

Ominous signs of incipient alcoholism include the need to drink to excess regularly, and the need for two or three drinks when one would previously do. Those who begin to drink earlier in the day are on their way to more troubles. Persons who have to be hospitalized, and are thus away from their regular drink, may become irritable, anxious, shaky or even paranoid; they may present almost by accident as dependent on alcohol.

With increasing age, a man becomes less and less sexually energetic. There is less ability to sustain an erection, and a sense of relative impotence ensues. His anxiety about masculine performance at work or in sports easily carries over into the sexual area. An illness, too much alcohol or too much anxiety may precipitate an occasional episode of impotence. All of these, for the male, are great sources of stress to which he must adapt. Extramarital affairs, most often with younger women, are a common response. These may take the form of a steady mistress, a series of sexual affairs and explorations in search of satisfaction or even a divorce out of fear of impotence, when the man recognizes that he may be more potent with other women than with his own wife.

The sexual sphere also offers many possibilities for maladaptive as well as adaptive solutions for women. Menopause may bring increased sexual capability interest, due to the lessened fear of pregnancy. The need to remain young, attractive and desirable may take the form of sexual escapades in search of youth. Although men continue to report greater interest and activity, increased interest in sex by the woman may contrast with an often decreased interest and ability in her spouse in such a way that any problems tend to become aggravated. The woman may now be ready to explore new sexual avenues and partners.

One-fourth of the divorces which occur annually are in marriages of 15 years' duration or longer. With their children grown and on their own, the marital partnership is re-evaluated by each member. Often one or the other decides to try it again with someone else. These changes are precipitated by a hope of finding a partner who will be more kind and considerate, more intellectual or more companionable sexually and socially. The needs now become more intimate and personal, as opposed to those which earlier influenced the selection of someone who could provide help in a career, or through family support. In seeking a new relationship, there is the sense that "this time it's just for *me* and for what *I* want." The increased value of a marital partner as both lover and companion predominates over other issues in middle adulthood.

Boredom constitutes an additional stress as well as a context for new solutions. In a setting of lack of job gratification or of dull routine in the home, many persons find themselves unable to make fruitful use of their leisure time and, indeed, unable to experience pleasure in their lives. This may lead to a lack of concern for others and to feelings that one is not a worthwhile person. This phenomenon has relevance for our discussion of maladaptive solutions, because persons with an inability to experience pleasure will sometimes turn to more exotic attempts to experience feelings. This phenomenon can be seen in the areas of sexuality and violence and may be related to some of the newer explorations in life-styles and relationships to be discussed later.

Prosen et al. studied men who had frequent extramarital affairs during middle age. A common pattern in such a man was the contrast between his mother, now old and wrinkled, and his fantasy of a mother still young, idealized and erotic, a psychological remnant of youth. Awareness of aging in the spouse and the struggle to deny the changes in one's own body image in this phase of life call for readjustment in all middle-aged couples. It is those who have not yet resolved earlier life tasks who are most likely to take this kind of readjustment least gracefully, as exemplified by the men in Prosen et al.'s study who frenetically sought out sexual activity as a now-or-never effor to hold onto childhood wishes.

Adaptive Solutions

Each new stress in life is a crisis not only in the sense of the need to regroup and meet a challenge, but also as an opportunity and challenge to make new decisions and find new solutions. The more affluent our society becomes, the more choices are open for new decisions in middle age. Increasing numbers of men and women find new outlets through second careers, which are generally more gratifying to them than their earlier choice. These may implement earlier interests or they may be new careers. As more people are offered the opportunity to retire after 20 years of work, second careers, both as outlets for leisure time and as vocations, become more important. Persons who retire from military and civil service have often prepared insufficiently for their "postretirement" careers and hobbies, just as those who retire at 65 may find a major crisis in their adjustment. Unless there has been adequate preparation for leisure and for the second career, much anxiety and readjustment may ensue once the worth-giving value of their work disappears.

A recent study by Lowenthal indicated that the prospect of grown children's leaving home seemed not to threaten many parents. She concluded that there is little evidence of an empty nest crisis; rather, this development may bring release.

The earlier discussion about extramarital affairs and divorces as examples of maladaptive solutions should also be considered in the light of their possibilities for adaptation. It is not the action per se, but the context in which the action occurs which is most important. A couple may have maintained a poor relationship for years out of a sense of responsibility for their children and for the public image. Divorce, with a more suitable object choice, or extramarital sexual activity may be adaptive and even growth-promoting, although they are in opposition to some moral points of view.

Many sources of satisfaction and security are more readily available in middle adulthood than in earlier life periods. The fact is that grandparents *do* have more money to spend and more time available, and they need not be worried about dirty diapers or a baby crying in the middle of the night. It is little wonder that they can be in better humor when they see the grandchildren.

Mechanisms of defense and modes of coping in middle adulthood range from the primitive ones of denial and projection to the most mature ones of altruism and identification. Herein lie the opportunities for the middle-aged. Many in middle age will find that their supervisors are younger persons. For the best adaptation, it is necessary that they relate to younger persons as adults, not as children but as peers in the full sense of the word. This mode of relating as adult to adult is as important with one's own now grown children as it is with associates at work. The middle-aged person can usefully share the benefits of his greater experience with younger colleagues. Rather than a sense of loss of youth, the person can thus have an increasing sense of pride about maturity.

Changes Associated with Middle Age

Much of the preceding discussion has considered the effect of adulthood on the marital relationship and the sexual behavior of the individual. Recent studies by Pfeiffer et al. on sexual behavior in middle age indicate dramatic differences between men and women of like age in regard to most indicators of sexual behavior. Men generally reported greater interest and activity at all ages studied, with both men and women showing a gradual decline beginning with middle age. It was also clear that sex continued to play an important role in the lives of the vast majority of those studied during the middle years.

New stresses tend to lead to a downing in activity and an upswing of anxiety before the development of a new, stable adjustment. Studies of the concerns of people in middle adulthood demonstrate a temporary period of increased anxiety in the early 40's, prior to a more lasting adjustment later. Gould, in a series of observations of both patients and nonpatients, found that the sense of time and the attitudes toward self and others in relation to time changed during the phases of adult life. He noted a series of temporary excursions from well established lifelong baselines, indicating a great deal of personal discomfort which abates to some degree in the mid-40's. His results dramatically affirmed the tenet that one's personality is largely set, and that life does not change from year to year. The results also indicated that marital happiness and contentment with the spouse continue to increase during middle life, along with renewed interest in friends and social activity and a continuation of concern for one's own family. In the 50's, he found the beginning of a lesser sense of responsibility for one's children and a greater awareness of the need for the children's approval. This concern for approval by one's children becomes equal with the needs for self-approval and approval by the spouse.

The frequency of divorce at this phase makes it imperative to clarify that divorced females more often remain unmarried. Divorced men, on the other hand, most often remarry. The same holds true following the loss of a spouse, with widows remaining so, and widowers most often remarrying. Incidentally, those who have never married must make renewed decisions in middle age, as the advantages of the unmarried state decrease as the parents die and the gratification of being the favored child lessen.

Among the casualties of the stresses and strains referred to above are a wide spectrum of people who develop psychosomatic symptoms, habituation to medication and a tendency to depression, and who disguise personal, marital and social problems in the form of somatic symptoms. Gynecologists see such women with all varieties of "pelvic congestion," associated difficulties in sexual relationships, backache and a spectrum of disabilities. The so-called "tired housewife" is known in many clinics and doctors' offices as an overworked person, often with economic difficulties and a large family responsibility, who only rarely gets out of the house. Nothing the doctor can do helps so much as a compassionate understanding of the social setting of the symptoms. Although antidepressants, sedatives and minor tranquilizers are used extensively, they often do not even remove the symptoms. Encouraging the patient to take time away from household obligations, suggesting that the husband help out, advising the patient to obtain household help if feasible and encouraging new interests are among the positive steps the physician can take.

Equally common and increasing in importance is the phenomenon of the "tired breadwinner." The similar spectrum of somatic complaints occurs in persons who have strong dependency needs which have previously been well defended. These are often men who started to work early in their lives, are often from lower socioeconomic groups and have worked at hard physical labor. They have a sense of responsibility to their families. But illness or an injury breaks their equilibrium, and they become chronic frequenters of doctors' offices. Although it is easy to feel that these men are mainly looking for a pension or a settlement of a lawsuit, they are not malingerers. The syndrome is, in part, a manifestation of an unconscious wish for early retirement by a person who cannot at the moment secure this retirement and relief in the usual manner. These are persons whose pride in their earlier work was hurt when they found they were not indispensable. They are those with physically taxing jobs who are locked into prospects of hard work, little money and no advancement. This phenomenon exists in the rich as well, if they lose their sense of importance in their job role. Finally, the impersonal nature of routine jobs in which there is little sense of creativity, and subsequent boredom, may lead the patient to the doctor's office with vague somatic complaints. The physician therefore needs to assess the environmental circumstances of patients with such complaints and, if possible, intervene in that arena, rather than reinforce a hypochondriacal semi-invalidism.

*   *   *   *

In this chapter, we have explored sexual development and function in detail. We have also discussed the topics of marriage, love, divorce and work. Our goal has been to permit a clearer understanding of the stresses of adulthood and of maladaptive and adaptive responses to those stresses.

REFERENCES

1. BACH, G., AND WYDEN, P. *The Intimate Enemy*. William Morrow, New York, 1969.
2. BARDWICK J. M. *Psychology of Women*. Harper & Row, New York, 1971.
3. BENEDEK, T. Sexual Functions in Women and their Disturbance, in *American Handbook of Psychiatry*, Arieti, S., ed. Basic Books, New York, 1959.

4. COMFORT, A. *The Joy of Sex*. Crown Publishers, New York, 1972. (A useful book for patients to read.)
5. DEYKIN, E. Y., JACOBSON, S., KLERMAN, G., AND SOLOMON, M. The empty nest: psychosocial aspects of conflict between depressed women and their children. *Am. J. Psychiatry 122:* 1422–1426, 1966.
6. FORD, C. S., AND BEACH, F. A. *Patterns of Sexual Behavior*. Harper & Row, New York, 1951. (A classical, socioanthropological study.)
7. GADAPAILLE, W. J. *The Cycles of Sex*. Charles Scribner's Sons, New York, 1975.
8. GOULD, R. L. The phases of adult life: a study in developmental psychology. *Am. J. Psychiatry 129:*521–531, 1972.
9. HUNT, M. *The Affair*. Signet Books, New York, 1969.
10. KAPLAN, H. S. *The New Sex Therapy*. Brunner/Mazel, New York, 1974. (A clear and sensible elucidation of treatment of patients with primary sexual dysfunctions.)
11. KINSEY, A. C., POMEROY, W. B., MARTIN, C. E., AND GEBHARD, P. H. *Sexual Behavior in the Human Male*. W. B. Saunders, 1948.
12. KINSEY, A. C., POMEROY, W. B., MARTIN, C. E., AND GEBHARD, P. H. *Sexual Behavior in the Human Female*. W. B. Saunders, Philadelphia, 1953.
13. LEVINSON, D. J., DARROW, C. N., KLEIN, E. B., LEVINSON, M. H., AND MC KEE, B. *The Seasons of a Man's Life*. Alfred A. Knopf, New York, 1978. (This and the Vaillant book indicate the potential for positive change and continuing development during adulthood.)
14. LIDZ, T. The Middle Years, in *The Person*. Basic Books, New York, 1968, pp. 457–475.
15. LOWENTHAL, M. F. Transition to the empty nest. *Arch. Gen. Psychiatry 26:*8–14, 1972.
16. MASTERS, W. H., AND Johnson, V. E. *Human Sexual Inadequacy*. Little, Brown, and Co., Boston, 1970.
17. MASTERS, W. H., AND JOHNSON, V. E. *Human Sexual Response*. Little, Brown, and Co., Boston, 1966.
18. PFEIFFER, E., VERWOERDI, A., AND DAVIS, G. C. Sexual behavior in middle life. *Am. J. Psychiatry 128:*1262–1267, 1972.
19. PROSEN, H., MARTIN, R., AND PROSEN, M. The remembered mother and the fantasized mother. *Arch. Gen. Psychiatry 27:*791–794, 1972.
20. RIESS, B. F. Changes in patient income concomitant with psychotherapy. *J. Consult. Clin. Psychol. 31:*430, 1967.
21. ROSENTHAL S. The involutional depressive syndrome. *Am. J. Psychiatry 124:*21–35, 1968.
22. SKOLNICK, A. S., AND SKOLNICK, J. H. (eds.). *Family in Transition*. Little, Brown, and Co., Boston, 1971.
23. SUTHERLAND, H., AND STEWART, I. A critical analysis of the premenstrual syndrome. *Lancet 1:*113–118, 1956.
24. TYLER, E. Introducing a sex education course into the medical curriculum. *J. Indiana Med. Assoc. 63:*898–901, 1970.
25. VAILLANT, G. E. *Adaptation to Life*. Little, Brown, and Co., Boston, 1978.
26. WALLIN, P. A study of orgasm as a condition of woman's enjoyment of intercourse. *J. Soc. Psychol. 51:*191–198, 1960.
27. WINOKUR, G. Depression in the menopause. *Am. J. Psychiatry 130:*92–93, 1973.

CHAPTER 19

THE CLOSING OF THE CYCLE: OLD AGE

GEORGE G. MEYER, M.D.

Who Are the Elderly?
Why People Age
Emotional Aspects of Aging
Sociocultural Factors of Aging
Suggestions for Treatment of the
Aged

Perhaps no phase of the life cycle has more expert commentators than aging. Although those who live through the phase of adulthood described in the last chapter may comment on their situation, few of them are as concerned with that phase of life as are the aged who are living through their years of retirement and impending death. One of the adaptive mechanisms utilized in aging is to comment on it and study it, so that many senior citizens comment at length on the plight of the aged. At a time when physicians who practice clinical medicine find much of their medical practice taken up with elderly patients, it is a cruel paradox that there are few courses in geriatrics and few specialists in geriatric care among physicians. Even psychiatrists, who increasingly are asked to help make decisions on matters such as placement and competence to handle funds, usually have little direct training in this special field. Experts on the aging process decry that, while their most important recommendations have to do with the need for a productive work life, continued social contacts and ready access to medical care, society denies the aged meaningful work opportunities, the mobility of family life decreases their opportunities for close, rewarding relationships with other family members and comprehensive medical care is difficult to afford on a restricted retirement income.

Who Are the Elderly?

Most definitions of the elderly are colored by the definer's fantasies and fears about aging—and death. All too often, these definitions conjure up a caricature of senility, and the elderly is equated with the institutionalized, dependent, forgetful invalid who constitutes only a small minority of this group.

We define the elderly as those over 65. They include a spectrum of individuals, from those who continue to be productive, active and healthy, to the extreme described above. They have increased from 4% of the population in the 1960 census to nearly 10% of the population in the 1970 census. Thus, the aged population today consists of just over 20 million people, of whom about one-third are 75 and older.

It is important to recognize that the span of life has not increased significantly in recent years. Rather, better medical controls of neonatal deaths, childhood deaths and deaths from infectious diseases have increased the number of persons who survive into middle age and beyond. Women survive to an older age more often than men. The survival rate of the sexes begins to diverge after age 40. After 65, there are seven women to five men; after 75, there are eight women to five men.

Two major inferences can be drawn from statistical data on the elderly. One is that our society needs to make a number of adjustments in facilities, programs and philosophy to accommodate the numbers expected. By the year 2000, the United States may have a population of over 300 million people, of whom about 30 million will be over 65. Our society must face the challenge of how to utilize and respond to this large group with unmet needs and untapped potential. The other important inference is that a man at 65 years of age can now expect to live to 79, and a woman at that age can expect to live to 81. Thus, while life plans have been geared to a retirement age at 65 with only a brief life-span following this, the current situation is that the person 65 years of age must plan what he will do for 15 years. The implications that this has for retirement planning, for the use of and provisions for leisure time and its impact on family life in a mobile society are just beginning to be explored.

Why People Age

Aging is a process which occurs throughout life. It is represented in the epithelial cells and blood corpuscles which are continually being replaced, beginning in infancy. It occurs in the conversion of muscle to fat and the diminished hormonal activity which begin in middle age. We distinguish between *senescence,* which implies the passage of time without the notion of decay, and *senility,* in which deterioration of brain and body functions lead to a variety of mental, physical and social problems.

Although not totally understood, the aging process involves an interaction of biological changes, rooted in the genetic make-up of the individual, with psychosocial factors. Primary aging occurs within the individual over time; secondary aging results from a variety of hostile agents or conditions which cause deterioration through trauma and disease. Some cells multiply throughout life but slow down their functions due to a variety of factors. These include the cells of the skin and the white blood cells. Other cells which cannot regenerate, such as brain neurons, are affected more dramatically by the progressive slowing over time. Noncellular factors, such as changes in the collagen tissues, have their own aging processes. In these components, aging involves cells which do not work as well, or the decline and loss of necessary numbers or an interference with the flow of materials for respiration.

The physical effects of aging include direct body shrinkage due to loss of cells and loss of elasticity, which amounts to 12% of the body mass. Taste buds atrophy, and the capacity to detect odors is decreased. Fifty per cent of the elderly have lost their teeth by age 65. Brain weight decreases by 10 to 15%, with the neurons in the cortex the most vulnerable, and the primitive brain the least affected. A listing of the systems involved becomes as detailed as the researcher chooses, but the over-all effect is one of decreased perception, mobility and coordination.

Decreased physical mobility and acuity have major effects on the life and interactions of the person. The musculoskeletal system is affected by calcification, fibrosis and osteoarthritis. As eyesight decreases and hearing becomes less acute, the person becomes less able to maneuver. He stays more to himself and has increased hesitancy about new contacts. With less acuity and alertness as his reflexes are slowed, his responses to danger signals are dulled and avoidance of accidents is more difficult. The person becomes aware of diminished energy for work and play, diminished tolerance for stress and diminished adaptability to new things. Action and outlook are increasingly conservative. There is an increased tendency to be self-centered as the world in which one functions tends to shrink.

With hearing loss, the person feels increasing anxiety at not understanding, which may progress to the point of paranoid delusional thought. Because the hearing loss is most noticeable when there are many stimuli, as in crowds or on the street, he tends to become more socially isolated.

Intellectually, the stresses of old age with its decreased activity lead to a situation analogous to the atrophy from disuse in the muscular system. The intellect must be stimulated to be continuously productive. Thus, reading, discussions and interests in the world around will enhance the intellectual abilities of an individual, whereas isolation, depression and lack of motivation will decrease these capacities. The previous life-style, intelligence, attitude toward learning, motivation to change and tolerance for the more sedentary pleasures all affect later adjustment. The best predictors of adequate adjustment are present much earlier in the life cycle, when reaction patterns to stress and the ability to interact with others and to live with oneself are already evident.

Memory loss is a cardinal sign of organic brain damage. In old age, recall of recent events is impaired, especially under stress. On the other hand, remote memory for past events remains quite clear. Many an elderly person aware of increasing memory difficulties will bore his listeners with repetitions of past events, which can be viewed as an attempt to reassure himself that his memory is intact. When memory erodes to the point that one's name and early life experiences are forgotten, basic identity is imperiled.

There is no direct correlation between loss of cells and loss of memory in the individual. Intellectual maintenance is associated with genetic endowment, good health, good socioeconomic status and previous pattern of living. Physiologically, there is a progressive slowing of the dominant frequency of the electroencephalographic (EEG) pattern. Busse's studies on cerebral blood flow demonstrate a direct correlation between oxygen consumption and EEG frequency, suggesting a decreased cerebral metabolic rate. The EEG's of elderly persons show a variety of other changes, many of which tend to disappear during sleep. Although the focal disturbances are not consistently related to changes in psychological functioning, it appears that a focus in the anterior left temporal area is associated with a decline in verbal abilities and that occipital diffuse slowing is associated with decreased visual-motor abilities. The correlation between EEG patterns and blood pressure has led Busse to argue that mild systolic hypertension is desirable in the elderly, because blood flow is dependent on blood pressure. Various studies have been done which demonstrate the importance of cerebral blood flow, regarding both the undesirable side effects of many medications in lowering blood pressure and the development of medications which attempt to increase cerebral blood flow and metabolism.

In summary, a number of factors can adversely affect the aged individual. Although more and more is known of what is involved, the specifics of the physiology of aging and the development of treatment and preventive approaches based on such knowledge are not yet complete.

Emotional Aspects of Aging

The physical factors outlined impinge on a personality with its own strengths, weaknesses and adaptability to stress. In the aged patient, the doctor most dramatically sees the interplay of physical, emotional and sociocultural factors. Thus, an understanding of previous reactions to stress, previous relationships with people and previous strengths and weaknesses are most necessary in working to establish new balance in the aged patient.

With aging, the person becomes more like himself. Indeed, he may become a caricature of himself, with his basic traits accentuated over time. Previously unsolved problems may resurface as earlier adaptations in the areas of work, mobility and supporting relationships collapse.

Psychological problems can be described separately from physical problems only if one remembers the great importance of interaction. Organic brain factors such as difficulties with memory, judgment, intellect and orientation are closely linked with psychological factors such as withdrawal, denial and depression.

Depressive feelings which have been well handled earlier in life may now be feared and magnified by the patient. The range of depressive feelings in the aged requires careful diagnostic work. There are, to begin with, normal and universal depressive feelings in the elderly. With the best of previous personality adaptations, with a minimum of stress and with a perfectly acceptable retirement and physical situation, old people are subject to sudden, unexplained depressive feelings lasting from hours to days. These are normal and nonpreventable and should be treated as such. Grief reactions are also universally experienced as the elderly person suffers the loss of a spouse, reacts to the loss of his job or hears repeatedly about the death of friends. The replacement of these real losses with new gratifications poses a challenge, especially in view of the reluctance to become deeply involved with new people who may also become lost to death and illness.

Depressive reactions of a more severe kind, with vegetative disturbances of sleep, appetite and bowel function, have been successfully treated with a variety of medications as well as with social interaction. These more serious depressions involve guilt over past failures, guilt over survival or range over lack of dependency gratifications. Elderly psychiatric patients tend to be volatile, decompensating to an ominous state of psychological disorganization or responding dramatically to treatment. Severe forms of psychiatric disturbance, with hallucinations, paranoid delusions and somatic delusions about bodily dysfunction, can also respond surprisingly well to treatment. In general, a more acute onset, better preservation of personality, the presence of a labile affect and an onset with dementia are more consistent with direct organic disease. Neurological findings may be more important than psychiatric ones in many such patients.

Hospital treatment of elderly patients for psychiatric or other causes can be difficult. One of the most important rights enjoyed by an individual is his right to submit to or to avoid treatment. This right is basic because it involves one's control over one's own body. However, in no society do absolute rights exist; in our society, there are sanctions under which others may decide for an individual whether or not he is to be treated or protected.

The legal rules under which people can be treated without their consent, or even in spite of their protests, vary from state to state, but the key issue is usually whether the individual in question can make an informed decision about the need for treatment. When the individual is adjudged incapable of such a decision by a court (largely on the basis of expert opinion from physicians), he may be committed to a guardian, who is sometimes the court or a hospital but often a relative, for the purpose of obtaining treatment. The most justifiable basis for commitment under mental health codes are that the person is regarded as an immediate danger to himself or others or that he is unable to perform the common activities necessary to support life.

In progressive states, the decision as to whether a person requires mental treatment is separated from the question of whether a person is competent to enter into binding contracts, make a will, vote, etc. When this determination is made separately from the commitment decision, the doctor is regarded as an expert. Particularly with the aged, the family physician will be expected to have an opinion as to whether an aged relative should be institutionalized and/or permitted to retain control of his or her property. Serious disorientation and major defects of recent memory on the mental status examination might appropriately be taken as evidence for questionable competence.

There are, however, several important factors to keep in mind. The first is that confusion and disorientation in aged patients, particularly those who have been hospitalized for physical or mental reasons, is often reversible by application of the principles of Folsom's treatment described in this chapter. The second is that, in addition to giving an expert opinion as to the patient's mental status, the doctor should expect to play a role in helping the family to deal with the problems of guilt often associated with taking such action. Finally, he should be aware that some states make special provision for the hospitalization of nonconsenting patients, senile or otherwise, which avoids unnecessary use of commitment or competency hearings. These are the so-called informal admissions under the terms of which a patient may be hospitalized and treated without signing admission papers but is free to leave at any time, his willingness to stay in the hospital being taken as tacit consent.

Removing the patient from familiar surroundings and immersing him in an all too often psychologically unresponsive milieu can lead to disorientation that may reach psychotic proportions. Fortunately, these reactions can be avoided and reversed by following fairly simple management guidelines, which have been described particularly by J. C. Folsom, M.D., and are sometimes referred to as "the Folsom treatment." Folsom quotes the instructions written by one of his nursing assistants:

> Introduce yourself to patients. Repeat your name as necessary. You may ask patients to repeat your name. Be sure he can pronounce it. Introduce patients to each other. Always call the patient by his name, and encourage him to call others by name.

> Try to set a calm, friendly and secure atmosphere. A patient who is confused will usually respond to a calm, friendly approach. Speak slowly and distinctly because many times older patients are hard of hearing. Speak in a friendly manner, but do not talk to him as though he were a child. Look directly at the patient when addressing him.

> Plan a simple activity—something that he has probably done before. Have the patient assemble a calendar notebook; be sure his name is on it. Make a calendar each month, and mark off the day each morning. Move to more complex and gratifying activity only after the patient has improved sufficiently—after he becomes more comfortable, and after he starts showing interest in his surroundings.

> Make minimal demands on the patient. Remember, he is already confused, upset, and possibly hostile. Give him one simple instruction at

a time. Spend as much time with the patient as possible—do not just get him started on his project and leave him. Return to him often and give instruction.

Keep in mind that it may not be the actual activity or project that the patient is doing, but more likely the social interaction with others that helps him return to reality as his self-confidence and dignity are restored.

Ask the patient to sign in on a daily roster; encourage him to do so. Use spelling sessions and discussion; this may be done while in a group around a large table. Keep words simple and close to reality. Ask the patient to spell the day, week, month, location of the hospital, next meal, etc.; anagrams may be used.

Reward patient immediately when he responds correctly; say, "Good," "That's right," "Fine," etc.

As soon as possible include the patient with others who have been in the reality orientation treatment.

The concepts of withdrawal and isolation are important in understanding the elderly. *Withdrawal* refers to the increasing self-absorption of the person and his avoidance of contacts with others. *Isolation* refers to the decreasing opportunities for interaction due to loss of mobility, relationships or facilities. The two concepts obviously overlap, as withdrawal may be initiated by others, and isolation by the individual himself. Withdrawal has social aspects. The elderly person who feels unwanted may indeed be unwanted by his children or by the workday world in which he becomes surplus. The social aspects of withdrawal are accentuated by our youth-oriented society, but there is a definite decrease in the tolerance for social interaction by the aged. Barnes has suggested that the lack of interest of many elderly people in church activities or golden age societies may be related to genuine withdrawal of interest in social activities, rather than a reaction to rebuffs, real or imagined, from the environment. Withdrawal may take the form of withdrawal of affection from others; the elderly have been described as misers with their affection. It may also take the form of preoccupation with self, with bodily preoccupations running the spectrum from healthy concern over illness all the way to delusional hypochondriasis. Withdrawal from sexual activity and other usual physiological functions may have to do with the amount of physical energy. The evaluation of such withdrawal as adaptive or maladaptive can be a great challenge. The phenomenon is clearly not an all or none situation. The person is, however, unable to withdraw selectively under stress, as would be normal for anyone who while physically ill becomes far more concerned with his immediate environment in the sick room and his bodily functions than with the outside world.

A number of factors contribute to isolation. The death of friends and family, the moods of the person and of others, the changes in vocational gratification and financial status all contribute. Illness decreases the chances for interaction, and may necessitate hospitalization and cessation of even desired activities. The loss of self-esteem which ensues leads to depressive feelings even when there were none earlier in the person's life. The realization of approaching death reawakens old conflicts about interaction with others and dependency on them.

The realities of being tired, physically smaller, vulnerable and ill are in marked contrast to a usual self-concept of being able to cope, and they set the stage for a denial of aging which protects self-esteem. Decreasing ability to maintain an erection, which is sometimes compounded by the psychological lack of interest, must find new outlets in fantasy or noncoital sex. When those who have previously prided themselves on physical strength or independent solution of problems must face weakness and dependency on others, conflicts are reactivated. Often the new adaptations are more primitive than the previous ones and lead, for example, to paranoid ideas that others are depriving them. In the elderly, stresses begin to overpower the resources for adaptation. In those previously fixated at an immature level of psychological function, who now have their backs to the wall psychologically, the only retreat is to the more primitive mechanism of defense.

Sociocultural Factors of Aging

The elderly person needs to be occupied, to be wanted and to be important. Different cultural groups have developed varied styles of dealing with their aged. In general, the smaller the number of persons who survive to old age, the more they are revered. The more static societies usually accord more respect to the wisdom of the elderly. The more mobile and fluctuating the society, the more its elderly are caught in the squeeze of social processes.

In some cultures, age is clearly equated with power, independence and influence over the affairs of others. Present-day Japan and many American Indian tribes are examples. The Japanese culture indulges its very young and very old but limits the freedom of its adult population; westernized society tends to do the reverse, keeping its young and old in dependent status.

Contemporary American benefits of better health facilities and better economic status for more people have been accompanied by rapid social changes and challenges to old cultural values in many subcultures, posing special problems for the aged. As an example, the flight to the suburbs in many large cities has drained the inner city of its middle-class support, both in health care and business activities. The elderly Jewish population of New York City is an example of a group deserted in this way. Those congregations that remain are attended by an ever smaller circle of elderly people, with limited financial ability to support religious activities. Similarly, the predominantly rural Mexican-American families of south Texas have suffered losses of family unity because the elderly could not maintain contact with their young, mobile families moving to the cities. In the suburbs around our cities, the phenomenon of elderly people living alone but unable to drive, and isolated from the resources which nurtured them, is common.

All lower socioeconomic groups have more disease. Thus, the "premorbid" history of an elderly person from a lower economic group will prepare him poorly for the stresses of aging. Nutritional problems, injury and strenuous physical work all take their toll. The best protections known against the ravages of aging are good intellect and education and favorable socioeconomic status. Happy marriages correlate directly with better adaptation in the aged. Such marriages are characterized by maintenance of close ties with kin, mutual affection and dependence, a stable family with tradition, positive social roles and mutual support under stress. Mentally healthy partners are better able to support each other. Continued sexual relations and tolerance for changing patterns of gratification in these relations are important. The frequency of intercourse may decrease while that of masturbation may increase, with gratification coming more from fantasy than action. Continuation of sexual interests is related to maintenance of interest in other people and other aspects of life.

Longevity is correlated with a good general physical function, social supports, visual-motor tests of intellectual function and greater participation in leisure time activities. Stresses brought about by retirement, especially for men, have pointed up the need for better preparation for this time of life. Better adjustment results from active leisure activities. More passive leisure activities, such as television viewing, may lead to loss of opportunities for interpersonal stimulation.

Eighty per cent of the elderly live in their own homes. As time passes, they need help in structuring their days and participating in useful activities. Retirement, illness and decreasing contacts all call for readjustment and response. The elderly, in some ways a disadvantaged minority, economically and socially deprived, are beginning to organize themselves politically through associations of retired people, groups of emeritus professors and golden age clubs which provide recreation and lobby for health benefits, hot meals and housing for the poor. The myth that age necessarily involves an inability to produce is challenged by the numbers of second careers and examples of influence maintained by prominent individuals late into their lives. The myth of inescapable brain damage must give way to the reality that some elderly persons do not show mental or physical signs of organic brain damage.

Although less than 5% of the elderly actually need total care, 30% of the annual first admissions to state mental institutions are of persons over 65, and state hospitals are increasingly becoming the geriatric warehouses of our society. The care of the individuals within institutions has received much more attention than the provision of care and facilities for the much larger group within the community. The principles of creating a milieu with participation, freedom, safety, individuality and contact with people have been described earlier in connection with the Folsom treatment. Unfortunately, transitional facilities which have helped in the community care of chronic mental patients are not yet available within most communities.

Attention to the nutritional needs of the elderly, facilities for socialization and ready access to health care are problems which can be best resolved through centralized planning. The development of such comprehensive care, a feasible goal ideally, awaits changes in social priorities.

The stresses described in this and the previous section influence the increasing rates of suicide among the elderly. Although especially common in those who are alone, diseased and alcoholic, suicide in the aged also reflects our inability to deal adequately with the problem of aging.

Suggestions for Treatment of the Aged

The physician needs to be aware of a host of factors which make treatment of aged patients problematical. Among these, denial of signs and symptoms is common in the aged. Relatedly, the aged tend to be less well educated than the young, and are thus more likely to use nostrums and sensational cures both because of the wish to hold out for a miracle and because of ignorance. The aged often have poor memories, hearing problems, or both, which affect their compliance with instructions. The slower responses of the aged, their overtalkativeness and their unappealing physical state can result in the physician's shunning close contact with them or abbreviating a treatment visit. This is especially so if the physician is unduly concerned with his own impending old age.

Instructions to patients and efforts to modify behavioral patterns will be more successful if the physician has an optimistic, but realistic, attitude. One can "teach an old dog new tricks" if it is done slowly, patiently and in cognizance of the elderly patient's fears of failure. Butler has called attention to the possibilities for treatment and change in older patients, pointing to the "life review" as a useful technique, part of a process of settling old issues within the person. An 80-year-old immigrant Russian-American woman's first attempts at poetry came in a nursing home as a result of contacts with a creative staff member. Among her poems she wrote:

> When I was young
> And love was easy
> And friends were constant and true,
> When the struggle
> To make a living
> Was taken in its stride
> When I woke up
> Every morning
> With renewed strength
> To keep on going,

I was glad to have
My children.
When they came
Life seemed to be
A labor of love.
Then the children grew up
And like birds
Left their nest

To make their own,
Leaving me lonely
To get old and dependent
On others for things
I was used to perform
Myself,
But plenty of time
For reflections.
Would I want
To have lived different
If I had a chance?
Would I have married
Another man?
Had different children (or different friends)
Definitely not.
I am thankful
For what I had.

The physician prescribing medication needs to reduce the usual dosage, for several reasons. First, the aged patient is a smaller patient. Lean body mass decreases with age, and renal function decreases in a linear fashion beginning about the age of 30. This latter fact is especially important because of the renal excretion of medications such as digitalis and most antibiotics. Second, the aged have altered end organ sensitivity. This is particularly important in increased anticholinergic sensitivity, which can result in urinary retention and in increased sensitivity to sedatives. Third, the aged person has diminished homeostatic efficiency, causing, for example, more postural hypotension from drugs which decrease blood pressure.

In particular, sedatives, tranquilizers and hypnotics should be prescribed with caution in the aged. In addition to the reasons discussed earlier, the underlying problem may be a different physical disorder. A careful history should clarify whether the basic problem in a patient presenting with insomnia is anxiety, depression, a full urinary bladder, itching or dyspnea accompanying mild congestive heart failure. Awareness of the frequent use of nonprescription drugs and folk remedies, as well as medication prescribed by more than one physician, should alert the doctor to the need for a careful medication history prior to instituting therapy.

Old people often make mistakes in taking their medicines, because of memory deficits, problems of attention and because they are likely to take so many. Therefore, instructions should be clear, simple and legible. Have a second person responsible for, or knowledgeable about, the medications when possible. Most important, do not prescribe any medication which is not necessary.

*   *   *   *

All of us must walk down this road. What we do to prepare occurs, in large part unconsciously, through the way we live, treat our patients and work in our daily lives. Physicians must cope with this stress of disability and death in their professional lives. They may deal with this through denial, through a coldly scientific approach to the patient or through an impassioned social crusade. But in the long run, we will lose every patient we ever care for. The psychological stresses this imposes account in part for the depressions suffered by large numbers of professional people as they mature in their careers.

Erikson has described conflict at various stages of life in terms of the alternative solutions. For the elderly, the conflict of ego integrity versus shame and despair is especially relevant. The grim inevitability of death should not distract us from the possibility of maintaining physical, psychological and social function into very old age. Sophocles, Emerson, Ben-Gurion and Adenauer are shining examples of productivity, respect and ego integrity in late life. Indeed, the most adaptive way to look at aging may be to put the accent on growth, variety and continued learning as part of the life process.

REFERENCES

1. Binstock, R. H., and Shanas, E. *Handbook of Aging and Social Sciences.* Van Nostrand Rinehold, New York, 1976.
2. Birren, J. E., and Schaie, K. W. *Handbook of the Psychology of Aging. Van Nostrand Rinehold, New York, 1977.*
3. Brikett, D. The psychiatric differentiation of senility and arteriosclerosis. *Br. J. Psychiatry 120:*321–325, 1972.
4. Busse, E. Biologic and sociologic changes affecting adaptation in mid and late life. *Ann. Intern. Med. 75:*115–120, 1971.
5. Busse, E. W., and Pfeiffer, E. *Mental Illness in Later Life; American Psychiatric Association Monograph.* American Psychiatric Association, Washington, D.C., 1973.
6. Butler, R. N. *Why Survive? Being Old in America.* Harper & Row, New York, 1975.
7. Finch, C. E., and Hayflic, L. *Handbook of the Biology of Aging.* Van Nostrand Rinehold, New York, 1978.
8. Folsom, J. C. Reality orientation for the elderly mental patient. *J. Geriatric Psychiatry 1:*291, 1968.
9. Stotsky, B. Social and clinical issues in geriatric psychiatry. *Am. J. Psychiatry 129:*31–40, 1972.

PART 3

"PHYSICIAN, HEAL THYSELF"

CHAPTER 20

ADAPTATION TO THE PHYSICIAN ROLE

CHARLES L. BOWDEN, M.D.

Throughout this book the focus has been that of physicians looking *out* at those whom they treat and at the host of factors which affect illnesses. In this last chapter, the physicians themselves are the focus of our concern—their health, professional role stresses, and preventive considerations which can optimize their well-being and satisfaction in their professional and personal lives.

The Physician's Health

Numerous studies have documented that physicians are, as a rule, abysmally poor patients. Although 90% of the physicians in one survey said that they recommended annual physical examinations for their patients, 70% acknowledged that they did not practice what they preached. Another study found that nearly one-third of the physicians who were particularly knowledgeable about cancer (based on their belonging to cancer-oriented medical societies) had *never* had an examination for asymptomatic disease. There is no comfort in the hope that perhaps the physicians knew that they did not need examinations. One study compared the results of physical examinations in well physicians and dentists with a comparable group of executives. Of the 61 physicians and 8 dentists, 45%, a percentage higher than that found among the executives, had significant asymptomatic problems, including 8

219

with cardiovascular disease and 2 with malignancies. Another study of physicians with diagnosed malignancies determined that most had ignored such symptoms as bloody stools, recurrent cramping abdominal pain, jaundice, dysphagia and hemoptysis for an average of 3 to 14 months. Another report showed that physicians, who should readily recognize symptoms of myocardial infarction, waited twice as long from the onset of symptoms to seek medical help as did laymen. Most persons waited an average of 6 hours after first symptoms before calling a physician, whereas the physicians did not call until an average of 12 hours had passed.

Drug abuse is much more common among physicians than among the general public. The incidence of narcotic addiction is higher among physicians than among any other occupational or socioeconomic group, including ghetto residents. It is estimated that approximately 1% of American physicians will become addicted at some point in their careers (primarily to meperidine (Demerol)), a rate 30 to 100 times that of the general population. The recovery rate when strict probationary rehabilitation programs are instituted is gratifyingly high—up to 92% in one study. On the grim side is the fact that about 10% of physician addicts commit suicide.

In a recent 10-year period, 3.2% of the registered physicians in Arizona and 2.3% in Oregon were brought before medical society disciplinary boards for alcoholism. Another study found that one-third of all the time during which physicians were hospitalized was caused by alcohol and drug use.

The suicide rate for physicians is moderately higher than that of the over-all male population. Within the profession, rates vary by specialty and sex. Radiologists have the lowest rates, psychiatrists the highest. The suicide rate for female physicians is at least three times that of the over-all rate for women and slightly higher than that for male physicians. Below the age of 45, the suicide rate for female physicians markedly exceeds that for male physicians. For physicians above 45 years of age, rates are somewhat higher for men. Blachly found that, of physicians who committed suicide, heavy drinking or alcoholism was recorded for 39%, 19% were drinking at the time of death and drug dependence or severe abuse was a factor in 19%.

These remarkable, troubling figures extend into practically every health-related area which has been investigated. For example, physician pilots are involved in fatal light plane crashes at a rate four times that of all civilian noncommercial pilots.

Factors Contributing to Physicians' Health and Role Problems

Role Strain. Sociologists define role strain as the result of disparity between the clear expectations about the role one is to perform and the inadequacy of social institutions and norms to support that role performance. The characteristics of the "good" physician emphasize suppression, perfectionistic attention to detail, conscientiousness, caring for others and deferral of gratification. All of these characteristics can be a superb and useful social adaptation, but they seem to predispose one toward depression, especially when the person is not concomitantly caring for himself. Related are the idealism and commitment of many physicians, which can lead to frustration and depression over awareness of the gap between what is actually provided in health care and in his practice.

Much prestige is often attached to the individual role performance of the physician. It can become seductively easy to use one's patients to become an authority figure, or to be loved by them or to make them feel dependent. When the patient praises his physician, it is easy for him to lose perspective and begin to believe that all of his patients who get better do so because of his care.

Added to this are the blandishments outside practice—inducements to buy land, take out loans or invest in expensive insurance plans. This attention and appeal to the financial status of the physician even affects the physician fatality rate from plane crashes. Most persons who learn to fly, including physicians, do so in basic planes. But the physician is often able and usually encouraged to buy a larger, more complex, more powerful plane which is beyond his full competence to handle.

This country's major system of payment on a fee for service basis creates insecurity in many physicians. A physician with a well established practice and an income in excess of $60,000 may fear that if he is away on a 2-week vacation his patients will leave him and he will be unneeded and impoverished. It is amazing to see this syndrome, which impels the person to work even harder than he wishes, because of his paradoxical insecurity in the face of plenty.

Medicine is hard work for anyone. But it is even harder for the physician who uses his practice to minister compulsively to and give solace to others (a kind of maladaptive altruism) while neglecting his personal needs. Vaillant found that the group of physicians whom he studied who were most prone to drug abuse were those who, in middle age, found that their self-sacrifice had not produced its fantasized rewards and that, as their energy waned, depression ensued.

The problems of physicians are also influenced by their preadult psychological adjustment. Having a disrupted childhood or being judged less sound in psychological adjustment in college appears to be an important predictor of life adjustment and drug abuse problems.

The area of specialization is another relevant variable. Those in direct patient-care specialities generally have the highest frequency of problems. There are two possible explanations for this. First, the physician elects to do something in order to be able to give what was not received in his own childhood; this is a poor basis for choosing a career. Second, the more intimate, intense and long term the therapeutic relationship, the more stress it may engender, and it may lay the physician more open to overinvestment and consequent depression. This is especially true among psychiatrists.

As has been described, the personality characteristics of the physician and the expectation of patients, colleagues and the public in general can enhance his sense of omnipotence. The more the specialty enhances the fantasy of omnipotence, the more it contributes to the likelihood of suicide. This is one reason for the especially high rates among anesthesiologists and psychiatrists.

In the area of drug abuse, two additional important factors are (1) the ready availability of narcotics and other drugs of abuse and (2) the remarkable ignorance concerning the addictive properties of drugs, especially meperidine. At times the physician gradiosely assumes that, because of his knowledge about drugs, he can take them and not risk dependence on them.

Difficulty Accepting the Sick Role. As has been shown, physicians have extreme difficulty accepting the sick role. They learn to dissociate themselves from the dangers with which they deal in patient care. For many doctors, one element in the motivational complex is an unconscious need to overcome illness and death. It is important for effective patient care that the physician generally hold the belief that "it can't happen to me." But this denial of potential liability and even of actual distress hurts the physician's own health. This denial is often reinforced by his feeling that he is indispensable to his patient. Illness, or the threat thereof, especially drug abuse and other emotional disorders, is often seen as a threat to his reputation and is rationalized or denied for that reason. The physician is more likely than the layman to use the adaptive mechanisms of turning against the self, altruism and hypochondriasis. The most common example of hypochondriasis is the physician who, in response to questions about his health, responds that "There is a lot wrong with me, but I will not inconvenience anyone else with it." This fear of imposing stems from several roots. On one hand, he may fear that an actual problem will be discovered. On the other, he may fear that nothing will be found and he will be unmasked as a hypochondriacal complainer or an incompetent diagnostician. Professional courtesy can also be a factor. Usually not paying for his care, the physician is therefore particularly reluctant to inconvenience his doctor and take away from his doctor's regular, paying patients.

A last common source of difficulty lies in the way in which they are treated by other physicians. Too often they are treated with special deference. Unpleasant procedures such as a rectal examination, questions about narcotic use and an examination for needle tracks are rationalized away as unnecessary. The mistake is made, often out of fear of embarrassing the physician, that just because he is a doctor he knows all about the problem at hand and does not require the patient instruction which would otherwise routinely be provided. In a related fashion, colleagues and medical societies are often embarrassed by what they may be implying or discovering in the physician, and respond by avoidance of firm action. One reason for this is that to see physical and emotional frailties in those similar to us can make us uncomfortably aware of our own vulnerability.

The Woman Physician

One-fourth to one-third of entering medical school classes are now composed of women, a percentage that has grown rapidly over the decade of the 1970's. Women physicians are estimated to practice approximately two-fifths fewer hours over their lifetime than do men, which works out to a still substantial 36 hours per week over a 33-year active practice. Complexities of mixing a career with family responsibilities are the primary unique stresses for women physicians. Women physicians are as likely to marry as other women, with half of them marrying physicians. The woman physician who commits suicide is more than twice as likely to be single, widowed or divorced than the over-all group of women physicians. Almost all leave practice temporarily at some point in their career, but currently most lose less than 12 months medical activity because of pregnancy and child care. Part-time graduate programs, retraining programs and more equitable division of household responsibilities should improve personal satisfaction and professional activity among women physicians. We do not believe that this unquestionably real, somewhat reduced professional activity of women should be used to discriminate against the interests of women who seek or are in medical careers; it should be recognized as a small price to pay for social equity.

Prevention and Care of Physicians' Health and Other Adaptational Problems

In the area of prevention, awareness of the reality of this problem is a necessary first step. It is easy for one to say that "All this is true but it doesn't apply to me." The truth is that the profession engenders some of this in all of us.

The physician should be "modest in his grandiosity." By this we mean that the mantle of the physician should be worn lightly. Do not take your status, your money or, most important, your importance to your patients too seriously. Expect and be willing to acknowledge your mistakes and errors. The ability to say "I don't know" is what science is all about.

Consider the aspects of normality described in Chapter 1 and periodically assess yourself in those terms. Pay attention to the business of *living well* rather than just business per se. Keep physically fit. Because physicians make such poor patients, it behooves you to do your best to avoid being one unnecessarily. Pay attention to the adage "Physician, heal thyself" in the positive sense of the statement. Take sufficient rest, exercise and time for your family and leisure pursuits. A functional understanding of the workings of transference and countertransference can be of immeasurable value in such continuing self-assessment.

Vaillant has well stated this admonition regarding drug use: "No physician, whatever his rationalization, should write a prescription for himself for anything that will make his brain feel better, sleep better or work better." Remember that self-medication with drugs and alcohol is the cause of one-third of the time physicians spend in the hospital.

Have a personal physician. It is essential that you establish an ongoing relationship with a physician which overcomes the general reluctance of one physician to impose on another. Do not let professional courtesy intrude.

Just as the preceding focuses on the physician as patient, so we need also to consider the doctor's doctor. Another reason for physicians' poor medical care is that other physicians are often afraid of treating them as a patient. They assume that they know more than they do, do not enforce limits with them and overlook obvious problems suggesting drug abuse because they do not know what to do with them and pronounce them cured before they are ready to resume their duties. Here, too, awareness of these problems can help the physician not to commit the same mistakes.

In the main, the same careful interview and examination should be conducted with the physician as with any other patient. They should receive the same specific instructions concerning medication and treatment. An attitude of friendly, collegial regard helps the sick physician to sustain and repair an already fragile self-respect. The same level of cooperation should be expected and the same limits set that would be with any comparable patient who is not a physician. The difference lies in the fact that in many areas the physician may be quite knowledgeable. Thus, to a greater degree than with most patients, it usually helps to make him or her an active collaborator in treatment. For example, physicians with schizophrenia apparently do best when they have some control over manipulating their own drug dosage. Similarly, a physician can often provide much more perceptive feedback than the average layman about symptoms, such as his exercise tolerance, and can help to arrive mutually at an appropriate treatment regimen. This policy works well only as long as it is clear that the treating physician is the authority responsible for the treatment.

Several caveats are important. Physicians who are on a professional disciplinary board, or who find that a colleague is in trouble should never rationalize that the person knows what to do and how to care for himself. He does not. They should recognize that this tendency to deny illness will make diagnosis and treatment difficult. The physician should be alert to signs of depression. Studies of physicians who committed suicide reveal that most showed unmistakable evidence of indecision, disorganization and depression in the 2 to 4 months preceding their suicide, but, in most cases, no colleague did anything to try to intervene in the difficulties he saw. Special pacts, secrecy or privileges have no more place in the care of the physician than in the care of the nonphysician. Sensitivity to this issue and firmness in handling it are important, because physicians often are skillfully manipulative, especially by making requests based on their feelings that they are indispensable to their patients. For example, it is not uncommon for a physician to plead to leave the hospital prematurely because he believes that his patients cannot adequately survive without him.

*   *   *   *

Significant risks accompany the life of the physician. Some physicians bring predisposing vulnerabilities to their lives in medicine. All are subjected to pressures which, as discussed in this chapter, can jeopardize both role function and personal health. Properly tending to the adaptational issues covered in this chapter will put physicians in a better position to approach their patients as Osler suggested in a statement that aptly summarizes the major aim of this book.

> The motto of each of you as you undertake the examination for treatment of a case should be: put yourself in his place. Realize so far as you can the mental state of the patient, enter into his feelings—scan gently his faults. The kindly word, the cheerful greeting, the sympathetic look—these the patient understands.

1. BLACHLY, P. H., DISHER, W., AND RODUNER, G. Suicide by Physicians, in *Bulletin of Suicidology*. National Institute of Mental Health, Bethesda, Md. December, 1968, pp. 1–18.
2. GREEN, R. C., CARROLL, G. J., AND BUXTON, W. D. Drug addiction among physicians. *J.A.M.A. 236*:1372–1375. 1976.
3. JUSSIM, J., AND MULLER, C. Medical education for women: how good an investment? *J. Med. Educ. 50*:571–580, 1975.
4. MODLIN, H. C., AND MONTES, A. Narcotic addiction in physicians. *Am. J. Psychiatry 121*: 358–365, 1964.
5. SARGENT, D. A., JENSEN, V. W., PETTY, T. A., AND RASKIN, H. Preventing physician suicide. *J.A.M.A. 237*:143–145, 1977.
6. SMALL, I. F., SMALL, J. G., ASSUE, C. M., AND MOORE, D. F. The fate of the mentally ill physician. *Am. J. Psychiatry 125*:1333–1342, 1969.
7. STEPPACHER, R. C., AND MAUSNER, J. S. Suicide in male and female physicians. *J.A.M.A. 228*:323–328, 1974.
8. VAILLANT, G. E., BRIGHTON, J. R., AND McARTHUR, C. Physician's use of mood altering drugs. *N. Engl. J. Med. 285*:365–370, 1970.
9. VAILLANT, G. E., SOBOWALE, N. C., AND McARTHUR, C. Some psychological vulnerabilities of physicians. *N. Engl. J. Med. 287*:372–375, 1972.

Index